Economics, Law, and Institutions in Asia Pacific

The Asia Pacific region is expected to steadily enhance its economic and political presence in the world during the twenty-first century. At the same time, many serious economic and political issues remain unresolved in the region. To further academic enquiry and enhance readers' understanding about this vibrant region, the present series, Economics, Law, and Institutions in Asia Pacific, aims to present cutting-edge research on the Asia Pacific region and its relationship with the rest of the world. For countries in this region to achieve robust economic growth, it is of foremost importance that they improve the quality of their markets, as history shows that healthy economic growth cannot be achieved without high-quality markets. High-quality markets can be established and maintained only under a well-designed set of rules and laws, without which competition will not flourish. Based on these principles, this series places a special focus on economic, business, legal, and institutional issues geared towards the healthy development of Asia Pacific markets. The series considers book proposals for scientific research, either theoretical or empirical, that is related to the theme of improving market quality and has policy implications for the Asia Pacific region. The types of books that will be considered for publication include research monographs as well as relevant proceedings. The series show-cases work by Asia-Pacific based researchers but also encourages the work of social scientists not limited to the Asia Pacific region. Each proposal and final manuscript is subject to evaluation by the editorial board and experts in the field.

All books and chapters in the Economics, Law and Institutions in Asia Pacific book series are indexed in Scopus.

Masayuki Murayama
Editor

The Japanese Legal Profession in Transition

Springer

Editor
Masayuki Murayama
Organization for the Strategic
Coordination of Research
and Intellectual Properties, Institute
of Law and Social Sciences
Meiji University
Tokyo, Japan

ISSN 2199-8620 ISSN 2199-8639 (electronic)
Economics, Law, and Institutions in Asia Pacific
ISBN 978-981-97-2691-2 ISBN 978-981-97-2692-9 (eBook)
https://doi.org/10.1007/978-981-97-2692-9

This Springer imprint is published by the registered company Springer Nature Singapore Pte Ltd.
The registered company address is: 152 Beach Road, #21-01/04 Gateway East, Singapore 189721, Singapore

Preface

This book is about the Japanese legal profession, its changes and its present situation. The Justice System Reform (JSR) from 2001 to 2004 was a very broad ambitious reform of the Japanese legal system to change the 'shape of the country'. It introduced lay assessors to sit with professional judges in criminal trials and made the rights of the accused more substantial by extending public defense to suspects. The JSR also tried significantly to improve access to justice by establishing the Japan Legal Support Center. The cornerstone of the JSR, however, is the large increase of legal professionals, particularly private attorneys. The JSR Council envisioned "to transform the spirit of the law and the rule of law into the 'flesh and blood' of Japan". Activities of a large number of lawyers would provide 'blood' to circulate in 'the flesh'. Without sufficient flow of 'blood', 'the flesh' would not be kept alive. Our research reported in this book is a present diagnosis of the 'blood' and its flow.

The significance of the JSR would not be well understood unless its vision is put in a wider historical perspective. In the process of modernization, the Japanese court system had developed a judicial infrastructure which produced 'small justice'. It was a product in which all the concerned found shared interests, though the meanings of shared interests were different among the concerned. As the judicial infrastructure was deeply rooted in the social, economic and political interests of the concerned, it would not be easy to change, in either a profound or even superficial way. However, we consider that the JSR has had certain significant impact on the Japanese legal system. What we need to do at this stage is to understand to what extent the JSR has achieved its vision and to recognize the conditions under which the JSR succeeded or failed. Focusing on the legal profession, we try to do this in this book.

Though the vision of the JSR seemed to be far-reaching 20 years ago, most of its plans have been implemented if not entirely as envisioned. One significant setback arose in its plan to sharply increase the number of lawyers in comparatively short time, in combination with the introduction of new post-graduate law schools styled on US models into Japanese law faculties with their pre-existing civil law mindset. The resulting challenge met resistance among professors, leaving doubt about just how much remained of that old way of thinking, including the substance and procedures of the Japanese bar examination. Notwithstanding, this new law school system has itself survived, despite significant elements of the old training system for legal professionals having been revived in the process. Additionally, as this book shows, the JSR has irreversibly changed the world of legal professionals, particularly attorneys, even if not as much as envisioned by the JSR Council, and lays the groundwork for still further change.

This book resulted from our collaboration for 7 years. I organized our research project in 2017 with five researchers, Shozo Ota, Isamu Sugino, Takayuki Ii, Kyoko Ishida, and Daisuke Mori, four of whom contributed to the book. Daniel H. Foote joined us from the second year and brought his rich knowledge of both the U.S. and Japanese systems to our discussion. Dan also read a part of the manuscript and gave us valuable comments as native researcher. We are grateful for his additional assistance. In the final year of the project, Hiroyuki Kabashima joined us and we benefited from his point of view as a legal practitioner.

I began to conduct research on the legal profession in the late 1980s. The topic was criminal defense work in the context of general legal practice. Since then, I have maintained my interest in the legal profession. I particularly benefited from joining the International Sociological Association Research Committee on Sociology of Law (ISA-RCSL), Working Group for Comparative Studies of Legal Professions. I first attended the RCSL annual meeting, organized by Vincenzo Ferrari, in Bologna, Italy, in 1988. I was a regular participant of the Working Group meeting from 1996 and learned a lot from lively discussions in intimate settings.

Since I began to work on the legal profession, I benefitted from reading many books and papers on legal professionals, only a part of which we could cite in this book. Many people also helped me to conduct research in Japan, the U.S., the U.K. and France. I thank Richard Abel, Benoit Bastard, Anne Boigeol, Antoine Garapon, Herbert Kritzer, Mavis Maclean, Heinrich Menkhaus, Kahei Rokumoto, Harry Scheiber, and Jean Van Houtte. My special thanks go to Susan Reid who read a substantial part of the book and gave us invaluable native comments.

Our research was made possible by funding from the Japan Society for the Promotion of Science Grant-in-Aid Scientific Research (A) (17H00964), Minji Hunso Shori Kenkyu Kikin (The Foundation for Research in Civil Dispute Resolution), Japan Law Foundation, and Shiho Kyokai. We are grateful for their generous support. Finally, and most of all, we are deeply grateful to all the questionnaire respondents and interviewees for sharing their experiences with us.

I am grateful to Juno Kawakami who provided editing assistance from the inception of this project. I am also grateful to Michael House for his native editing.

I thank Yoshie for making all projects of our life possible.

Tokyo, Japan
November 2023

Masayuki Murayama

Introduction

In Japan, as in other parts of the world, it is necessary to pass the bar examination to become a judge, prosecutor, or attorney at law (*bengoshi*; hereinafter also "lawyer").[1] An increase in the number of bar examination passers in Japan, implemented in 2006 as a part of the Justice System Reform (JSR), resulted in a large increase in the number of lawyers, and their world has been changing as a result of this increase and other developments. For decades, the annual number of bar examination passers had remained around 500, though it was increased a little in the 1990s. As a result, the lawyer population was small. As of 1990 there were only 13,800 lawyers in Japan. Even after the modest increases in the 1990's, the number remained at 17,126 in 2000. The Justice System Reform Council (JSRC), which was established in 1999 and issued its final report in 2001, recommended to increase the annual number of bar exam passers to 3000 by 2010 and to bring the size of the lawyer population to 50,000. Due to the resistance of the Japan Federation of Bar Associations (JFBA) and its constituent bar associations, this recommendation was not fully realized. Yet, following the introduction of a new system of law schools in 2004 and a new bar exam system in 2006, the annual number of passers increased to more than 2000 in 2007. In the face of strong resistance by the bar, the number of passers subsequently declined, but it has remained at about the 1500 level. This has resulted in the increase of the lawyer population from 23,119 in 2007 to 44,101 in 2022, a 91% increase over those 15 years.

This was not the first time in Japan that the lawyer population increased and lawyers objected to it. The profession of lawyers was born in the process of importing the French legal system soon after the Meiji Restoration in 1867. The Meiji government tried to transplant the French law and French judicial system into Japan, and created two professions, advocate (*daigen-nin*), for representation in court, and scrivener (*daisho-nin*), for preparing documents for submission to the court. Initially, no formal qualification was required to become an advocate, but this

[1] While judges and prosecutors are also included under the heading of "legal professionals" in Japan, only attorneys are members of bar associations.

changed in 1876 when advocates were required to pass a qualifying examination. From this point, the professional project of advocates[2] began.

Although only advocates were allowed in principle to represent a party in court, there were exceptions. When an advocate was not available and a party could not attend, a party's close family member could represent a party, and when a close family member was not available, a proxy with a seal of recognition of a head of ward or district[3] could represent a party (Hashimoto, 2005, p. 191). People without a license to practice as advocate took advantage of this exception and represented parties in many cases.[4] The Code of Civil Procedure (Act No.29 of 1890) also recognized a wide range of exceptions. At the District Court, when a lawyer[5] was not available, a litigant's family member or employee could represent a litigant and, when none of these existed, anyone that had the capacity to sue or be sued could represent a litigant. At the Summary Court, even when a lawyer was available, a litigant's family member or employee could represent a litigant. In 1893, the Attorneys Act was passed, changing the official name of advocates (*daigen-nin*) to lawyers (*bengoshi*), but it did not prohibit representation in court by people without license. Non-lawyers' representation in court seemed to continue until around 1900 (Hayshi, 2009, p. 641).[6]

As the Attorneys Act had no provision concerning legal practice outside of litigation, people without license continued to work outside of litigation side by side with lawyers even after non-licensees were driven out of litigation. These people were more easily accessible for local people and helped them to solve disputes. They also provided legal services, including legal consultation, and played the role of an intermediary to bring clients to lawyers. As the Attorneys Act allowed lawyers to establish branch offices, lawyers often left management of branch offices to those people without license. Therefore, lawyers and people without license did not always have conflicting interests and the widespread legal practice without license indicates that lawyers could not provide enough legal services to satisfy legal needs among local people (Hashimoto, 2005, pp. 36–40; Misaka, 2011).

---

[2] Larson argued that an occupation tried to become a profession by achieving its market monopoly and upgrading its social status, which she called a 'professional project' (Larson, 1977, p.104). The professional project of the legal profession seeks to establish control over production of legal service and the number of people permitted to provide legal services (Abel, 1988, pp.186–187).

[3] In terms of administrative jurisdiction, a prefecture consisted of districts and a district consisted of wards.

[4] It is not known how many of such people represented litigants, but recent studies revealed that people without a license worked for litigation in areas studied, such as Shizuoka, Kyoto and Shiga (Hashimoto, 2005, pp. 193–195; Misaka, 2017, pp. 317–335).

[5] The Code of Civil Procedure includes the term "*bengoshi*" (lawyer), indicating that the word was in common usage prior to its enactment, despite the job title not yet having been officially changed from advocate to lawyer.

[6] Representation in court by people without license began as proxy's representation. Hayashi considers that this practice of representation by people without license ceased after the Rules of Proxy (Dajokan Ordinance No.215 of 1873) was abolished in 1898.

The bar examination for advocates and later for lawyers was conducted separately from the examination for judges and public prosecutors. Over the 17 years from 1876 to 1892, 2084 persons passed the advocates exam, an average of 123 advocates per year.[7] The bar exam for lawyers was more competitive, as the pass rate was very small, 5% from 1897 to 1908. The total number of bar exam passers was only 1801, an average of just 65 persons per year over 27 years from 1894 to 1921. The examination for judges and prosecutors and the examination for lawyers were combined in 1923. In 1922, the year before they were combined, 1104 persons had passed the bar examination.[8] Thereafter, from 1923, the annual number of passers of the combined judicial and bar examination remained in the 200 to 400 person range,[9] and this led to a steady increase in the lawyer population.[10] It is apparent that the Ministry of Justice which controlled the entry of persons into the legal profession felt that increasing demand would justify the increase of lawyers, noticing that a large number of people without the professional license in fact provided legal services outside of litigation.[11] The growth of the Japanese economy, particularly after the First World War, and new settlement procedures such as conciliation increased demand for legal work outside of litigation (Hayashi, 2009, p. 642). The Ministry of Justice and some lawyers considered the possibility of establishing a new profession like solicitor, but outcries among lawyers against people without license prevailed.[12] The Attorneys Act (Act No.53 of 1933), which was amended in 1933, expanded the scope of lawyer's work from legal services concerning litigation

---

[7] Calculated from the table in Appendix G, Spaulding, 1967, p. 346.

[8] As we just saw, the bar examination was very competitive. It seemed that the new combined examination for judges, prosecutors and private attorneys was expected to be more difficult than the bar examination and, in 1922, just before the introduction of the combined examination, an unusually large number of applicants passed the bar examination. Hashimoto considered that the Ministry of Justice intentionally increased the number of bar exam passers to satisfy increasing legal needs during the period from 1913 to 1922.

[9] Each year 100 or so among the passers were appointed to be judges or prosecutors and the rest became private attorneys (Spaulding, 1967, pp. 347–348). Even though the new combined examination had started, a special bar examination was conducted, from 1923 to 1941, for people who had applied for the bar examination before 1923 in order to "rescue the applicants to the bar examination for lawyers" (Ohno, 1970, p. 92). This special examination might have been believed to be the cause for the increase in the number of lawyers. But the statistics show that the combined examination passers were more responsible for the increase (Spaulding, 1967, pp. 347–348).

[10] A lawyer complained that the lawyer population increased from 3300 in 1921 to 5900 in 1926, which he called about a 90 percent increase (in fact 79 percent) even though these were years of economic depression (Tasaka, 1929, p. 5). Members of the bar also demanded that the annual number of passers of the combined examination should be reduced and that more judges should be appointed so as to increase the number of litigation cases (Tasaka, 1929, p. 5; 1930, pp. -2–3).

[11] Lawyers estimated that there were 20,000 persons working without license in Tokyo and 50,000 nationwide (Tasaka, 1930, p. 47).

[12] Complaints of insufficient income or even impoverishment and blaming non-lawyers and the excessive number of lawyers appeared in journals (Tasaka, 1929, pp. 11–16), though some lawyers argued that the large number of non-lawyers working without license indicated that the lawyer population was not large enough (Masumoto, 1930, pp. 90–96).

to legal services in general. It prohibited lawyers from having more than one office. Additionally, in 1933, legislation entitled the Act to Supervise Dealing with Legal Practice (Act No.54 of 1933) excluded people without license from all law- related work.[13] In this way, Japanese lawyers achieved their professional project for the control of their "product", legal services (Abel 1988, p. 186). This also marked the establishment of "the small justice system"[14] which continued to exist throughout the twentieth century in Japan.

A substantially revised Attorneys Act (Act No.205 of 1949) was enacted pursuant to a proposal by Diet members with GHQ[15] support, in 1949. Article 72 of the Act prohibits non-attorneys from providing legal services. Lawyers who had vivid memories of the pre-war situation of "excessive lawyer population"(Tasaka 1929, 11) opposed increasing the number of lawyers, and any significant reform was not possible without the agreement of the so-called "three branches" of the legal profession: The Supreme Court (SC), for judges; the Ministry of Justice (MOJ), for prosecutors; and the JFBA, for lawyers. Thus, the Japanese bar succeeded in controlling

[13]As law-related work increased after WWI, lawyers who were members of the Imperial Diet worked to establish new occupations for law-related work by legislation: Judicial scrivener in 1919, patent lawyer in 1921 and public accountant in 1927. Each of these occupations could do only a narrowly defined area of work, while lawyers could do all areas of the work. Thus, lawyers were ranked at the top of the law-related professions (Hayashi, 2009, pp. 643–646).

[14]Sato Koji who would later become Chair of the JSRC characterized the traditional Japanese Justice system as 'small justice' which had remained from the pre-war period under the Meiji Constitution (Iimuro et al., 1999, p. 44). "Small justice" meant, above all, the small role of the court system in governing society. The Meiji state was a development-focused administrative state. Under the Meiji Constitution, constitutional rights could be and were circumscribed by statutes. The law was used as the instrument of governance to develop industry and keep public order. The state tried to constrain claims based on legal rights and to limit the scope of litigation by setting up conciliation procedures in civil justice conducted at the courts. The whole court system was a branch of the Ministry of Justice and the judicial power was represented by the Ministry of Justice, a Ministry of the Executive Power (Mitani, 2001, p. 48). As the prosecutors' political influence increased after 1905, judicial independence began to include prosecutors. The Penal Code (Act No.45 of 1907) gave wide discretion to indictment, sentencing and implementation of sentence, helping the judiciary to be politicized (Mitani, 2001, pp. 61–62). For the part of the court system that mostly dealt with 'ordinary people', reduction of the cost of legal services was sought. For instance, in 1913, the government expanded the subject matter jurisdiction of Summary Court and drastically reduced the number of the Summary Courts by abolishing more than 130 Summary Courts (about 40 percent of them) nationwide. This made access to the court more difficult for local people and intensified their dependence upon people without license (Hashimoto, 2005, pp. 244–245). 'Small justice' is the product of the confluence of interests among the three branches of the legal profession (judges, prosecutors, and attorneys), whose interests happened to overlap. The state wanted to minimize the cost of the courts and the lawyers wanted to control legal services and the number of lawyers who provided legal services. Official conciliation procedures and the Penal Code continued to exist after the second World War. On the development of conciliation in Japan, see Murayama, 2000, and on discretion in criminal justice in Japan, see, Murayama, 1992. The structure of criminal justice process in 1920 resembled that in 1985 with a wide exercise of discretion and a very high conviction rate (Murayama, 1998, pp. 30–35)

[15]General Headquarters of the Supreme Commander for the Allied Powers. The occupation of Japan by the Allied Powers continued until 1952.

the market by excluding non-lawyers and also by suppressing the number of bar examination passers.

The increase of the lawyer population in the twenty-first Century is, in a sense, remarkable, as it was started in the face of professional control of the legal market by lawyers, although the JFBA could not ignore the changing environment for their legal practice.[16] Yet, as was the case around 1930, the sharp increase of the lawyer population from 2007 incurred outcries against the "excessive increase in the number of lawyers". As has been the case ever since reform to the legal training system shortly after the second World War, bar exam passers must complete training at the Legal Training and Research Institute (LTRI) before working as legal professionals, but it was publicized on mass media that some graduates of the LTRI could not find jobs[17] and that lawyers began to engage in instances of malfeasance or other misdeeds because of excessive competition.[18] Local bar associations began to demand the decrease of bar exam passers[19] and, in 2011, the JFBA changed the policy from supporting the JSRC recommendation, to decreasing the number of bar exam passers, although the JFBA did not immediately specify the reduced number of bar exam passers. (JFBA, 2011a).[20]

Because of this backlash against the planned increase in bar exam passers, the number never reached the 3000 figure announced by the JSRC. Neither did it ever come back to the previous low number of 500, and the total number of lawyers has been growing steadily, if not so rapidly as planned.

[16] Under the mounting political pressures for deregulation, there was a long process toward the Justice System Reform (Murayama: 2020, pp. 751–757). There was an expression, "20 percent justice", which meant that the Japanese courts handled only 20 percent of all the legal problems that should have been dealt by the courts. The JFBA president from 1990 to 1992 criticized this small capacity of the judiciary and argued for increasing the number of bar exam passers (Iimuro et al., 1999, p. 47). He had become well known after representing consumers in a toxic powdered milk case and a fraudulent gold trade case. On the dark side of the small capacity of the judiciary, see, Milhaupt and West, 2000.

[17] Most LTRI graduates used to enter employment at law firms after completing the LTRI training. During this period, some graduates could not find employment at law firms, as we will see in Chap. 1. When the number of bar exam passers was restrained to 500, success in the bar examination almost guaranteed lifetime income. On the financial aspect of this situation, see Nakazato et al., 2006.

[18] The JFBA began to announce record high numbers of disciplinary dispositions against lawyers' misconduct. In 2007, the number of disciplinary dispositions increased to 70 cases for the first time and further increased to 98 in 2013 and 101 in 2014. A newspaper article wrote that the period of increase overlapped that of increasing number of bar exam passers, implying the causal relation between the two (Asahi, 2015).

[19] For instance, the Tokyo Bar Association sent its opinion on the Population Problem of Legal Professionals to the JFBA, arguing that the JSRC policy of increasing the number of bar exam passers to 3000 by 2010 was too hasty and that it would be appropriate to consider setting the number of passers within the range from 2100 to 2500 (Tokyo Bar Association, 2009).

[20] The following year the JFBA proposed reducing the number of bar exam passers to 1500 (JFBA, 2012a).

The increase of the lawyer population in the twenty-first century has already caused structural changes in the Japanese legal profession: stratification in terms of income and prestige and diversification of legal practice.

Business law firms handling international transactions and finance were small until the 1990s, but now five law firms, the so-called Big Five, have grown to have 500 to 600 lawyers each.[21] As of 2022, there were 11 law firms with more than 100 lawyers and the number of lawyers at those law firms comprised 9% of all the lawyers in Japan (JFBA 2022a, pp. 53–54). As this reflects, the large business law firms have become conspicuous.

The increase in the lawyer population also brought competition into legal practice not only for corporate clients but also for individual clients. In the past, Japanese lawyers did not like to take cases of clients without a personal introduction. According to a JFBA survey in 2000, the respondents had some kind of introduction or had prior consultation with the lawyer in 92% of cases (JFBA Bengoshi Gyomu Kaikaku Iinkai 2002a, p.77). But the practice of relying on personal introductions to obtain clients has been gradually changing in the case of individual clients. In the early 2000's law firms began to advertise their practice for consumer loan cases on TV, and since then law firms have begun actively to advertise on the Internet their practices handling divorce, traffic accidents, compensation for hepatitis B, and criminal defense as well as consumer loans. These advertisements clearly assume that general members of the public are consumers of the firms' legal services. The report of a JFBA survey conducted in 2010 indicated that the use of advertisements significantly increased the percentage of new clients without introduction (JFBA 2011b, p. 101).

As more people seek information on the Internet, an increasing number of lawyers have created home pages for their offices. In 2005, a lawyer who had worked at one of the Big Five law firms set up a venture business managing a portal site for potential clients to search for lawyers, Bengoshi Dot Com. The company grew rapidly, and was listed on the Tokyo Stock Exchange Mothers in 2014. It now boasts having over 20,000 lawyer members (Bengoshi Dot Com 2023). Bengoshi Dot Com not only provides information for member lawyers but also helps them create their own home pages on the Internet. Bengoshi Dot Com also created a free legal advice page, called "legal consultation for everybody", where any person can write in a legal question, to which any lawyer, as a volunteer, can give a legal answer free of charge. In this way, lawyers can make their name more visible among visitors to the website. Since Bengoshi Dot Com had to be careful not to violate the Attorneys Act, they provided their service on the website free of charge in the early years. Now they charge a membership fee for member lawyers (Motoe, Uesaka 2015, p. 1, pp. 76–77, pp. 101–105, p. 127).

As more people searched for information on lawyers on the Internet, lawyers began to advertise particular fields as their strength, virtually indicating it as a

[21] Initially there were four large firms, the so-called Big Four: Nishimura Asahi, Anderson Mori Tomotsune, Nagashima Ono Tunematsu, and Mori Hamada Matsumoto. TMI caught up them later, resulting in the current Big Five.

specialized field on their home pages.[22] It is now common that most lawyers mention particular fields of law as their frequent practice.

The public view of the role of lawyers is also changing. In the twentieth century, both lawyers and the general public viewed the role of a lawyer to be a litigator. People went to see a lawyer when they considered litigation.[23] That narrow view is gone. When people have some problem or dispute, they go to meet lawyers, not always thinking about suing others.

This book focuses on the structural changes of the Japanese legal profession and their consequences by relying on, mainly, our research data on careers of individual lawyers from 1950 to 2019.[24] We also rely on interview data with lawyers[25] as well as statistics compiled by the JFBA, SC and MOJ.

In Chap. 1, Stratification and Diversification in the Japanese legal profession, Masayuki Murayama looks at the changing landscape for private attorneys and their practice. The rapid increase of the lawyer population in the twenty-first century has had a significant impact on legal practice at law firms, and it has also allowed lawyers move to other sectors such as in-house positions and public offices. Among law firms, there appeared the Big Five firms for business clients and "mass process" law firms for individual clients. General practice has been getting more focused and traffic accidents and divorce matters have become the major sources of income for many lawyers. The budget for legal aid and public criminal defense was increased and came to represent a significant source of income for some young lawyers. Legal practice at law firms has changed from a profession largely aloof from common people to more general legal service providers. The increase in lawyer population also significantly increased the number of in-house lawyers. Along with the rise in business law firms, law departments of corporations have been expanding in the business law field. Lawyers from law firms also have begun to take leave from their firms to work at national ministries on fixed term appointments. Lawyers also have begun to work as part-time judges for civil and family cases on fixed term appointments.

The following chapters analyse select themes more intensively. Chapter 2, Number of Lawyers and Lawyer Career Mobility in Japan, looks at how professional mobility has changed. Shozo Ota analyses annual changes in individual lawyer's mobility since qualification as a legal professional, and also changes of

[22] Most lawyers do not use the term "specialized field", as the JFBA recommends against it. This is because there is no institutional guarantee on specialization.

[23] "Proposal to go out to activities out of court has been repeated since the Meiji period, yet lawyers of our country stayed in court-centered activities.... Even today, representation or defense at the court is at the center of activities in legal practice" (Kawabata, 1981, p. 14).

[24] For the survey and data, see Appendix A. The questionnaire is in Appendix B.

[25] Nineteen interviews were conducted during the period from June 2017 to August 2018. Two additional interviews were conducted in August 2023. Three interviews among the nineteen were conducted by Daniel H. Foote and Masayuki Murayama together, and one interview was conducted by Daisuke Mori. Others were conducted by Masayuki Murayama. Only the month and year are shown for each interview to avoid identification of an interviewee.

mobility for a 10-year term since qualification as a legal professional. These analyses indicate that the mobility among lawyers began to increase in the middle of the 1990s when the number of legal professionals registered at the JFBA exceeded 500 for the first time since 1974. This finding indicates that the current level of annual increase in the number of lawyers will maintain such mobility among lawyers in future.

Income is often the most important element for any occupation, and that is particularly the case with the legal profession, as high income often comes together with high social prestige. It was long believed that once having passed the bar exam, life-time good income was guaranteed. In Chap. 3, Work History Factors Affecting Lawyers' Incomes: Firm Size, Clientele, and Legal Apprenticeship Cohort, Isamu Sugino considers whether and to what extent such factors as sector of practice, clientele, office management style, law school graduation, gender, years of practice, etc. affected income, relying on multiple regression and longitudinal analyses. He finds the larger the firm size and the longer the years of service, the higher the income. But this is not the case with women lawyers. He also finds that recently qualified lawyers earn less than experienced lawyers.

Kyoko Ishida examines characteristics of women lawyers' careers in Chap. 4, Japanese Lawyers' Career Through the Lens of Gender. She finds that though income disparity between men and women lawyers has persisted, it is less in the younger generation. For women lawyers, their salaries reduced often between the first and second law firms. This was not the case for men lawyers. She does not find such a gender disparity among in-house lawyers, however. She predicts that, as work-life balance was chosen by many women for a reason for changing jobs, many women lawyers will move to in-house positions.

It has been often said that graduation from a best law school opens a way to a job at a top law firm. Daisuke Mori tests whether this prediction is a valid one in Chap. 5, The Relationship between Education Institutions and Legal Careers. He compares the periods before and after the establishment of the law school system. He finds that, regarding the number of lawyers at their first law firm, both within-school and between-school inequalities widened after the establishment of the law school system. Moreover, between-school inequalities considerably widened between the first 5 years and the second 5 years in the period after the establishment of the law school system.

In the concluding chapter, From Professionalism to Consumerism, we summarize our findings and see how the latest backlash has affected the JSR. Competition and stratification that the JSR brought about undoubtedly triggered the backlash. However, despite the negative campaigns, the public image of lawyers has improved, and people now look for lawyers as legal service providers for all. Although lawyers are deeply divided with their different occupational interests anchoring in different groups of clients, it is probable that the JFBA will still be able to influence the number of lawyers in the future.

Tokyo, Japan Masayuki Murayama

References

Abel R (1988) United States: The Contradictions of Professionalism. In Abel R, Lewis P, eds., Lawyers in Society: The Common Law World, University of California Press, Berkeley, Los Angeles, London.

Asahi (Asahi Shinbun) (Asahi News) (2015) Bengoshi Chokai Saita 101ken Azukarikin Ryuyo Medatsu Sakunen (Record High 101 Lawyers Disciplined Chiefly for Misappropriation of client funds in 2014), February 21, morning ed., 37.

Bengoshi Dot Com (2023) https://www.bengo4.com/lawyer/service_plan/?utm_source=google&utm_medium=cpc&utm_campaign=brand&gad=1&gclid=Cj0KCQjwvL-oBhCxARIsAHkOiu2yoeoDsZFqd-HANNI1JZ1gepQtxzvQ305pyCQ3sbMMlx1zCig-2yMaAvU5EALw_wcB. Retrieved September 23, 2023.

Hahimoto S (2005) Zaiya "Hoso" to Chiiki Shakai (How Working "Legal Professionals" Interact with Their Communities), Horitsubunkasha, Kyoto.

Hayashi M (2009) Nihon ni okeru Hoh Senmonshoku no Kakuritsu—Shokuiki no Keisei to sono Dokusen (Establishment of the Legal Profession in Japan: Formation of Professional Work and Its Monopolization) , Suzuki H, Takatani C, Hayashi M, Yashiki J, eds., Hoh no Ryuhtsuh (Circulation of Law), Jigakusha, Tokyo, pp 639-665.

Iimuro K, Nakabo K, Yasuoka O, Sato K, Horino O, 21 Seiki no Shiho wo Kataru, Jiyu to Seigi 50(1): 42-69.

JFBA (Japan Federation of Bar Associations) (Nihon Bengoshi Rengokai) (2011a) Urgent Recommendations on Policies for the Number of Legal Professionals, March 27. https://www.nichibenren.or.jp/en/document/opinionpapers/220317.html. Retrieved September 16, 2023.

------ (2011b) Bengoshi Gyomu no Keizaiteki Kiban ni kansuru Jittai Chosa Hokokusho (Survey Report on the Economic Basis of Legal Practice), Jiyu to Seigi, 62 (6).

------ (2012a) Hohsoh Jinkoh Seisaku ni kansuru Teigen (Proposal Concerning Policy on Numbers of Legal Professionals)," March 15, 2012. https://www.nichibenren.or.jp/library/ja/opinion/report/data/2012/opinion_120315.pdf. Retrieved August 29, 2023.

------ (2022a) Bengoshi Hakusho (White Paper on Attorneys), Nihonbengoshirengokai, Tokyo

JFBA Bengoshi Gyomu Kaikaku Iinkai (JFBA Committee for Reforming Lawyers' Practice) (2002a) Nihon no Horitsu Jimusho 2000—Bengoshi Gyomu no Keizaiteki Kiban ni kansuru Jittai Chosa Hokokusho (Law Firms in Japan in 2000: Survey Report on the Economic Basis of Legal Practice), Jiyu to Seigi, 53 (13).

Kawabata, K. (1981) Shokugyo tosite mita Bengoshigyo—Bengoshi Service no Juyo to Kyokyu no Doko (Lawyering Seen as an Occupation: Changes in Need and Provision of Legal Services), Horitsu Jiho 53 (2): 13–22.

Larson, M. (1977) The Rise of Professionlism: A Sociological Analysis, University of California Press, Berkeley, Los Angeles, London.
Masumoto, S. (1930) "Bengoshi ha hatashite kajoka? (Are There Really Too Many Lawyers?), "Hohsoh Kohron, 34 (2): 90–96.
Milhaupt C, West M (2000) The Dark Side of Private Ordering: An Institutional and Empirical Analysis of Organized Crime, The University of Chicago Law Review, 67: 41-98.
Misaka Y (2017) Kindai Nihon ni okeru "Zendan no Shiho" to sono Ninaite—1880 Nendai Shigaken Hikone Chiiki no Minji Hanketsu Genpon ni arawareta Daigennin to Dainin wo Sozai to shite ("Prior Stage for Justice" and People Who Worked There in Modern Japan: Based on Advocates and Proxies Who Appeared in Civil Judgment in the Hikone District of Shiga Prefecture in the 1880s). In Nakamura K, Kiriyama T, Yamamoto K, eds., Shakai Henkaku to Shakai Kagaku—Jidai to Taiji suru Shiso to Jissen (Social Transformation and Social Science: Thought and Practice Confronting the Times in Which We Live), Showado, Kyoto.
Mitani T (2001) Seiji Seido toshiteno Baishinsei: Kindai Nihon no Shihoken to Seiji (Jury System as a Political Institution: Judicial Power and Politics in Modern Japan), The University of Tokyo Press, Tokyo.
Motoe T, Uesaka T (2015) Bengoshi Dotto Komu: Komatteiru Hito wo Sukuu Bokutachi no Chosen (Bengoshi Dot Com: Our Challenge to Save People in Trouble), Nikkei BP, Tokyo.
Murayama M (1992) Postwar Trends in the Administration of Japanese Criminal Justice: Lenient but Intolerant or Something Else? J Japan-Netherlands Institute, 4: 221–246.
------ (1998) Nihongata Keiji Shiho Katei no Tokucho (Characteristics of Japanese Criminal Justice Proceedure). In Shibahara K, Nishida N, Inoue M (eds), Matsuo Koya Sensei Kokishukuga Ronbunshu (Festschrift for 70th Birthday of Professor Koya Matsuo), Gekan (Vol. 2), Yuhikaku, Tokyo, pp. 25–46.
------ (2010) The Origins and Development of Family Conciliation in Japan: A Political Aspect, Journal of Social Welfare & Family Law, 32 (2): 143–153.
------ (2020) Japan: Toward Stratification, Diversification and Specialization. In Abel R, Hammerslev O, Sommerlad H, Schultz U, Lawyers in 21st-Century Societies, Volume 1: National Reports, Hart Publishing, Oxford, New York, pp. 753–774.
Nakazato M, Ramseyer J, Rasmusen E (2006) The Industrial Organization of the Japanese Bar: Levels and Determinants of Attorney Incomes, Discussion Paper No. 559, Harvard Law School.
Ohno M (1970) Shokugyo Shi toshiteno Bengoshi oyobi Bengosikai no Rekishi (History of Lawyers and Bar Associations as an Occupational History). In Ohno M, ed., Gendai no Bengoshi (The Contemporary Lawyer). Vol. 2: Bengoshi no Dantai (Associations of Lawyers), Nihon Hyoronsha, Tokyo, pp. 1–116.
Spaulding, R (1967) Imperial Japan's Higher Civil Service Examinations, Princeton University Press, Princeton.

Tasaka S (1929-30) Shakai Mondai to shiteno Bengosshi no Seikatu oyobi sono Taisaku (Life of Lawyers as a Social Problem and Countermeasures for Same), Hohsoh Kohron, 33 (10): 2–18; 33 (11): 2–16.
Tokyo Bar Association (2009) Hoso Jinko Mondai ni kansuru Ikensho (Opinion on the Problem of the Population of Legal Professionals). https://www.toben.or.jp/message/libra/pdf/2009_03/p54-58.pdf. Retrieved August 15, 2023.

Statutes

Bengoshi Ho (Attorneys Act) (Act No.7 of 1893; Revised, Act No.53 of 1933; Revised, Act No.205 of 1949)
Dai-nin Kisoku (Rules of Proxy) (Dajokan Ordinance No.215 of 1873)
Horitsu Jimu Toriatsukai no Torishimari ni kansuru Horitsu (Act to Supervise Dealing with Legal Practice) (Act No.54 of 1933)
Minji Sosho Ho (Code of Civil Procedure) (Act No.29 of 1890)

Contents

Contributors

Mori Daisuke Kumamoto University Faculty of Law, Kumamoto, Japan

Sugino Isamu Ochanimizu University, Tokyo, Japan

Ishida Kyoko Waseda Law School, Tokyo, Japan

Murayama Masayuki Institute of Law and Social Sciences, Organization for the Strategic Coordination of Research and Intellectual Properties, Meiji University, Tokyo, Japan

Ota Shozo Meiji University School of Law, Tokyo, Japan

Abbreviations

ANOM	Analysis of means
Asahi	Asahi Newspaper
DPJ	Democratic Party of Japan
JFBA	Japanese Federation of Bar Associations
JILA	Japan In-House Lawyers Association
JLSC	Japan Legal Support Center
JSR	Justice System Reform
JSRC	Justice System Reform Council
LAC	Legal Access Center, JFBA
LDP	Liberal Democratic Party
LLA	Legal Aid Association—Japan
LOESS	locally estimated scatterplot smoothing
LTRI	Legal Training and Research Institute
MEXT	Ministry of Education, Culture, Sports, Science and Technology
MHLW	Ministry of Health, Labour and Welfare
MOJ	Ministry of Justice
Nikkei	Nihon Keizai Shinbun [Japan Economic Newspaper]
SICJS	Special Investigation Commission on Justice System
SC	Supreme Court
Yomiuri	Yomiuri Newspaper

Chapter 1
Stratification and Diversification in the Legal Profession

Masayuki Murayama

Abstract Justice System Reform has increased the number of lawyers significantly. Although the Justice System Reform Council's recommendations were not fully realized, the increase of the lawyer population brought stratification of law firms and diversification of legal practice. The Big Five firms emerged as the largest business law firms attracting best Legal Training and Research Institute graduates. For individual clients, mass process law firms began to advertise on TV and the Internet. Traffic accidents and family matters appeared as the major focused fields. The division of legal practice for individuals and for corporations is becoming clear but many law firms do both types of work. The majority of firms other than solo practitioners have cost sharing arrangements. Income differences are large among lawyers. Lawyers began to advertise their services as a method of obtaining new clients, changing themselves from "profession" to "legal service business". The number of in-house lawyers has increased in this century. Most in-house lawyers are now assigned to law departments. The growth of business law firms and that of law departments went side by side and expanded the business law field. New temporal career paths emerged between law firms and national ministries.

1.1 Production of Lawyers

1.1.1 Tight Control Over Numbers of Lawyers

The post-World War II Japanese legal profession was established in 1949, by the Attorneys Act. To become legal professionals, people must pass the bar examination administered by the Ministry of Justice, and bar examination passers must take legal training at the Legal Training and Research Institute (LTRI) administered by the

M. Murayama (✉)
Organization for the Strategic Coordination of Research and Intellectual Properties, Institute of Law and Social Sciences, Meiji University, Tokyo, Japan

M. Murayama (ed.), *The Japanese Legal Profession in Transition*, Economics, Law, and Institutions in Asia Pacific,
https://doi.org/10.1007/978-981-97-2692-9_1

Supreme Court (SC).[1] Lawyers are required to register at the Japan Federation of Bar Associations (JFBA) and a local bar association where they practice.[2] Both the JFBA and local bar associations are given autonomy to establish lawyers' ethics and discipline their members. Private attorneys are legally equal to judges and prosecutors and receive the same legal training at the LTRI.

Under the pre-war recruitment and training system of private attorneys from 1933, those who aspired to become private attorneys had to take training at law firms without pay for 2 years. Those who were recruited by the Ministry of Justice (MOJ) as judges and prosecutors could get paid during their training period for 1 year and 6 months.[3] Under the post-war training system, all the bar examination passers were treated equally and paid the first-year salary of the national career track public employees. They were also paid allowances for commuting, housing and family support. In this way, all future legal professionals' life was financially stable once they passed the bar examination. A survey result indicated that the financial situation of private attorneys was not bad in the late 1950s.[4]

This shared experience among the legal professionals at the LTRI had significant impact upon the subsequent relationship among the judicial three, but it would be felt much later.[5] In the post-war period from the 1950s to the 1960s, the majority of

[1] Initially the training period was 2 years. But when the number of bar examination passers rose to more than 900 in 1999, the training period was shortened to 18 months. From 2006 to 2011, it was further shortened to 16 months. When law school graduates began to take the new bar exam and the number of bar exam passers further increased in 2006, the training period became just 1 year.

[2] There are three local bar associations in Tokyo, though the geographical jurisdiction is the same. When the lawyer population increased from 2957 in 1919 to 5266 in 1923, there appeared a structural division between senior lawyers and junior lawyers. Some of the former were Imperial Diet members and established themselves as social elites. The division originated from their educational backgrounds, English law taught at imperial universities and French law taught at private universities. Senior lawyers established Daiichi Tokyo Bar Association, divided from Tokyo Bar Association, in 1923. Lawyers dissatisfied with the two bar associations established the third, Daini Tokyo Bar Association in 1926. The National Bar Association, a lawyers' voluntary nationwide association, was also divided and senior lawyers established the Imperial Bar Association in 1925 (Ohno 1970, pp. 67–75). After the Second World War, the JFBA was established as the only national bar association, while the three Tokyo bar associations continued to exist side by side.

[3] In 1939 the Judicial Research Institute of the Ministry of Justice was established to train future judges and prosecutors, as both the courts and the public prosecutors belonged to MOJ before WWII. This institute became the LTRI of the SC in 1947.

[4] According to a survey of lawyers without date but presumed to be conducted in1960, the average monthly income of lawyers was 98,939 Yen. Lawyers in their 1950s earned 117,542 Yen, and those in their 1920s 40,454 Yen (Shimizu 1960, p. 759). Among the Japanese people, declared annual tax return was on average 49,167 Yen per month and an employee's monthly income was 21,667 Yen according to National Tax Agency (Kokuzeicho 2021).

[5] As all the bar exam passers were treated equally, the LTRI program helped to cultivate the sense of unity as the legal profession rather than the division between private attorneys on one hand and judges and public prosecutors on the other. It is not an accident that Justice System Reform could not begin in the 1960s but it could in the 1990s.

private attorneys were those who had practiced in pre-war Japan.[6] They brought the pre-war self-definition of themselves as "lawyers in the field" in opposition to "lawyers in the government" (Shimizu 1960, p. 757). They also had vivid memories of "excessive number of lawyers" in the 1920s and 1930s. It was difficult for "the three branches of the legal profession" to agree on an increase of the lawyer population.

In the early 1960s, the SC found it difficult to recruit a sufficient number of young judges, and the Provisional Justice System Investigation Council was established by law (Act No. 122 of 1962) to make recommendations on increasing the number of legal professionals and the remuneration of judges and public prosecutors. The Council recommended to increase the number of legal professionals, while focusing on preventing the diminishment of the quality of legal professionals. It pointed out that the lawyer population was too small in Japan: just 10 lawyers per 100,000 persons, while for each 100,00 people there were 162 lawyers in the U.S., 62 in West Germany, 46 in England and 26 in France, respectively (Rinji Shiho Seido Chosakai 1964).

This proposal by the Council was rejected by the JFBA, as the Council did not adopt judicial appointment from among private attorneys just like the Anglo-American system (JFBA 1967), one of the major demands of the JFBA since the pre-war period (Ono 1970, pp. 88–91). During the 1960s, the number of bar examination passers increased from 350 to 500, but, since then and up until 1990, it remained at the level of 500.[7]

Because the supply of legal professionals was tightly controlled, the bar examination was "notoriously competitive" (Rokumoto 1988, p. 165). The pass rate of the bar examination was 10.3% in 1949, but soon went down to 4% in the period from 1954 to 1964, and further down to 1.8% in 1979. Although the number gradually increased in the 1990s, the pass rate stayed around 3% until 2000. As a result, as Table 1.2 shows, the number of private attorneys increased only between 200 to 300 every year until the middle of 1990s.

1.1.2 Justice System Reform: A New Training System Designed to Drastically Increase the Number of Lawyers

Political and economic trends toward deregulation prompted the establishment of the Justice System Reform Council (JSRC) in 1999. It issued its final report in 2001 (Murayama, 2020, pp. 755–757). The JSRC declared "Justice system reform should be positioned as the 'final linchpin' of a series of various reforms concerning

[6] The number of lawyers who had graduated from the LTRI became more than a half of those registered at the JFBA in 1970. Calculated from the data in JFBA (2022a), p. 24; (2010), p. 27.

[7] Foote argued that the backlash against the JSRC proposal to increase the lawyer population was a repetition of this 1960s incident. In both cases 'excessive competition' and 'lowering the quality of the legal profession' were key words in the argument against the population increase (Foote 2019, pp. 153–174).

Table 1.1 Population per private attorney in five countries (1990–2020)

Country	Year			
	1990	2000	2010	2020
Japan	8696	7155	4423	3000
France	3161	1897	1235	934
Germany	1132	788	535	501
England and Wales	857	612	442	369
United States	366	295	279	249

Source: For 1990 and 2000, JFBA (2012), p. 81. For 2010, JFBA (2010), p. 82. For 2020, calculated from the number of lawyers of the five countries in JFBA (2022), p. 48, and the population data of the five countries from Kokuritu Shakai Hosho Jinkoh Mondai Kenkyujo 2020, Table 2–16

restructuring 'the shape of our country'",[8] in order "to transform the spirit of the law and the rule of law into the 'flesh and blood' of Japan" (JSRC 2001, Chap. 1). The JSRC considered that the current legal profession "can hardly be regarded as being capable of sufficiently responding to the legal demands of the society in any respect" and recommended to secure 3000 successful applicants for a new national bar examination per year by about 2010 (JSRC 2001, Chap. 1) so that the number of legal professionals was expected to reach 50,000 by 2018 (JSRC 2001, Chap. 3). The Council planned to increase the Japanese lawyer population to the level equivalent to the French lawyer population, though it was never realized as is shown in Table 1.1.

Although the JSRC specified the increased number of new entrants to the legal profession, it did so intending to deliberately increase the number of legal professionals, and made it clear that continuing to allow the three branches of the legal profession to decide the number of bar examination passers was "already a relic of the past" and that the number of legal professionals was "to be decided by the market principle, which is based on social demands" (JSRC 2001, Chap. 3).

In order to increase the number of bar examination passers drastically, the JSRC recommended the establishment in 2004 of new law schools at the graduate level. These professional law schools would offer a two year program for law faculty graduates and a three year program for those who had not studied law at an undergraduate level.[9] Only graduates of the new law schools were qualified to take the bar examination until 2012, when passers of the preliminary bar examination (discussed in Sect. 1.1.3) began to take the bar examination. The JSRC envisaged that the pass rate of the new bar examination would be 70–80% of the law school graduates, who would then take legal training at the LTRI for a year.[10]

[8] The JSRC wanted not only to strengthen the judiciary but also to reduce prior administrative regulations, including regulations to constrain lawyers from taking positions in public office and in business (JSRC 2001, Chap. 3, Section 3 (2)).

[9] The 3 year program was considered important as legal professionals should be recruited from people with various backgrounds other than law.

[10] One year was considered enough, as the new law school and the LTRI were expected to share legal professional training. One of the official reasons against an increase of bar examination passers had been the limited capacity of the LTRI. As the number of bar examination passers increased gradually, the training period at the LTRI began to be shortened. See also footnote 1.

In fact, as too many new law schools were allowed to be established by Ministry of Education, Culture, Sports, Science and Technology (MEXT), the pass rate of the new bar examination was 48.3%, in 2006, much lower than what the JSRC expected, although it is significantly higher than the pass rate of the old bar examination. Yet the number of bar examination passers began to increase to 2099 persons, more than 2000 for the first time, in 2007, the second year of the new bar examination. This was exactly what the JSRC had recommended: 2000 passers of the bar examination in 2007. However, as the number of applicants increased, the pass rate went down to 40.2%. This low pass rate began to be picked up as the evidence of poor education at the new law schools. An article of a major national newspaper argued that even though the number of the bar examination passers had not become 3000, there was a lowering of quality evident in the recent passers, stating that some could not find employment, and thus practicing without pay. The article questioned whether 3000 passers would be justified in this context (Nikkei 2007, p. 19).

It was pointed out that fear of excessive competition and a belief in the lowering of the quality of legal professionals justified the restrictive policy of the bar examination in the eyes of lawyers (Foote 2019, p. 153). What we observed in the mass media's criticism of the increase of legal professionals reflected this fear and belief.[11] Despite this fear and belief, the number of bar examination passers further increased to 2209 persons in 2008 and remained at the level of 2000 persons until 2013.

When the JSRC recommendations were announced, the JFBA agreed with the JSRC's policy to increase the number of legal professionals, changing "small justice to large justice" (JFBA 2001), and, in 2005, JFBA adopted the declaration to implement the Justice System Reform at the general meeting (JFBA 2005). Though oppositions to the increase of bar exam passers were rising, the JBFA did not immediately change its policy to support the Justice System Reform. In 2009, the JFBA proposed to reconsider the appropriate number of legal professionals. Then, in 2012, the JFBA proposed to decrease the number of bar exam passers to 1500 (JFBA 2012). Therefore, despite the JSRC's recommendation, which the JFBA had endorsed, the number of bar examination passers has never reached 3000. From 2014, the number began to decrease gradually to 1403 persons in 2022.

Table 1.2 shows the recent decline of annual increase of private attorneys. Yet the total number of private attorneys who registered under the new exam and training system was 21,596 persons, 49.0% of all the registered private attorneys.[12] Since 2006, the lawyer population became almost two times larger in 16 years. This increase triggered competition in legal practice both for corporate clients and individual clients. Business law firms became larger, making the stratification of law firms visible, while law firms for individual clients began to advertise for nationwide networks of branch offices.

[11] As we will see later, the increase in competition has been real, though the diminution in the quality of legal professionals has been debatable. On the latter, see, "Hoso no Shitsu" Kenkyukai (Research Group on the Quality of Legal Professionals) 2008.

[12] One thousand ninety-two persons passed the old bar examination during the transitional period from 2006 to 2010. If they are included, the percentage is 50.1% of all the lawyers.

Table 1.2 Annual number of Private Attorneys and bar examination passers[a] (1950–2022)

Year	Number	Old bar exam passers	Annual increase	Year	Number	Old bar exam passers	New bar exam passers	Through preliminary bar examination (included in the passers)	Annual increase
1950	5827	269	0	1987	13,074	489	–	–	244
1951	5804	272	−23	1988	13,288	512	–	–	214
1952	5822	253	18	1989	13,541	506	–	–	253
1953	5836	224	14	1990	13,800	499	–	–	259
1954	5837	250	1	1991	14,080	605	–	–	280
1955	5899	264	62	1992	14,329	630	–	–	249
1956	5967	297	68	1993	14,596	712	–	–	267
1957	6009	286	42	1994	14,809	740	–	–	213
1958	6100	346	91	1995	15,108	738	–	–	299
1959	6217	319	117	1996	15,456	734	–	–	348
1960	6321	345	104	1997	15,866	746	–	–	410
1961	6439	380	118	1998	16,305	812	–	–	439
1962	6604	459	165	1999	16,731	1000	–	–	426
1963	6732	496	128	2000	17,126	994	–	–	395
1964	6849	508	117	2001	18,243	990	–	–	1117
1965	7082	526	233	2002	18,838	1183	–	–	595
1966	7343	554	261	2003	19,508	1170	–	–	670
1967	7645	537	302	2004	20,224	1483	–	–	716
1968	7918	525	273	2005	21,185	1464	–	–	961
1969	8198	501	280	2006	22,021	549	1009	–	836
1970	8478	507	280	2007	23,119	248	1851	–	1098
1971	8797	533	319	2008	25,041	144	2065	–	1922
1972	9106	537	309	2009	26,930	92	2043	–	1889
1973	9541	537	435	2010	28,789	59	2074	–	1859
1974	9830	491	289	2011	30,485	–	2063	–	1696
1975	10,115	472	285	2012	32,088	–	2102	(58)	1603
1976	10,421	465	306	2013	33,624	–	2049	(120)	1536
1977	10,689	465	268	2014	35,045	–	1810	(163)	1421
1978	10,977	485	288	2015	36,415	–	1850	(186)	1370
1979	11,206	503	229	2016	37,680	–	1583	(235)	1265
1980	11,441	486	235	2017	38,980	–	1543	(290)	1300
1981	11,624	446	183	2018	40,066	–	1525	(336)	1086
1982	11,888	457	264	2019	41,118	–	1502	(315)	1052
1983	12,132	448	244	2020	42,164	–	1450	(378)	1046
1984	12,377	453	245	2021	43,206	–	1421	(374)	1042
1985	12,604	486	227	2022	44,101	–	1403	(395)	895
1986	12,830	486	226						

Source: JFBA (2022), p. 24; JFBA (2021a, b), p. 56; MOJ (2010)

[a] Passers of the bar examination become legal professionals after training at the LTRI

1.1.3 *Preliminary Bar Examination: Creating New Elites Among Legal Professionals*

The JSRC recommended offering an option to take the new bar examination for those who could not afford tuition for learning at a new law school, or who had years of life experience. For this purpose, the preliminary bar examination was created in 2011. There is no requirement to take the preliminary bar examination, which tests whether applicants have academic knowledge, are capable of using that knowledge and have basic professional qualification concerning the law, equivalent to law school graduates. If successful, passers of the preliminary bar examination can take the bar examination the following year.

The preliminary bar examination provides a way to bypass the ordinary course of attending a law school and, in so doing, it could make law school education redundant. The old bar examination did not require any prior legal education. Just like the old bar examination, if successful in the preliminary bar examination, training at the LTRI might be the only occasion for bar exam passers to engage in formal legal education. The JSRC envisioned a process of professional training of 2–3 years at a new law school and 1 year at the LTRI. But the preliminary bar examination could make training at the LTRI the only occasion for bar examination passers to receive a formal legal education. This virtually goes back to the old bar examination scheme.

What has made the preliminary bar examination stand out is the contrast between the very low pass rate of the preliminary bar examination and the very high pass rate of the bar examination among those who had passed the preliminary bar examination. The preliminary bar examination is extremely competitive. When it began in 2011, the pass rate was only 1.8% (MOJ 2011). It is increasing, yet still very competitive, 4.0% in 2021 and 3.6% in 2022 (MOJ 2021, 2022a). Those passers could take the bar exam next year. The pass rate of the bar examination for those passers of the preliminary bar examination was very high, 97.5% in 2022 and 92.6% in 2023 (MOJ 2022b, 2023).

Undergraduate law students and law school students alike have been increasingly taking the preliminary bar examination, taking advantage of its lack of prerequisites. In the first year of the preliminary bar examination, 2011, undergraduate and graduate students represented 22.1% of the applicants and 41.4% of those who passed. In 2022, the percentage of undergraduate and graduate student applicants was 37.5% and 67.8% of those who passed. In contract, in 2011 the percentage of applicants with only high school education or who otherwise had no formal education in law was only 2.5% and of these, none passed the exam. In 2022, the former was 3.6% and the latter 0.8%. The preliminary bar examination has become a super-express way to enter the LTRI among undergraduate students. Passing the preliminary bar examination has become a symbol of superiority for successful undergraduate students and provides opportunities for getting employed by the Big Five firms or the court. As the number of the preliminary bar examination passers has been gradually increasing from 116 in 2011 to 472 in 2022, the number of bar exam passers through the preliminary bar exam has been the increasing trend (Table 1.2). If the number of the bar exam passers decreases further, or that of preliminary bar exam passers increases, the preliminary bar examination will become a clear alternative to attending a law school for undergraduate students.

1.1.4 Experience of Studying Abroad

Studying abroad could provide opportunities to find particular jobs as it could provide the lawyer with extra skills, e.g. fluency in another language, or work in cross-border matters. Among the lawyers in our data, 7.1% studied abroad. But of that 7.1%, 7% of them studied abroad *before* obtaining the qualification of a legal professional. All of them studied in the U.S. when they were juveniles. Such study thus does not seem to confer any particular advantage in passing the bar exam

93% of those who studied abroad did so after having become legal professionals. Most of them studied abroad as private attorneys (94.5%), a few judges (1.1%), public prosecutors (2.2%), and in other capacities (2.2%). The overwhelming majority studied in the U.S. (76.7%), but others studied in U.K. (11.1%) or other countries (12.2%). All these legal professionals were selected for the opportunity to study abroad, based on their professional performance.

Japanese lawyers are concerned about the internationalization of legal practice, feeling it necessary to increase the capacity to deal with cross-border cases. The fact that only 7% of the legal professionals studied abroad and that most of them studied abroad after getting qualified as legal professionals, seem to support this concern. Lawyers who studied abroad can use English for communication, but the number of those lawyers is limited. Under the current school curriculum, young people are not expected to use English fluently.[13]

1.1.5 Gender Disparity

The effects of gender on lawyers' careers are discussed in detail in Chap. 3 and, in particular, in Chap. 4. As is shown by Ishida in Chap. 4, the participation of women in the legal profession began late and expanded very slowly. Three women were qualified as lawyers in 1940 for the first time and the number increased to 42 in 1960, 0.7% of lawyers. The percentage of women lawyers finally reached to 10% in 2001, yet it has not reached 20% in 2022 (JFBA 2022a, b, c, p. 24).

When we look at the percentage of women legal professionals, the disparity is just a little better. The percentage of women LTRI graduates was 12.9% in 1990,

[13] Lawyers in the corporate business law field all agreed that competence in English was the largest challenge for Japanese lawyers in business law fields (Foote 2021, pp. 131–138).

27.2% in 2000, 26.3% in 2010 and 25.5% in 2022. It was highest, 27.7%, in 2011 (JFBA 2022a, b, c, p. 44), but it has not shown a steady growth since then.

Among the three branches of legal professionals, the percentage of women is highest among judges, 28.2%, followed by public prosecutors, 26.4%, and lawyers, 19.6% in 2022 (JFBA 2022a, b, c, p. 44).[14,15]Law firms do not always seem to provide favorable work environments for women lawyers. As is discussed in Chap. 4, if more women lawyers move to in-house positions, the percentage of women lawyers could increase in future.

However, it is to be noted that the rather low percentage of women among the legal professionals is not peculiar to the profession. According to the statistics provided by the Ministry of Health, Labour and Welfare (MHLW), the percentage of women was 47.1% of all employees in 2021. But more than half of the women employees were not full-time employees. The percentage of full-time women employees was 25.1% of all the employees in Japan in 2021.[16] The percentage of women legal professionals is similar to that of full-time women employees. This indicates that legal professional work is not particularly avoided or preferred by women and that the low percentage of women legal professionals rather reflect the low percentage of women's full participation in the labor market.

1.2 Composition of Practice Sectors, Move of a Workplace, Reason for Move

Most Japanese legal professionals had three main initial career choices: private attorneys, judges and prosecutors. Although corporate business law firms began to expand in the latter half of the 1990s, the career choices and future prospects were still overwhelmingly what they used to be. Though the number of bar exam passers increased from 500 to700 in the late 1990s, career choices seemed to reflect the traditional way. During the 1990s, on average, 611 persons became legal professionals after graduation from the LTRI each year. Among them, 93 were appointed to as judges, 62 as prosecutors while 448 became private attorneys and 8 found their

[14]The fact that more women legal professionals are found among judges and public prosecutors might look similar to the situation of France and some other countries and the reason might be also similar: more amenable to work-life balance. However, Japanese judges and public prosecutors move from one jurisdiction to another along the course of promotion. This practice could deter married legal professionals from becoming judges or public prosecutors and could impose more difficulties on women than men, as women are often considered to be second earners.

[15]On the present SC, there are three women justices among fifteen. Including all the retired justices, women are only 9 among 188 (4.8%). No woman has been the chief justice of the SC or the Attorney General, but a woman lawyer was just elected to be the president of the JFBA from April, 2024.

[16]The percentages are calculated from the data of the MHLW (MHLW 2021, p. 17).

positions outside of the judicial world, in public offices or academia.[17] Since the Meiji period, judges and prosecutors, after quitting or retiring from their official positions, became private attorneys. In the last century, the direction of their career move was almost always one-way, from a judge or a prosecutor to a private attorney.

Although Japanese lawyers wanted to adopt the Anglo-American system of appointing judges from among private attorneys, the SC never agreed with such an appointment system. Yet in the 1990s, the courts began to appoint a few lawyers to permanent judicial positions and in the period 1992 to 2022, 127 private attorneys have been appointed to judge's positions. In 2004 the courts also began to appoint private attorneys to part-time judicial positions dealing with civil and family cases, including conciliation, totaling 583 in 2022 (JFBA 2022a, pp. 138–139).[18]

The traditional overall picture of legal professionals and in particular private attorneys changed in the twenty-first century. Based on the JSRC recommendation to liberalize legal practice, the Attorneys Act was changed in 2003 to allow private attorneys to work in public offices or in private companies without the permission of their bar associations. These changes enlarged opportunities for lawyers to find their jobs outside of law firms. Part-time judicial appointments of lawyers were also facilitated by this deregulation.

It was during the 1990s that private attorneys began to work as in-house lawyers in business corporations. Such employment started at a large U.S. company in Japan. In 2001 there were 66 in-house lawyers at 39 companies. But there were only eight companies where more than one lawyer worked. Those companies were mostly U.S. companies in the financing or IT industries. Among these eight companies, there was only one Japanese company. After the amendment of the Attorneys Act in 2003, the number of in-house lawyers grew rapidly to 3184 lawyers at 1429 companies in 2023. Among the top ten companies, seven companies were Japanese (JILA 2023b).

In 2022, 92% of 44,101 lawyers practice at law firms while 7% of lawyers work in-house, 1% in public office and just 0.3% teach as specially appointed law professors.[19]

Table 1.3 shows how registered lawyers have moved since they became legal professionals following their graduation from the LTRI. The table shows only movement between sectors. When lawyers changed their workplace within the same sector, the change is not shown in the table except movements only between law firms.

---

[17] Calculated from the data of the JFBA (2022a, p. 44).

[18] Part-time judge positions are not considered as a path to judgeship, but rather as opportunities to experience the work of judges. A similar system for judges and prosecutors to experience the work of private attorneys began in 2007 and 286 judges and prosecutors worked as private attorneys by 2022 (JFBA 2022a, p. 139).

[19] Calculated from the data from the JFBA (2022a), pp. 24, 126, 133, 136.

Table 1.3 Movements of lawyers (1950 ~ 2017)[a] between sectors (Career Survey 2018–2019)

Movement among sectors[b]	Percent	No. of respondents
Law firm Never moved 39.6% Once moved 30.1% Twice moved 9.8% Three times or more 4.1%	83.6%	1194
Law firm→In-house	3.9%	55
Law firm→Public office	0.5%	7
Law firm→Other	0.2%	3
Law firm→In-house→Law firm	0.6%	8
Law firm→Public office→Law firm	1.3%	19
Law firm→Public office→In-house	0.3%	4
Law firm→Other→Law firm	0.4%	5
Law firm→Public office→Other→Law firm	0.1%	2
Law firm→Public office→Law firm→Public office	0.1%	1
In-house	3.2%	45
In-house→Law firm	0.9%	13
In-house→Law firm→In-house	0.1%	1
Public office	0.1%	1
Public office→Law firm	4.3%	62
Public office→In-house	0.1%	1
Public office→Other→Law firm	0.3%	4
Public office→Law firm→In-house	0.1%	1
Public office→Law firm→Public office→Law firm	0.1%	1
Other	0.1%	1
Other→Law firm	0.1%	1
Total	100.0%	1429

[a] Respondents were qualified as legal professionals from 1950 to 2017
[b] Law firm, In-house, Public office, and Others include movements within a given sector, such as from one law firm to another

1.2.1 Move Between Law Firms

Most lawyers, 84% of them, have not moved out of practice at law firms. Moreover, 40% of them have never moved, staying at the law firm where they found a job after graduation from the LTRI. Thirty percent of them moved just once. Ten percent moved twice. The percentage of lawyers who moved from a law firm to another three times or more is only 4%. Practice at law firms seems stable and the career of most lawyers practicing at law firms is without much upheaval. Yet there are some indications that lawyers entering the job market at law firms in recent years may change their law firms more quickly. This will be analyzed in more detail in Chap. 2.

Table 1.4 Reason for move from the first law firm to the second law firm (Career Survey 2018–2019)

	Year of LTRI graduation			
Reason for move	1950 ~ 1996	1997 ~ 2006	2007 ~ 2016	Total *N*
Better income[a]	3.8%	4.5%	19.6%	651
Worthwhile work[b]	11.4%	21.2%	23.2%	651
Human relations[b]	16.7%	20.5%	29.8%	651
Work-life balance[b]	7.1%	14.7%	18.6%	651
Have my own law firm[b]	60.0%	48.1%	38.9%	651
Other[b]	16.2%	26.3%	29.1%	651

[a]Fisher's exact test, $p. < 0.001$.
[b]χ^2 $p. < 0.01$

We asked the reason for move to lawyers who changed their jobs.[20] The reason for moving from the first law firm to the second law firm seem to reflect changes of legal practice over years. We divided the lawyers into three groups by the year of the LTRI graduation, up to 1996, from 1997 to 2006 and from 2007 to 2016. The first group began their practice in a stable environment without many upheavals. The second group saw the rise of business law firms and the emergence of mass process law firms. It was the period of gradual increase of bar exam passers. The third group faced the sharp increase of bar exam passers and competition among lawyers in seeking clients. As Table 1.4 shows, the percentage of the reason for move increased from the first group to the third group, except "Have My Own Law Firm". "Better Income" was not a frequent reason for move from a law firm to another by the middle of 2000. The percentage of "Better Income" was only 3.8% for the reason for move in the first group and also only 4.5% in the second group, while it increased to 19.6% in the third group. This change shows that, after the bar exam passers exceeded 2000 in 2007, more lawyers were dissatisfied with their income and moved between law firms seeking "Better Income". Yet, the percentage is small, just 1% more than the lowest 18.6% for "Work-Life Balance".

11.4%, more than one in every ten lawyers who moved to another law firm did so for "Worthwhile Work" in the first group. The percentage doubled in the second group, and further slightly increased in the third group. This increase of moving for "Worthwhile Work" after 1997 may reflect a transition in legal practice from general practice to more specialized practice. Our hypothesis is that younger lawyers were increasingly assigned to specialized work: a discrete part of a larger piece of work, or work in a narrow area. As a result, these younger lawyers might increasingly want to do another piece of specialized work, or move away from such specialized work to experience a broader practice.

The fact that "Human Relations" has been a most divisive factor for a law firm is shown by its high percentage in the first group. As sizes of law firms became larger

[20]We listed as main reasons for move "better income", "worthwhile work", "human relations", "work-life balance" and "others" and asked respondents to choose as many as they considered relevant.

and the number of solo practitioners decreased, more lawyers had problems with relations with colleagues and moved to another law firm for "Human Relations".

"Work-Life Balance" became important for lawyers rather recently. The period of the economic growth until the 1980s was also the period when the gender roles for men and women were firmly fixed. 1996 was the year when the percentage of women among LTRI graduates reached 20% for the first time in the history of the Japanese legal profession.[21] As Ishida discusses in Chap. 4, law firms have not been women-friendly workplace. Even in the youngest group, the percentage of "Work-Life Balance" for the reason for move is the lowest among the six reasons.

The percentage of "Have My Own Law Firm" has been the highest in every group. In the first group, in which solo practice was very common in legal practice, the percentage is 60.0%. Lawyers considered their profession as free and independent. This image reflects their desire to control their work on their own.[22] However, as the number of law firms with associates increased, more lawyers tended to stay in their law firms. Therefore, it seems natural that the percentage of "Have My Own Law Firm" for the reason for move decreased in the second and third groups, as sizes of law firms became larger. Yet, the percentage for this reason is the largest among the six reasons even in the third generation from 2007 to 2016. At the time of the survey, the lawyers in this group had 2–11 years of experience. For many lawyers in this group, years of practice were not long enough for them to become independent and have their own law firm. Therefore, more lawyers will have their own law firms as time passes. As we will see later on the management type of law firms, cost sharing is more common than income sharing. This tendency may reflect the self-image of the profession as free and independent.

"Other" is a residual category for reasons other than the five reasons. This reason could include reasons for which lawyers themselves did not decide to move, such as break-up, dissolution, and merger.[23] Partners who decided to break-up, dissolve or merge their law firm with another law firm would have one or some of the five reasons, but associates did not have a choice to move to another law firm or a merged law firm in such a case. The increase in the percentage of this reason from the first group to the second and third group reflects increasing circumstances under which law firms faced organizational challenges in competition.

Among the lawyers who moved from a law firm to another law firm twice, the most frequent reason for the second move was "Have My Own Law Firm", 37.4%, indicating that lawyers' desire to have their own law firm was still strong. The second frequent reason was "Other", 28.6%. "Human Relations" was the third, 24.8%, followed by "Worthwhile Work" 16.5%, "Work-Life Balance" 11.2%, and "Better Income" 9.7%. There was no significant difference among the three groups, except

[21] Calculated from the data in JFBA (2010), p. 77.

[22] An experienced lawyer who worked long time in the field of international transactions characterized the image of lawyers in his generation as "lone wolf". He considered that the rise of Big Five had changed the image of elite lawyers more amenable to organizational authority. Interview with a partner of a large business law firm in August 2023.

[23] I thank Hiroyuki Kabashima for suggesting this point.

Table 1.5 Move of lawyers by size of law firm (Career Survey 2018–2019)

N of lawyers at the law firm	Registered lawyers (2018)		Lawyers moved to in-house	
	Percent	Number	Percent	Number
1 ~ 10 lawyers	77%	30,983	43%	20
11 ~ 50 lawyers	14%	5557	28%	13
51 ~ 100 lawyers	1%	536	7%	3
101 lawyers ~	7%	2990	22%	10
Total number	[a]99%	40,066	100%	46

[a] Rounding error

"Work-Life Balance". The percentage of "Work-Life balance" was significantly small, only 4.5%, in the first group. However, it increased to 12.8% in the second group and 18.2% in the third group (Fisher's exact test, $p. < 0.05$). This increase was due to the increase of men lawyers who moved to the third law firm for "Work-Life Balance". Among men lawyers, the percentage of "Work-Life Balance" was only 1.3% in the first group, but it increased to 10.0% in the second group and 16.4% in the third group (Fisher's exact test, $p. < 0.01$). However, among women lawyers, the percentage of "Work-Life Balance" was already high, 23.1%, in the first group, and the overall percentage was 22.0% with no significant generational difference.

1.2.2 Move from Law Firm to In-House

The most frequent move from law firm to another sector is the one to in-house positions. Table 1.5 shows that lawyers practicing at larger law firms tend to move to in-house position much more often than those at smaller law firms. Although the percentage of lawyers working at law firms with one to 10 lawyers was 77% of all registered lawyers, the percentage of lawyers at the same size law firms who had moved to in-house positions was only 43%. In contrast, the percentage of lawyers working at largest law firms with more than 100 lawyers was only 7% of the registered lawyers, but the percentage of such lawyers who moved to in-house positions is 22%.

These findings indicate that lawyers with focused fields[24] related to corporate business tend to move to in-house positions. Our data confirm this tendency: 28% of those having moved to in-house positions had practiced in finance as a focused field, 12% in intellectual property, and 8% in mergers and acquisitions. Yet 10% of those having moved to in-house positions practiced in traffic accidents as a focused field and 6% in family law. Lawyers whose areas of practice included both individual and corporate clients also moved to in-house positions.

[24] When a particular field of practice brings one third of income or more, it is called a focused field. See, Sect. 1.3.3.

As the move from law firms to corporations was a recent phenomenon, we compared the group of LTRI graduates from 1997 to 2006 and that from 2007 to 2016 for reasons for moves. As Ishida discusses in detail in Chap. 4, in-house positions have been considered to be friendly for women lawyers. In fact, more women lawyers tended to move to in-house positions. Among lawyers registered at the JFBA, the percentage of women lawyers was 23.2% in the group of the LTRI graduates from 1997 to 2006 and also 23.0% in that from 2007 to 2016. However, we found that, among the lawyers who moved from law firms to corporations, the percentage of women lawyers who were LTRI graduates from 1997 to 2016 was 44.0%. Therefore, the percentage of the reason for move from a law firm to a corporation is influenced by the high percentage of women lawyers.

There was no significant difference between the two LTRI graduate groups above, one from 1997 to 2006, the other 2007 to 2016, in any of the reasons. The most frequent reason for move was "Work-Life Balance" with the percentage being 57.4%. "Worthwhile Work" was the second most frequent reason for move with the percentage being 44.3%, followed by "Other" 24.6%, "Better Income" 21.3%, and "Human Relations" 14.8%. It is conspicuous that more than half of the lawyers who moved from law firms to corporations did so for "Work-Life Balance". The high percentage of "Worthwhile Work" is also remarkable, indicating that those lawyers were dissatisfied with legal practice at their law firms. The percentage of "Better Income", 21.3%, is not particularly high, but this indicates that corporations could pay more to in-house lawyers than law firms. In fact, as we will see later, recent incomes at law firms were varied and high income was not always guaranteed, while corporations could provide stable and moderate income to in-house lawyers.

1.2.3 Move from Law Firm to Public Office

The move from a law firm to a public position is the second main move from a law firm to another sector. Lawyers at middle to large law firms tend to move to public positions much more than those at smaller or the largest law firms. In 2018, the percentage of lawyers who moved to public offices from law firms with more than 10 to 100 lawyers was 30%, while the percentage of lawyers belonging to those law firms was only 15%. Interestingly 21% of the lawyers who moved from law firms to public offices had mergers and acquisitions as a focused practice, 13% finance, and 8% intellectual property and international transactions. Large and middle size law firms specialized in corporate business law fields tend to develop relationships with national Ministries to provide human resources. But these moves are usually not permanent but temporal, and associates at law firms are sent to positions at Ministries just for a few years.[25]

[25] Ministries value not only their expertise in law but also their knowledge of what is going on in business fields. It would be difficult for Ministries to appoint to official positions employees of private companies, because they are often considered subjects of their regulation, but lawyers are

The reason for move reflects the organizational network between law firms and public offices. When we compare the three groups of LTRI graduates, the first group from 1950 to 1996, the second from 1997 to 2006, and the third from 2007 to 2016, there is no significant difference in the reasons for move among the three groups, except "Other". No lawyer moved from a law firm to a public office in the first and second group for "Other", but 53% of the third group did so (Fisher's exact test, *p.* = 0.068). This indicates that the move from law firms to public offices for organizational reasons became established practice rather recently.

Another characteristic of the reason for move from law firms to public offices is the very high percentage of "Worthwhile Work", 73%, though there is no significant difference among the three groups. This indicates that work at public offices looked attractive to lawyers, or that lawyers who moved could choose the kind of public work they would like to do.

1.2.4 Move from Public Office to Law Firm

In Table 1.3, the most frequent move between sectors is from public offices to law firms. But this is not a new path, rather it is a traditional one. As we saw above, since the Meiji period, retired judges and prosecutors have moved into private practice at law firms. In our data, 48% of them were judges, 44% public prosecutors and 8% public officials at national ministries. Judges, public prosecutors, and ministry officials do not always stay in public office until their retirement age but move to law firms in their middle of their career. Eighty one percent of legal professionals who moved from public offices to law firms were younger than 40 years old, most of them quitting public positions in their 20s. This indicates that judges, public prosecutors, and ministry officials are quick to decide whether they suit public service and quit quickly if they find it does not suit them.

As the move from public offices to law firms is an established career route, there has been no significant increase in move from public offices to law firms over years. There is no significant difference in the reason for move among the three groups of LTRI graduates, from 1950 to 1996, 1997 to 2006, and 2007 to 2016. Although the income of public officials was lower than that of private attorneys and it was often believed that former judges and public prosecutors became private attorneys to obtain higher income, the percentage of "Better Income" is only 2%, the lowest among the six reasons. In contrast, the percentage of "Worthwhile Work" is high,

considered independent of business interests. Lawyers also get benefits from their work experience to understand official practice at Ministries, as corporations as their clients often want to know mind-sets of Ministries. Associates are also sent to private corporations temporarily. Interviews with associates of the Big Five firms, July 2017 and May 2018.

24%, following "Other", the highest, 44%.[26] Another conspicuous characteristic of the reason for move from public office to law firms is that 23% of the public officials in the first group who moved to law firms did so in order to establish their own law firms, while none of the public officials in the second and third groups did so. Apparently, it became more common for former judges and public prosecutors to join law firms as partners or counsel rather than to establish their own offices.

1.2.5 Hope to Change a Present Job?

We asked respondents whether they hoped to change their present job and, if so, to which sector they would like to move. We excluded the sector of "other", as the number of respondents in the other sector is very limited. The responses indicated to what extent the work situation of lawyers is fluid, from which sector lawyers will move to another sector, and on what aspects of their present jobs lawyers are concerned with when they consider the possibility of changing their job.

More than two thirds, 79%, of lawyers working at law firms, did not hope to change. Among the in-house lawyers, the percentage was 43%, while it was 38% of lawyers working in public offices. The percentage of lawyers who hoped to change was only 6% of the lawyers at law firms, 19% of the in-house lawyers, and 25% of the lawyers in public offices. The percentage of lawyers who could not say either way was rather high, 38% among the in-house lawyers and the lawyers in public office, respectively (Fisher's exact test, $p. <0.01$). Apparently, lawyers at law firms were most satisfied with their current employment among the three sectors at the time of the survey, at the end of 2018 to the beginning of 2019, despite claims of increasing competition among lawyers. Among lawyers at law firms, managing lawyers were much more satisfied (88% of them did not hope to change) than employed or other lawyers (62% of the employed lawyers did not hope to move, and 70% of the other lawyers did not hope to move) (Fisher's exact test, $p. <0.01$). In-house lawyers and those in public office were rather skeptical of their current positions, and the majority of them either hoped to change or could not say clearly whether they hoped to change or not.

However, most of them who hoped to change their job wanted to move to the same sector where they worked: 57% of lawyers at law firms and 86% of in-house lawyers hoped to change their jobs in the same sector.[27] 20% of lawyers at law firms

[26] As career paths for judges and public prosecutors have been more or less established, one can foresee, in the middle of one's career, to which level of the judicial or prosecutorial hierarchy one can get promoted. The high percentage of "Other" indicates that judges and prosecutors moved to law firms after considering the possibility of their promotion in the judicial or prosecutorial hierarchy.

[27] Fifty percent of the lawyers in public office hoped to move to the same sector. But the number of the respondents was very limited.

hoped to move to in-house positions, while 10% of in-house lawyers hoped to move to law firms (Fisher's exact test, $p. < 0.01$).

Among the six reasons for hoping to change their present job, "To Increase Income" was chosen by 38% of lawyers at law firms and 67% of in-house lawyers (Fisher's exact test, $p. < 0.05$). Among lawyers at law firms, the majority of employed lawyers, 53%, wanted to move for increasing income, while 17% of managing lawyers and 11% of other lawyers wanted to move for the same reason (Fisher's exact test, $p. < 0.01$). "More Worthwhile Work" was chosen by 35% of lawyers at law firms and 57% of in-house lawyers (Fisher's exact test, $p. < 0.05$). Thirty percent of lawyers at law offices hoped to change their jobs because they wanted to have their own law firms, while no in-house lawyers wanted to have their own law firms. There was no significant difference between lawyers at law firms and in-house lawyers in "Human Relation", 29% on average, "Work-Life Balance", 30% on average, and "Other", 22% on average, respectively.

1.3 Law Firms

1.3.1 Stratification of Law Firms

In the twentieth century, there were high income lawyers and law firms with high prestige, but high-income lawyers were scattered among small law firms and prestigious law firms were often identified with well-known lawyers. As Table 1.6 shows, sizes of law firms were small, and high-income or prestigious lawyers were more or less individual phenomena until the 1990's. But in the twenty-first century, law firms with high income lawyers and prestige emerged to make a stratum, if small, among the business law firms. First, let's take a look at how law firms expanded.

Table 1.6 shows how the number of lawyers working at law firms has changed since the 1950s. Changes were slow and incremental until the 1990s. The increase of office sizes occurred in the late 1990s to the early 2000s, though the overall expansion of office sizes is not very large with the median not really increasing.

Until 1990, when the annual number of bar exam passers was around 500, most passers entered the LTRI to become legal professionals, and around 350 to 400

Table 1.6 The number of lawyers at a law firm in the first year of practice (Career Survey 2018–2019)

Total *N* of lawyers	Year of LTRI graduation					
	1950 ~ 1966	1967 ~ 1976	1977 ~ 1986	1987 ~ 1996	1997 ~ 2006	2007 ~ 2016
Mean	5	4	5	7	15	28
Smallest	2	2	1	1	1	1
Largest	15	25	40	50	240	540
Median	3	3	3	4	5	5
N	24	54	92	108	227	662

passers became lawyers, while around 100 to 150 became either judges or prosecutors. Yet 70 to 90 retired judges, prosecutors and notaries[28] became lawyers each year. Therefore, around 420 to 490 or so new lawyers were added to the lawyer population. During this period, future lawyers found their positions as associates at small law firms, in many cases, where they had been accepted as trainees during the training program at the LTRI.[29] Most lawyers chose the profession as they believed it to be free and independent (JFBA Bengoshi Gyomu Kaikaku Iinkai 2002, pp. 213–214). Thus, many associates planned to have their own law firms in 5–10 years after working as associates. Typically, their master lawyers allowed them to take some of the clients, particularly some company clients, which was considered important to have stable management of their law firms.[30] In this way solo-practitioners and small offices were reproduced over decades.

Although the number of bar exam passers increased to between 700 and 800 in the 1990s, the rather static situation did not really change. The percentage of solo practitioners occupied 50% in 1980, 56% in 1990 and 50% in 2000. The percentage of lawyers who belonged to offices with 2 to 9 lawyers was 47% in 1980, 41% in 1990, and 46% in 2000. The percentage of offices with 20 or more lawyers was only 1% throughout this period (JFBA Bengoshi Gyomu Taisaku Iinkai 1981, p. 54; 1991, p. 14, p. 16; JFBA Bengoshi Gyomu Kaikaku Iinkai 2002, p. 20). This situation changed profoundly with the emergence of large business law firms in the twenty-first century.

1.3.1.1 Emergence of the Big Five Firms and Corporate Law Practice

Law firms specializing in international transactions and corporate business matters existed from the 1950s,[31] but their sizes were small, 20–40 even around 1990 (Nagashima et al. 2011, p. 28). It was said that Japanese law firms could not grow

[28] There are about 500 notaries at 300 notary offices in Japan. Notaries are appointed by the Minister of Justice and their fee is fixed by the government. Most notaries are appointed from among retired judges and prosecutors. Japan National Notaries Association, https://www.koshonin.gr.jp/system/s02/s02_02, accessed on 15 August 2023. As the retirement age for a notary is 70 years old, retired notaries could become private attorneys.

[29] The training program at the LTRI was divided into five parts, lectures at the LTRI, training at court, a prosecutor's office and a law firm, and again lectures at the LTRI.

[30] Corporate clients would bring work to a lawyer steadily, and if a lawyer gets a position of legal counsel for a company, the monthly fee for legal counsel would help to make the financial management of a law firm stable. A lawyer who just establishes her/his own law firm tends to get concerned about the possibility that few clients would come. The author met lawyers who had had nightmares that no client would have come to their law firms after they established their firms in the early 1990s.

[31] Under the Attorneys Act of 1949, foreign lawyers were allowed to practice in Japan by obtaining the recognition of the Supreme Court. Three of the Big Four firms originated from two law firms which were founded by U.S. lawyers, "Anderson, Mohri and Rabinovitz", and "Blakemore". Japanese associates at these law firms studied at U.S. law schools and gradually expanded their practice (Nagashima et al. 2011, pp. 57, 129, 171).

to more than 50 as they tended to break up.[32] However, as banks and insurance companies went bankrupt under the new de-regulation policy from around 1996,[33] opportunities for business lawyers increased and large business law firms had to further expand in order to take on big cases such as mergers and acquisitions. In the 2000s, law firms specializing in corporate matters merged with those specializing in financing. Nagashima Ohno merged with Tsunematsu to become the first law firm with more than 100 lawyers. In 2003, Mori merged with Hamada Matsumoto to have 169 lawyers, obtaining lawyers for international transactions. Anderson Mohri already had 138 lawyers in 2004 and merged with Tomotsune in 2005. Nishimura Sanada merged with Tokiwa to have 150 lawyers in 2004 and again merged with the international group of Asahi to become Nishimura Asahi with 316 lawyers. These largest law firms were called the Big Four.

The late comer is TMI Associates, which spun out from Nishimura Sanada with ten lawyers in 1990. By actively recruiting graduates from the LTRI, it had more than 100 lawyers in 2006. TMI Associates has a large number of patent lawyers and actively sought relationships with foreign law firms. In 2022, Nishimura Asahi had 633 lawyers, TMI Associates 527, Anderson Mohri and Tomotsune 523, Mori Hamada and Matsumoto 522, and Nagashima Ohno and Tsunematsu 514, and they were called the Big Five. Lawyers at the Big Five firms comprise more than 6% of all the Japanese lawyers.

The rapid expansion of the Big Five firms was assisted by the increase in the number of bar exam passers. Under the new bar examination, each of the Big Five firms recruited 20–40 graduates from the LTRI almost every year, except 2011 and 2012.[34] They attracted the best LTRI graduates with high income, more than 10 million Yen a year,[35] and recently 12 million as the number of bar exam passers decreased.[36] Because of this high entry income, it has become prestigious for LTRI graduates to find a job at a Big Five firm.[37] The Big Five firms tend to recruit the youngest LTRI graduates, as associates are sent to foreign elite law schools typically in the U.S. or U.K. after working for 4–6 years.[38] Studying at an elite U.S. law

---

[32] Mori Sogo with 53 lawyers broke up as a top lawyer set up a boutique law firm in 1998 (Nikkei 1998).

[33] The Japanese financial industry was protected under the regulations of Ministry of Finance. The regulated protection was called as "convoy system". This protection was gone in the Japanese "big bang" beginning in 1996.

[34] Business law practice slowed down in these years impacted by the bankruptcy of Lehman Brothers. Also Great East Japan Earthquake occurred in March 2011.

[35] Interview with a former associate at a Big Five firm, May 2018. The entering income that the JFBA wants to guarantee has been six million Yen, which the JFBA considers equivalent to the income of a judge for the first year.

[36] The annual income is guaranteed for the first few years, then moves to a commission system. Interview with a former associate at a Big Five firm, May 2018.

[37] Either judge or associate at a Big Five firm is an alternative for the best LTRI graduates. Interview with an associate of a Big Five firm in July 2017.

[38] Associates are sent to a foreign country for 2 years. They study at law schools for the first year and work as trainees at foreign law firms for the second year. Recently some associates study at business schools instead of law schools. Interview with a former associate at a Big Five firm, July 2017.

school is important for their career as most senior partners once studied at U.S. law schools.

Other large law firms with more than 100 lawyers do not always pay an annual salary equivalent to that of a Big Five firm. It is well known that working hours at a Big Five firm are long[39] and can be unexpected.[40] One of the large law firms pays less to associates but working hours are shorter. The pay system is also different, as the firm pays a fixed amount based on seniority and bonus, depending upon total estimate of associate's work.[41]

Income-sharing provides stable management of law firms, provided that the partners agree on how the income is to be split, as is shown by splits of law firms in the 1990s. Income sharing has two types of distribution of profit: lock-step system and commission system. A lock-step system is a way to pay income based on seniority, and a commission system is a way to pay income based on how much profit a lawyer brought to a law firm. Nishimura adopted a lock-step system in 1996, while Asahi adopted a commission system based on pure merit in 1992. When Nishimura and Asahi merged in 2007, lawyers of Asahi who did not accept the lock-step system did not join the new law firm (Nagashima et al. 2011, pp. 141–142, p. 165). But Japanese large law firms tend to have a commission system to prevent competent partners from leaving. Even if law firms have a lock-step system, there must be a supplementary procedure to pay bonuses to partners who bring profits.[42]

The legal service market for the Big Five firms is said to be tight. The Big Five firms actively try to take large cases for very competitive prices.[43] The Big Five firms try to expand their practice for cross-border cases by setting up branch offices in China and ASEAN countries, but it takes time to establish their practice in foreign countries.

The Big Five firms also face internal challenges. The work of associates is hard and unpredictable. Their work is more and more specialized. A senior lawyer of a top ten law firm questioned how long young associates could endure such hard work. He also questioned how long Japanese law firms would accept lower time charges than U.S. law firms (Foote 2021, p. 114).

Even large law firms, including some of top ten law firms, do not exclude general practice and individual clients. At a Big Five firm, a young associate works with a senior associate and a partner, and insofar as a junior associate works with the same

---

[39] A partner of a Top 10 firm said that, as associates at a large law firm had to work really hard, it was not a question whether they could catch the last train, but the question was whether they could catch the first train. Interview, July 2017.

[40] A former associate of a Big Five firm compared the work at a national ministry with that of the law firm. At the ministry, one could be very busy, working overnight, but it was predictable. At the law firm, the lawyers were not only busy during weekdays, but a weekend could be gone when a partner put a pile of documents on the desk, asking the lawyer to work on them over the weekend. Interview with a former associate at a Big Five firm in July 2017.

[41] Interview with a partner at a Top Ten law firm in May 2018.

[42] Interview with a partner at a Top Ten law firm in July 2017. As most law firms have a commission system also for associates, associates can earn more than partners at such law firms.

[43] Interview with an associate at a Big Five firm in July 2017.

partner, s/he works in the same specialized field as the partner does. But one of the top ten law firms have much less specialized work assignment, and another law firm lets junior associates move from one specialized field to another almost every year. In this way, those law firms try to let their associates develop competence to handle various different cases rather than highly specialized competence.[44]

Top ten law firms other than the Big Five do not always seek large cases. According to a partner at a top ten law firm, there are needs of commoditized legal service for them to satisfy.[45] As corporate law departments grow and control their legal needs, commoditization of legal service for corporations will increase, though commoditization of legal services has not yet spread so much in the corporate business law sector.[46]

Large law firms tend to take on large corporate clients, but large corporations retain middle-size law firms and even small boutique legal firms as well as large law firms, depending upon the cost of their legal service and the specialization of their legal practice (Hamano 2015, p. 94).

1.3.1.2 Mass Process Law Firms

Among the top ten law firms, Adire and Verybest are different from the other law firms, as their main clients are individuals. They have another differentiating characteristic: these law firms utilize a large number of supporting staff and process many cases in uniformed ways. The origin of so called 'mass process' law firms goes back to small law firms specialized in settling individual consumer loan cases. In 2006 the Supreme Court ruled that debtors could asked loan companies to return an amount that had been overpaid in the past.[47] The Supreme Court rulings awoke lawyers to the possibility that consumer loan cases could be opportunities for lawyers to obtain profits rather easily.[48] The number of overpaid and other consumer

[44] Interviews with a partner at a top ten law firm in May 2018 and a former partner at a Big Five law firm in August 2023.

[45] Interviews with a partner at a top ten law firm in May 2018. Commoditization of legal service and outsourcing to non-lawyers occurred in various fields in the U.S. (Kritzer 1998). But because of the Attorneys Act's prohibition, outsourcing of commoditized legal service can be made only to lawyers in Japan.

[46] Interview of a partner of a large law firm in August 2023.

[47] This is one of the series of SC decisions on overpaid cases. In one of the early important cases, in 1968, the SC held that a debtor could ask a loan company to return an amount a debtor had paid in excess of the upper limit that the Interest Rate Restriction Act (Act No.100 of 1954) imposed (Saiko Saibansho, November 13, 1968). In 2006, the SC held that an acceleration clause of a loan contract was a de facto compulsion so that overpayment could not have been made voluntarily (Saiko Saibansho, January 13, 2006). A debtor cannot ask a loan company to return an overpaid amount which the debtor had paid voluntarily, but this judgment virtually eliminated this possibility.

[48] When we visited a local bar association for research on legal advice centers in August 2007, a senior lawyer of the bar association told us that they advised first year lawyers to take overpaid cases as they would not require experience of legal practice.

loan cases increased sharply at the district courts during the 2000s: 42,614 cases in 2005, 93,286 cases in 2007, and 144,468 cases in 2009. Then, the number began to decrease to 38,636 cases in 2018. During the 2000s, a law firm began to advertise its practice for overpaid cases on radio and then on TV. A few law firms followed this example and Adire and Verybest expanded themselves to the largest law firms of this kind.

Adire became a Top Ten law firm with 88 lawyers in 2012. They established their branch offices in most of the prefectures and advertised their practice both on TV and the Internet. TV advertisements can be broadcasted in particular areas, but advertisements on the Internet can be seen anywhere nationwide. Thus, Adire established local offices in almost every prefecture though they sometimes met resistance from local bar associations.[49] Adire appointed a lawyer as the head of a local office, working mainly as an intake officer. Most cases are then sent to the headquarters in Tokyo for processing. When litigation is conducted, a lawyer is sent from the Tokyo office and s/he works together with the branch lawyer.

Although advertising for legal practice was allowed by the revision of the JFBA rules in 2000, lawyers were slow to begin advertising. One law firm broke the ice by advertising their practice for consumer loans and overpaid interest cases on radio. Adire dared to advertise on TV and the Internet for mass marketing. Such a marketing method did not give prestige to Adire and they had difficulties in recruiting lawyers. Yet entry income was better than the JFBA baseline, though it could decrease according to the labor market situation of lawyers. But a head of a local office was paid well around ten million Yen, or even more.[50]

On the Internet advertisement, Adire wrote that the initial fee would be free if a client made a contract with Adire during the particular month, although in reality Adire waived the initial fee all the time. The Consumer Affairs Agency ordered Adire to remove the false advertisement in 2016. In 2017, the Tokyo Bar Association disciplined Adire by suspending its practice for 2 month and its head partner for 3 months.[51] As Adire had to discontinue its contracts with the clients, it lost most clients particularly in debt cases. Adire survived the suspended period but reduced the number of its lawyers to 145 in 2019. Yet Adire has remained a major 'mass process' law firm with 222 lawyers in 2022.

Verybest became a Top Ten law firm with 105 lawyers in 2016. While Adire was trying to recover from the suspension, Verybest expanded its practice in a similar way, though it mainly advertised on the Internet. It also set up branch offices in most prefectures nationwide. In 2020, Verybest was disciplined by the Tokyo Bar Association for having violated the Attorneys Act: it paid a judicial scrivener's office in exchange for the introduction of overpaid cases which a

[49] In order to set up a branch office, a lawyer must be admitted to the local bar association by obtaining recommendations of two members of the bar association. When Adire could not find the necessary two members' recommendation, it sued. Such an incident shows that Adire was not welcomed by many local lawyers.

[50] Interview with a partner of a mass process law firm in June 2017.

[51] The length of this suspension was later reduced to 2 months by the JFBA.

judicial scrivener could not continue to work since the quantum of the cases was more than judicial scriveners were allowed to work on, i.e. 1.4 million Yen.[52] Verybest was suspended from practice for 6 months. Appealing to the JFBA, Verybest argued that it did not pay for the introduction of clients, but for the work that the judicial scrivener had already done for the cases. The JFBA shortened the length of suspension period from 6 to 3 months, but maintained the disciplinary decision itself. Verybest appealed the case to the Tokyo High Court in 2022 and the litigation is still ongoing.

1.3.1.3 Issue of Immediately Going Solo

When the number of bar exam passers increased, lawyers began to complain that some of the LTRI graduates could not find employment at law firms and were forced to practice alone. This was considered a serious problem because new graduates could not get on-the-job training or supervision that new graduates usually obtained in their employment at law firms in the past. This problem was publicized to emphasize the "excessive increase of bar exam passers". There were two types of "immediately going solo". First, a new graduate began solo-practice by opening one's own office. Second, a new graduate "borrowed" a space for practice in a law firm. As the second looked like practicing under the eaves, such a lawyer was called "an eaves lawyer". But it is not new that a new LTRI graduate established one's own office all by oneself or that a new graduate practiced at a law firm without employment. Before 2007, when the number of newly registered lawyers exceeded 2000, 0.9% of the lawyers who began to practice at law firms during the period from 1950 to 2006 established their own office without prior employment. From 2007, and up to 2017, that percentage increased to 2.0%. "An eaves lawyer" was not new, either. Among the lawyers who began to practice from 1950 to 2006, 1.4% of them could be "eaves lawyers". In the period 2007 to 2017, that percentage increased to 2.4%.

In 2008 the JFBA began to give financial support to LTRI graduates who would go solo in areas with few lawyers within a year from the graduation (JFBA 2016a), and also technical support by publishing a manual for going solo immediately.[53] Local bar associations have also begun to give support to LTRI graduates who go solo immediately or soon after graduation (JFBA 2022c).

Whether these lawyers are competent enough or not is debatable.[54] But the issue has been less and less visible, as there has been no reports of malpractice by such

---

[52] Attorneys Act Article 27 prohibits lawyers collaborating with non-attorneys.

[53] The JFBA published a technical manual and a collection of experiences of lawyers who went solo soon after their graduation from the LTRI (JFBA Wakate Hoso Center 2012; JFBA Wakate Bengoshi Support Center 2015).

[54] On the Internet, a senior lawyer recommended to avoid such a lawyer: https://www.nishino-law.com/publics/index/47/detail=1/b_id=80/r_id=817/.

lawyers and simply the number of unemployed lawyers significantly decreased as the number of bar examination passers decreased.[55]

1.3.2 Diversity in Law Firm Management

1.3.2.1 Management Forms of Law Firms

Management forms of Japanese law firms can be classified into five main categories: (1) Solo-practice, (2) a master lawyer with associates, (3) cost sharing among partners, (4) income sharing among partners, and (5) professional legal corporation. When a solo-practitioner becomes busier, obtaining an increasing number of clients, s/he employs an associate to expand her/his practice. The Solo-practitioner then becomes a master lawyer with an associate. At cost-sharing offices, partners share the costs of running the law firms such as rent, supporting staff salaries, telephone bills, etc. However, at a cost-sharing law firm, each partner practices alone. Therefore, a cost-sharing law firm is in effect solo-practice with a number of solo practitioners. At an income sharing law firm, the equity partners share both the costs of running the firm and the income stream and seek clients for the law firm.

One characteristic of Japanese law firms is that there are cost-sharing law firms which are not very small. Here are three examples. After two friend lawyers set up a cost sharing office, the office grew to a law firm with ten lawyers, and then 15 lawyers in 2023. All of the lawyers are partners who share in the costs of the law firm; this law firm does not have any associates. If an associate is needed, a partner lawyer is to employ the associate by her/himself. A secretary or other supporting staff member is also to be employed by that partner. When asked why the law firm did not become an income sharing law firm despite the increasing size, a partner answered that, once partners did not disclose their income to each other, no partner wanted to disclose income to others. That's how the cost-sharing management continued.[56] Another law firm started as solo-practice and the lawyer began to employ an associate as his work expanded. After his associate worked with him for 5–6 years, he proposed him to become a cost-sharing partner. In this way, his law firm now has 11 lawyers, 7 of whom are cost-sharing partners. Unlike the first example, this law firm employs secretaries and support staff.[57] The third example is a law firm with more than 50 lawyers: more than 30 partners, more than ten associates, several counsel, a foreign lawyer and a few patent attorneys. Most of their work includes corporate matters and international transactions, and this law firm is presented as a corporate business law firm on the Internet. But among the partners, there are a few lawyers who handle traffic accident cases for victims or

[55] The JFBA recognized that the difficulty of employment among LTRI graduates had improved greatly in 2022 (JFBA 2022b).

[56] Interview with a partner of this law firm in October 2017.

[57] Interview with a partner of this law firm in August 2017.

who handle family matters. When asked why such a large business law firm is a cost sharing firm, a partner answered that the partners did not want to take responsibility for what other partners did.[58]

At these three law firms, clients are mixture of companies and individuals. But clients often designate particular lawyers. When a client comes without designating a particular lawyer, such a client is to be assigned to a lawyer according to the rules of the firm. Each of these firms hold a meeting of partners to decide how to manage the law firm. But unlike an income sharing law firm, each of the partners does not know how much other partners earn and do not take responsibility for what other partners did.[59] This is very different a mind-set to the one that partners are supposed to have at an income sharing law firm.

Legal professional corporations have been allowed from 2002, following the recommendation of the JSRC. A legal professional corporation is formed by a lawyer or partners. A lawyer or partners have full responsibility for the corporation. A legal professional corporation can employ lawyers and set up branch offices. A lawyer at a branch office must be a partner who registered at a bar association where the branch office is located.

When the idea of a legal professional corporation appeared, local bar associations opposed to the idea, because local lawyers were afraid that urban lawyers would set up branch offices and take clients away from local lawyers. Therefore, the main purpose in allowing a branch office was understood as increasing the presence of lawyers in areas with few lawyers. But, as we saw, law firms in urban centers established branch offices to expand their practice in large cities or nationwide. In 2022, 2017 legal professional corporations existed and 18% of the lawyers belonged to the legal professional corporations. Of these 2107 legal professional corporations, only 472 or 23% had set up branch offices. Most of them, 316, had set up only one branch. Four law firms had set up more than 30 branches. Since 2002, the percentage of lawyers belonging to legal professional corporations increased by a little less than 1% every year and can be expected to continue growing (JFBA 2022a, pp. 56–57). Since the internal management structure could be similar between an income sharing office and a legal professional corporation, larger law firms, including the Top Ten, often established both a partnership and legal professional corporation with the same name.[60]

Table 1.7 shows the present distribution of lawyers among different types of law firm management according to generations and in total. The percentage of individual management law firms decreased over time, while that of cost-sharing law firms increased. As the number of lawyers increased and more law firms employed new LTRI graduates, it was natural for solo practitioners to decrease and for master lawyers to increase. In the youngest generation, the percentage of solo-practitioners and

[58] Interview with a partner of this law firm in August 2023.

[59] In a cost-sharing law firm, contract with a client is made by a partner, not by a law firm.

[60] As the largest legal professional corporation has 254 lawyers which is much fewer than the number of lawyers at any of the Big Five, some of the lawyers belonged to legal professional corporations and the rest to partnership law firms (JFBA 2022a, p. 58).

Table 1.7 The percentage of lawyers practicing at different types of law firm management by the first year of practice (Career Survey 2018–2019)[a]

Management style	Year of LTRI graduation						Total
	1950 ~ 19566	1967 ~ 1976	1977 ~ 1986	1987 ~ 1996	1997 ~ 2006	2007 ~ 2016	
Individual (Solo or Master)	80%	56%	62%	46%	45%	43%	48%
Cost sharing	18%	22%	28%	30%	35%	32%	31%
Income sharing	7%	13%	11%	18%	16%	8%	11%
Professional corporation	2%	12%	6%	10%	10%	24%	17%
Others	2%	5%	0%	2%	0%	2%	2%
N	45	82	108	121	240	675	1306

[a] Multiple answers for a legal professional corporation, as it can be chosen together with individual management or income sharing

Wmaster lawyers combined is 43%, less than half. As the number of lawyers increases and the size of a law firm expands, one might expect that income-sharing firms would increase. But Table 1.7 shows a contrary tendency: Cost sharing law firms increased, while income sharing law firms decreased. It is possible that some of the income sharing partnership law firms were changed to legal professional corporations.

1.3.2.2 Practice with Registered Foreign Lawyers

From 1987, foreign lawyers were allowed to practice in legal matters of their mother country's law, but employing a Japanese lawyer and joint enterprise with a Japanese lawyer were both prohibited. In 1988, 31 foreign lawyers were registered. In 1995, foreign law joint enterprise with a Japanese lawyer was allowed. But until the late 1990s, the number of registered foreign lawyers was around 80 and did not really increase as "the bubble economy" burst. In the late 1990s, the number of registered foreign lawyers began to increase, as the corporate business law practice was expanding. Since then, the number of registered foreign lawyers gradually increased to 267 in 2008, 412 in 2018 and 456 in 2022 (JFBA 2022a, p. 59).

In 2005, the prohibition for a registered foreign lawyer to employ a Japanese lawyer was lifted, and income sharing in a joint enterprise was allowed between a Japanese lawyer and a registered foreign lawyer. In 2020, 46 foreign law joint enterprises existed. In total, 146 Japanese partners and 80 registered foreign partners employed 688 Japanese associates and 72 registered foreign associates in these joint enterprises. Among the foreign law joint enterprises, the largest was one of the Big Five firms, Anderson Mohri and Tomotsune. This is a foreign law joint enterprise between its Japanese law firm and the registered foreign law firm, which had 170 Japanese partners, one legal professional corporation, 4 registered foreign partners, 307 Japanese associates and 8 registered foreign associates. The second largest was between Yanssen (a registered foreign law firm) and Atsumi Sakai Law Firm, which had 5 Japanese partners, 1 legal professional corporation, 1 registered foreign partner, 154 Japanese associates and 6 registered foreign associates. The third was Baker and McKenzie which had 26 Japanese partners, 10 registered foreign partners, 61 Japanese associates and 2 registered foreign associates (JFBA 2022a, pp. 61–62).

It is to be noted that among the Big Five firms, Nishimura Asahi, Nagashima Ohno and Tsunematsu, and Mori Hamada and Matsumoto do not have foreign law joint enterprises. But both the Big Five firms and the large foreign law joint enterprises have tried to expand their ability to deal with cross-border cases by establishing offices in China, ASEAN, EU and the U.S.

1.3.2.3 Practice with Quasi-Legal Professionals

Diversity of law firm management can be also seen in the way how lawyers work together with quasi-legal professionals. The Justice System Reform Council recommended to actively promote cooperation among lawyers and quasi-legal professionals in order to realize "one-stop service" (JSRC 2001, Chap. 3, Part 3, 7). Lawyers have been increasingly working together with quasi-legal professionals. There were disputes between lawyers and judicial scriveners over the limits of their jurisdictions, but now lawyers and judicial scriveners seem to work in cooperation rather than in conflict.[61]

Article 72 of the Attorneys Act prohibits lawyers from establishing Alternative Business Structures (ABSs) through which non-lawyers bring cases to law firms. The Basic Rules of the Duties of Practicing Attorneys, Article 12, prohibits lawyers from sharing profit with non-lawyers unless there is a justifiable reason, and the JFBA has indicated that it would be highly probable that this article would be violated if a lawyer and a law-related legal professional manage an income sharing law firm. Yet the JFBA has also indicated that it would be possible not to violate this article, if a lawyer and a law-related legal professional manage a cost sharing law firm by setting up rational criteria for splitting profits.[62] According to this regulation, a quasi-legal professional is not prohibited from becoming a partner of a cost sharing law firm or a non-equity partner of an income sharing law firm.

Law firms specializing in corporate business law fields often have patent attorneys and tax accountants. Most salient is TMI, which, in 2023, has 90 patent attorneys, 19 of which are partners. Nishimura Asahi has 13 patent attorneys and 5 tax accountants. Anderson Mohri Tomotsune has 15 patent attorneys, while Mori Hamada has 2 patent attorneys and 4 tax accountants.

There are law firms which have origins different from most of the big law firms. Yuasa and Hara started as a law firm specialized in intellectual property and international transaction in the Meiji period and has become a specialized law firm with 57 patent attorneys, 13 lawyers, 4 certified public accountants and 2 tax accountants in 2022. Deloitte Tomatsu legal professional corporation, a legal division of Deloitte Tomatsu certified public accountant firm, has 43 lawyers.

[61] Judicial scriveners could be qualified from 2003 to represent civil cases at the summary court after taking special training. Judicial scriveners are allowed to deal with civil cases worth up to 1.4 million Yen. The percentage of cases represented by judicial scriveners hit the highest point of 21.2% in 2010, but since then it has been decreasing to 5.2% in 2020. The Japan Federation of Shiho-Shoshi Lawyer's Association urged members to get qualified and represent cases at the court, but the movement did not last long. The percentage of lawyers who were concerned with competition with judicial scriveners significantly decreased from 42.8% in 2010 to 21.7% in 2020 (JFBA 2021a, p. 165).

[62] The JFBA has stated that the necessity of setting up one-stop service that the JSRC had recommended could be a justifiable reason (JFBA Bengoshi Rinri Iinkai 2017, pp. 28–29). I thank Kyoko Ishida for indicating the JFBA's view on the prohibition of profit sharing with non-lawyers.

Table 1.8 The number of lawyers by the number of full-time office employees

	Number of full-time office employees					
Number of lawyers	None	1 ~ 5	6 ~ 10	11 ~ 20	21 ~ 30	31~
Mean	2.6	3.9	13.8	24.5	28.9	248.7
Smallest	1	1	1	3	1	4
Largest	70	30	200	133	85	630
Median	1	3	10	21.5	27	145
N	90	576	89	52	15	95

There seem to be two strategies of cooperating with quasi-legal professionals: one is to include them inside a firm; the other is to establish each professional firm, such as a patent attorney firm and a tax accountant firm under the same name of a law firm.

1.3.2.4 Varing Reliance on Full-Time Employees

The relatively large percentage of cost sharing law firms indicate the diversity of legal practice among partners. As they are, in a sense, a group of solo practitioners, a strategy outlook of a law firm can be varied, depending upon what kind of clients each partner seeks and which focused field each partner tries to concentrate on.

Similarly, we can see the diversity of legal practice strategy in huge differences in the ratio of full-time supporting staff per lawyer. In many law firms, one to three lawyers have one or two supporting employees, and the number of supporting employees increases as that of lawyers also increases.[63] But there are outliers. As Table 1.8 shows, a law firm with 70 lawyers does not employ any full-time staff. It is not surprising that some solo practitioners do not employ supporting staff, but it is unusual that such a large size law firm does not employ full-time staff. Most likely, such a law firm employs part-time employees. At the opposite end, there are law firms where there are only one or a few lawyers while there are 20–30 supporting employees. Law firms of this type are likely to be engaged in "mass process" legal practice of some type.

1.3.3 Focused Practice: Emerging Specialization

A 1980 survey showed that "Japanese lawyers depend heavily on debt collection and real estate matters, in which resort to court often is unavoidable" and that "problems that arise in the everyday lives of most people" and "those bodies of law

[63] According to a JFBA survey result, 6.6% of the lawyers did not employ a supporting staff and 43.4% employed less than one staff, indicating part-time employees. The average number of supporting staff per lawyer was 1.01 (JFBA 2021a, p. 43).

that affect the daily affairs of larger business enterprises" were not important sources of business for Japanese lawyers (Rokumoto 1988, p. 170). This situation has changed greatly. As we saw in Sect. 1.3.1, since business law firms expanded from around 1996, larger business enterprises have become important clients for the Big Five firms. Problems in the everyday lives of many people also became an important source of work for Japanese lawyers.

The JFBA does not recognize any specialization in legal practice. There is no program in which specialization is institutionally guaranteed by the JFBA or local bar associations. The JFBA Guidelines for Advertisement recommends not to use the word "specialized field" (JFBA 2012, Chap. 3, 12 (1)). In our survey in 2018–19, we asked respondents whether they have a particular field the income from which occupies one third or more, and if any, which field it is, listing 14 legal fields, as is shown in Table 1.9.

Family problems have the largest percentage of focused legal fields. Family problems include inheritance and divorce, and inheritance was a main source of lawyers' work in the 1980s. But the increase of family cases mainly arose from divorce cases. The Japanese judicial system traditionally has discouraged involvement of lawyers in divorce and a divorce can be obtained with a simple administrative procedure. The main judicial forum for divorce is conciliation at the Family Court, but, in the past, the Family Court never encouraged divorcing spouses to consult or retain lawyers in divorce cases. Yet an increasing number of divorcing spouses began to consult lawyers and the involvement of lawyers in divorce conciliation increased from 25% in 2007 to 60% in 2021 (JFBA 2022a, p. 113).

Traffic accidents is also a growing field of legal practice. Traditionally, Japanese people mostly relied on insurance companies to negotiate a settlement when they were injured or their cars were damaged in car accidents (Murayama 2008, pp. 1141–1142). However, over time such people did not accept the estimates of the insurance companies, and this, coupled with the increase of insurance policies covering costs of lawyers, no doubt helped motor vehicle accident victims to consult and retain lawyers. In 2001, the JFBA established the Legal Access Center (LAC) to introduce lawyers to insured accident victims and also record the lawyers who worked on insurance cases. So far in 2003 the LAC has handled only three cases but, in 2019, LAC handled 40,879 cases. Insurance cover for legal costs has apparently expanded the legal service market for traffic accidents.

Family problems and traffic accidents are now main sources of lawyers' work, as reflected in the increase of the number of lawyers with family problems or traffic accidents as a focused field from around 2000, with a marked increase from 2006. The size of law firms focusing on family problem is significantly smaller than those without such focus (6.5 lawyers v. 35.7 lawyers, $p < 0.01$). That is also the case with traffic accidents (6.1 lawyers v. 35.7 lawyers, $p < 0.01$).

Personal bankruptcy and consumer loans are also handled by small size law firms: personal bankruptcy (7.5 lawyers v. 32.0 lawyers, $p < 0.01$) and consumer loans (9.5 lawyers v. 31.7 lawyers, $p < 0.01$). These cases are also being handled by mass process law firms. Lawyers with personal bankruptcy as a focused field existed for decades and their number began to increase from 2004. Lawyers who worked in

Table 1.9 The percentage of lawyers who had a focused field at the first law firm and present (Career Survey 2018–2019)

Focused field	Year of LTRI graduation						Present[a]
	1950 ~ 19566	1967 ~ 1976	1977 ~ 1986	1987 ~ 1996	1997 ~ 2006	2007 ~ 2016	
Familyb	9.4%	13.6%	11.3%	13.3%	14.2%	12.9%	17.5%
Traffic accidents[b]	6.3%	9.1%	7.2%	12.4%	10.1%	17.4%	16.5%
Real property[c]	15.6%	9.1%	13.4%	5.3%	8.9%	5.1%	6.5%
International transactions[d]	–	3.0%	1.0%	7.1%	8.5%	5.1%	5.8%
Labor law	3.1%	7.6%	3.1%	0.9%	3.2%	6.1%	5.6%
Business bankruptcy	–	6.1%	3.1%	4.4%	7.3%	3.6%	5.2%
Personal bankruptcy[b]	3.1%	4.5%	1.0%	5.3%	7.7%	5.7%	5.1%
Criminal[b]	3.1%	1.5%	3.1%	1.8%	3.6%	5.4%	4.9%
Finance[d]	9.4%	3.0%	5.2%	6.2%	5.7%	5.6%	4.6%
Consumer loans[b]	3.1%	3.0%	1.0%	1.8%	8.9%	5.1%	4.1%
M & A[d]	–	–	1.0%	4.4%	6.5%	4.3%	3.5%
Intellectual property[c]	3.1%	3.0%	6.2%	1.8%	3.6%	2.6%	3.1%
Medical malpractice[b]	3.1%	3.0%	4.1%	0.9%	1.6%	0.8%	2.2%
Tax	–	–	1.0%	0.9%	0.8%	0.4%	0.3%
Others[d]	15.6%	4.5%	7.2%	10.6%	13.0%	8.8%	10.1%
N	32	66	97	113	247	719	1178

[a] At the time of the survey, from November 2018 to January 2019
[b] The average number of lawyers with the focused field is significantly smaller than that of lawyers without the focused field at significance level < 0.01
[c]The average number of lawyers with the focused field is significantly larger than that of lawyers without the focused field at significance level < 0.05
[d] The average number of lawyers with the focused field is significantly larger than that of lawyers without the focused field at significance level <0.01

consumer loans as a focused field began to appear from 2001. These two focused fields are correlated (0.43, $p < 0.01$), showing that lawyers working in personal bankruptcy also often work in consumer loans matters.

Family problems as a focused field has significant correlations with other focused fields: personal bankruptcy (0.28, $p < 0.01$), consumer loans (0.16, $p < 0.01$), traffic accidents (0.15, $p < 0.01$), real property (0.13, $p < 0.01$) and criminal (0.11, $p < 0.01$). This indicates that family problems are a common source of legal work coexisting with another focused field, mostly for small law firms. Here an exception is real property. It is also handled by larger law firms (81.3 lawyers v. 27.7 lawyers, $p < 0.05$), though large law firms do not always have real property as a focused field. Real property has been a major field of legal practice for lawyers.

Among focused fields, criminal cases have some significant correlation with personal bankruptcy (0.13, $p < 0.01$), family problem s(0.11, $p < 0.01$) and traffic accidents (0.10, $p < 0.01$). But it must be noted that most criminal defense work for defendants has been done by court-appointed lawyers. The percentage of defendants with court-appointed counsel at the District Court was 73% in 2001 and 84% in 2021. In contrast, the percentage of defendants with privately retained counsel was 26% in 2001 and 18% in 2021. Until 2006, suspects had to personally retain lawyers if they wanted representation, but the court began to appoint counsel for some detained suspects from 2007 and, in 2021, for all detained suspects. The remainder of the suspects may retain defense lawyers by themselves, though it is unlikely that defendants do not have defense lawyers.[64]

The significant correlation between criminal and family matters indicates that lawyers take criminal cases as a usual source of legal work, which has been a traditional pattern of privately retained criminal defense work. There were generalist lawyers who also had a passionate interest in taking criminal cases for decades in the last century.[65] But, after 2007, there emerged some law firms that took only criminal cases. They disclosed their fees for each procedure in the criminal process, but a client did not always know how much it would cost in total, which led to complaints to a local bar association. One law firm, specialising in criminal cases and accidents, set up branch offices, trying to make a nationwide network. As a traffic accident can incur both civil and criminal responsibilities, traffic accidents and criminal defense as focused fields may correlate, as we saw above.

Medical malpractice is a focused field predominantly at small law firms. The average size of law firms with medical malpractice as a focused field is 3.6 while that of a firm without medical malpractice as a focused field is 31.4 ($p < 0.01$). Even when the number of lawyers increased from 2007, the number of lawyers who had medical malpractice as focused field did not increase. The average age of lawyers with a focused field tends to be younger, but the average age of lawyers who take medical malpractice cases as a focused field is significantly older than that of

[64] Most defendants are defended by lawyers in trial: 99.5% of the defendants at the District courts and 98.1% of those at the Summary courts in 2022 (SC Jimusokyoku 2022, Tables 23 and 24).

[65] In 2000, there was only one lawyer who took only criminal cases but nothing else in Japan. But there were individual lawyers at small law firms who liked to do criminal defense work.

lawyers who do not have medical malpractice as focused field (57 years old v. 47 years old, $p < 0.01$).

Although the percentage of lawyers is not large, focused fields relevant to corporate business law firms have similar tendencies and correlate with each other. The average size of law firms where lawyers practice in international transactions, finance, M&A and intellectual property is significantly larger than that of law firms where lawyers do not have such a focused field: for international transactions 174.7 lawyers v. 22.5 lawyers, $p < 0.01$, finance 171.4 lawyers v. 23.9 lawyers, $p < 0.01$, M&A 191.2 lawyers v. 23.3 lawyers, $p < 0.01$, and intellectual property 97.7 lawyers v. 28.7 lawyers, $p < 0.05$. As a focused field, international transactions significantly correlated with M&A (0.29, $p < 0.01$), finance (0.16, $p < 0.01$) and intellectual property (0.13, $p < 0.01$). Finance also correlated with M&A (0.20, $p < 0.01$) and real property (0.17, $p < 0.01$).

In Table 1.9 we can also see that international transactions and business bankruptcy did not appear as focused field among lawyers who began to practice in 1950 to 1966. M&A as focused field appeared further later in 1977 to 1986. These changes reflect the rise of corporate business law firms.

What is conspicuous is that few Japanese lawyers handle tax cases. Lawyers who work on tax cases as a focused field tended to practice at middle size firms, but the sample is too small to get any statistically significant result.[66]

Japanese large business law firms usually have two kinds of internal divisions, vertical and horizontal. Vertical division has three sectors of specialization: (1) corporate matters including M&A, (2) finance, and (3) litigation/bankruptcy. Horizontal division is that of area and language.[67] Each legal field can be further divided. For instance, finance is further divided into capital finance and structure finance. The former is divided further such as stocks or energy.[68] The Big Five firms can make further specialization and expand foreign regions, though the Big Five differ in their efforts to set up branch offices both in Japan and foreign countries.[69] But other large, yet smaller than the Big Five, law firms have to choose a small area of practice as it is impossible to cover all the narrowly specialized fields.[70]

The focused fields can be classified into those of practice mainly for individual clients and those mainly for corporate clients. Labor law can be both for individual workers and corporate employers. All the other fields can be either for individual or

[66] Though tax law has been an important field of practice in the U.S., it is considered as a new legal field among lawyers in Japan. (Foote 2021, p. 95).

[67] Interview with a partner at a Top Ten firm in July 2017.

[68] Interview with an associate of a Top Ten firm in July 2017.

[69] Nagashima Ohno and Tsunematsu does not have any branch office inside Japan and seven offices in 6countries. In contrast, TMI Associates has five branch offices in Japan and 11 offices in nine countries. Nishimura Asahi has four branch offices in Japan and 11 offices in nine countries. Mori Hamada and Matsumoto has four branch offices in Japan and eight offices in six countries. Anderson Mohri and Tomotsune two branch offices in Japan and nine offices in six countries. All Big Five have their offices in China and ASEAN.

[70] Interview with a partner at a Top Ten firm in July 2017.

corporate clients.[71] Focused fields mainly for individual clients include family matters, traffic accidents, personal bankruptcy, criminal defense, consumer loans and medical malpractice. Focused fields mainly for corporate clients include real property, international transactions, business bankruptcy, finance, M&A, intellectual property, tax and others. The percentage of lawyers who have the former group of focused fields (i.e. for individual clients) is 50.3%, while the percentage of those with the latter group of focused fields (i.e. for corporate clients) is 39.9%. Insofar as we see through the focused fields, Japanese lawyers work for individual clients more than corporate business clients.

1.3.4 Large Difference in Annual Income

How much Japanese lawyers earn annually is shown in Table 1.10. Oldest and youngest generations tend to earn less for obvious reasons. Oldest generations are in their retirement ages and they do not work as much as they used to. Many of the youngest generation are employed and have less opportunities to earn a lot.[72] Declared income tax amount which managing lawyers earned was on average 6.6 million in 2018 and an employed lawyer's annual income was on average 3.7 million yen in the same year. But there are large differences in the amount of annual income among lawyers with 10–40 years experience.

Table 1.11 shows how much the annual income changed from the first year to the last year at the same law firm. Table 1.11 is made, based on the categories of income levels shown in Table 1.10. If a lawyer's income in the first year was level 3, 5 to less than seven million Yen, and that in the last year was level 5, 10 to less than 15 million Yen, the difference in income in Table 1.10 is +2. If the first year income was level 4 and the last year income was level 2, the difference in income is −2. As intervals between levels in Table 1.10 are not the same, this is very rough estimate. But it helps to understand how much lawyers' incomes could change. Table 1.11 shows that the oldest two generations never experienced a decrease in income but some had huge increase, though an income increase was not large for most lawyers of these generations. This is due to the low-income level in Japan during this period.

For the subsequent generations, the income difference became larger, and some lawyers experienced a serious reduction of annual income. But the percentage of

[71] Some focused fields can be both for individual and corporate clients, such as accident victims and insurance companies in traffic accidents and patients and hospitals in medical malpractice. But the number of lawyers who work for corporate clients does not seem to be large in these cases.

[72] Associates usually receive a monthly salary in first years and whether they can work for commission on a personal basis depends upon policies of law firms. Even when associates are allowed to take cases on the individual basis, they may be too busy to find time for such works. Therefore, incomes of young lawyers tend to be limited.

Table 1.10 Distribution of present annual income before tax among lawyers at law firms (Career Survey 2018–2019)

		Year of LTRI graduation						
	Annual income (Japanese Yen)	1950 ~ 1966	1967 ~ 1976	1977 ~ 1986	1987 ~ 1996	1997 ~ 2006	2007 ~ 2016	Total
1	Less than three million	44.1%	20.0%	4.3%	2.8%	3.9%	2.6%	5.4%
2	3 to less than five million	11.8%	8.3%	9.7%	8.4%	2.6%	10.5%	8.5%
3	5 to less than seven million	5.9%	3.3%	4.3%	6.5%	9.6%	23.3%	16.1%
4	7 to less than ten million	20.6%	18.3%	8.6%	11.2%	19.3%	24.7%	20.5%
5	10 to less than 15 million	2.9%	15.0%	24.7%	21.5%	18.4%	22.4%	20.8%
6	15 to less than 20 million	2.9%	16.7%	17.2%	11.2%	14.5%	8.3%	11.0%
7	20 to less than 30 million	2.9%	5.0%	14.0%	12.1%	16.2%	6.3%	9.1%
8	30 to less than 50 million	8.8%	6.7%	11.8%	17.8%	10.5%	1.2%	5.9%
9	50 to less than 100 million	–	6.7%	2.2%	3.7%	3.9%	0.5%	1.9%
10	100 million or more	–	–	3.2%	4.7%	0.9%	–	0.8%
Total		99.9%	100.0%	100.0%	99.9%	99.8%	99.8%	100.0%
N of respondents		34	60	93	107	228	647	[a]1195

[a] The total number of respondents from 1950 to 2016 is 1169. 26 respondents did not answer when they graduated from the LTRI training program

Table 1.11 Difference in income between the first and last year at law firm (Career Survey 2018–19)

Difference in income	Year of LTRI graduation					
	1950 ~ 1966	1967 ~ 1976	1977 ~ 1986	1987 ~ 1996	1997 ~ 2006	2007 ~ 2016
−4	–	–	–	–	–	0.3%
−3	–	–	–	–	0.4%	0.1%
−2	–	–	–	0.9%	1.2%	1.1%
−1	–	–	2.0%	5.4%	2.8%	2.5%
0	51.7%	41.9%	36.7%	30.6%	36.0%	45.9%
+1	20.7%	27.4%	22.4%	22.5%	26.8%	30.7%
+2	10.3%	9.7%	14.3%	18.0%	16.8%	11.9%
+3	6.9%	8.1%	11.2%	11.7%	7.6%	5.4%
+4	3.4%	9.7%	5.1%	4.5%	5.2%	1.4%
+5	–	1.6%	4.1%	4.5%	2.8%	0.4%
+6	–	–	4.1%	1.8%	0.4%	0.1%
+7	3.4%	–	–	–	–	–
+8	3.4%	1.6%	–	–	–	–
Total	[a]99.8%	100.0%	[a]99.9%	[a]99.9%	100.0%	[a]99.8%
N	29	62	98	111	250	716

[a] Rounding error

those who experienced an income decrease is not large, 2.0% of the 1977–86 generation, 6.3% of the 1987–96 generation, 4.4% of the 1997–2006 generation and 4.0% of the 2007–2016 generation. The widening differences indicate the increasing competition among lawyers, seeking better income.

1.3.5 Preliminary Bar Examination Passers

As we saw above, the preliminary bar examination created a new route by which undergraduate students could quickly become legal professionals. But it also provides an opportunity for people with relevant social experience to become legal professionals without going to law school. Therefore, people taking the preliminary bar examination are mixed in terms of their ages, though passers are predominantly young people. In 2022, among 472 passers, those up to 24 years old occupy 59.5% and those between 25 and 29 years old 14.2%, while those in their 30 s 15.5%, in their 40 s or older 10.8%. Those in their teens or 20 s are an overwhelming majority: 73.7% (MOJ 2022a).

According to our survey data, preliminary bar examination passers tend to find positions at much larger law firms (122 lawyers on average) than those who have not passed the preliminary bar examination (18 lawyers on average) ($P. < 0.001$).

It is also characteristic that, when comparing preliminary bar examination passers with those who have not passed the preliminary bar examination, preliminary bar examination passers tend to find their jobs in Tokyo (67% v. 37%) but very few in Osaka (6% v. 14%), none in Nagoya (0% v. 6%). Similarly, preliminary bar examination passers tend to find jobs in cities with a High Court (15% v. 13%), and fewer in cities without a High Court (12% v. 29%) (Fisher's exact test = 0.015). When the preliminary bar exam passers moved to other law firms, they tended either to move to big cities with High Court, including Nagoya but none to Osaka (57%), or to stay in Tokyo (43%) (Fisher's exact test = 0.072). It is clear that preliminary bar examination passers tend to work in Tokyo or in other big cities with High Courts.

Both the preliminary bar examination passers and non-passers tended to be employed at law firms, but management styles of their law firms tended to be different. More non- passers tended to practice at solo-practitioner's offices (45%) than passers (24%) (Fisher's exact test = 0.026), while more passers tended to be associates at income-sharing law firms (24%) than non-passers (5%) (Fisher's exact test = 0.001). Law firms where preliminary bar exam passers work as their first offices were most often legal professional corporations (46%).

As preliminary bar examination passers tended to practice at large law firms in Tokyo or big cities much more often than non- passers, there are also differences in their focused fields: passers much more often work on international transactions (19% v. 5%, Fisher's exact test = 0.012) and finance (22% v.3%, Fisher's exact test = 0.000), while non- passers much more often work on traffic accidents (20% v. 3%, Fisher's exact test = 0.015).

Preliminary bar examination passers tended to earn more than non- passers, as shown in Table 1.12. The largest income group of non- passers (41%) is between 5 and seven million Yen and the second largest (34%) between 3 and five million Yen, which, combined is 75%, while the largest income group of passers (27%) is both between 3 and five million Yen and 10 and 15 million Yen. The percentage of non-passers who earned between 10 and 15 million Yen is only 5%. There are two peaks

Table 1.12 First year annual income before tax of preliminary bar examination passers and non- passers at their first law firms (Career Survey 2018–2019)

	Preliminary bar examination	
Income of the first year at the first law firm	Passed	Not passed (Not taken)
Less than three million	3%	9%
3 to less than five million	27%	34%
5 to less than seven million	21%	41%
7 to less than ten million	21%	11%
10 to less than 15 million	27%	5%
Total	[a]99%	100%
N	33	248

Fisher's exact test = 0.000

[a] Rounding error

Table 1.13 The last year annual income before tax of preliminary bar examination passers and non-passers at their first law firms (2018–2019)

Income of the last year at the first law firm	Preliminary bar examination	
	Passed	Not passed (Not taken)
Less than three million	3%	7%
3 to less than five million	12%	19%
5 to less than seven million	27%	35%
7 to less than ten million	18%	23%
10 to less than 15 million	27%	12%
15 to less than 20 million	9%	4%
20 to less than 30 million	3%	[a]0%
Total	[b]99%	100%
N	33	248

Fisher's exact test = 0.081
[a]0.4%
[b]Rounding error

in the distribution of passers' income but there is only one peak in the distribution of non- passers' income.

Last year annual income at the first law firms increased after years of practice for both preliminary bar examination passers and non- passers (Table 1.13), but just like the first year income, passers' income tended to be higher than for non- passers. The shape of the income distribution is the same as the first year income distribution with two peaks for the passers' income.

1.3.6 Public-Interest Legal Service

1.3.6.1 Civil Legal Aid and Public Criminal Defense

The Justice System Reform increased the budget for civil legal aid and public criminal defense for the indigent, which helped expand the work of lawyers, particularly young lawyers.

The civil legal aid program used to be a small program carried out by lawyers. The Legal Aid Association (LAA) was established in 1952 by the JFBA and the state subsidies were small, 74 million Yen in 1980 and 116 million Yen in 1990. Expecting the future expansion of civil legal aid, the Civil Legal Aid Act (Act No.55) was only enacted in Japan in 2000. The LAA was transformed into an agency supervised by the Ministry of Justice and, in 2000, the state subsidies were increased to 2.16 billion Yen.

The Justice System Reform Council recommended an expansion of civil legal aid, indicating that the right to a trial was not sufficiently guaranteed, and suggested a comprehensive reform including an expansion of public criminal defense from defendants to suspects (JSRC 2001, II, No.1, 7 (2)). Following this recommendation, the Comprehensive Legal Support Act was legislated in 2004 (Act No. 74) and, in 2006, the Japan Legal Support Center (JLSC) was established under the jurisdiction of the Ministry of Justice to provide civil legal aid and court-appointed defense counsel for criminal cases.

The establishment of the JLSC sharply increased the state subsidies for civil legal aid. The LAA received 2.16 billion Yen in 2000, but the JLSC received 15.54 billion Yen in 2010 and 15.82 billion Yen in 2020 (JLSC 2011, p. x; 2021, p. 12), though it is difficult to expect a further significant increase of the budget.

The most publicized service of JLSC for the general public was to provide free advice over the phone, later also by email. It set up a call center at its headquarters in Tokyo to give answers to simple questions or referral to other agencies,[73] and local offices established throughout Japan provided a similar service. The headquarters in Tokyo received 370,124 queries from all over Japan by phone or email in 2010 and 349,533 in 2020 while the local offices received 234,614 queries in 2010 and 202,211 in 2020 (JLSC 2011, p. xi; 2021, p. 13).

For civil legal aid, the JLSC provided three kinds of services: preparing documents, legal consultation, and representation. Legal documents are prepared by judicial scriveners, while legal consultation and representation are given by lawyers. The volume of these services sharply increased as the result of the transition from the LAA to the JLSC. The number of legal consultation cases was 35,505 in 2000 (JFBA 2002), and it increased to 256,719 in 2010 and 290,860 in 2020 (JLSC 2011, p. 13; 2021, p. 13). The number of representation cases was 20,098 in 2000, and it also increased to 110,217 in 2010 and 105,630 in 2020.[74] The number of legal document cases was smaller, but it also increased from 163 in 2000 to 7366 in 2010 but decreased to 3476 in 2020. The number of contracted lawyers was 15,037 in 2010 and 24,028 in 2020, while that of contracted judicial scriveners was 5617 in 2010 and 7500 in 2020 (JLSC 2011, p. 13; 2021, p. 13). The expansion of civil legal aid benefited lawyers, particularly young lawyers who had not yet established their legal practice.

The public criminal defense lawyers were appointed by the court, but, before the Justice System Reform, the system of public criminal defense, including making a list of lawyers and assigning cases, was managed by local bar associations. When bar associations defined themselves as the "legal professionals in the field", as opposed to "legal professionals in the government", criminal defense had a special significance for them, as criminal defense was allowed to be conducted only by private attorneys, and, particularly before the Second World War, it could present an opportunity for a private attorney to defeat a public prosecutor. Therefore, criminal defense was considered as an essential element of Japanese private attorneys which should be able to be done by every private attorney, though the gap between the professional ideal and the

[73] At the call center a few lawyers stand by to give legal advice when operators cannot answer to questions.

[74] Legal aid representation in court was not, and still is not, free, though legal advice was free. Those who received legal aid for representation have to return what they received, but particular indigent people are eligible for exemption. In 2020, 32.4% of what should be paid back for representation and preparing judicial documents was exempted. The percentage was calculated from the data of the JLSC, 2021, pp.83, 85, 86.

reality of legal practice was widening in urban centers like Tokyo. While almost all active members of small local bar associations were obliged to take court-appointed criminal defense cases in turn because of the small number of lawyers, only 19% of the lawyers in Tokyo actually took public criminal defense cases in 1990.[75]

Despite the perception of criminal defense as the essential element of their profession, the increase in public defense cases caused a devaluation of criminal defense work. This was because the fees for such public criminal defense work were low and many lawyers were reluctant to take such cases on. The percentage of public defense cases at the District Courts increased from 60% in 1990 to 72% in 2000 and the percentage at the Summary Courts increased from 79% in 1990 to 87% in 2000.[76] Because of the small fee, public criminal defense cases were often taken by junior lawyers without much experience or generalists who tried to catch up with current practice of criminal trials (Murayama 2002).

Prior to 2000, the legally aided public criminal defense work was not extended to suspects, persons not yet formally charged with a crime by the prosecutor. It was estimated that only 20% to 30% of defendants had retained defense lawyers before indicted in cases where defense lawyers were legally required for trial. Pre-indictment criminal defense work was actively conducted in some labor and public security cases, but, with the exception of traffic accident cases, generally public access to pre-indictment criminal defense counsel was limited (JFBA 1989, pp. 207–208).

The first impetus to expand defense works for suspects came from lawyers themselves. In 1990, the Oita Bar Association, a small local bar association in the Kyushu Region, began to dispatch a lawyer, called "duty lawyer", to suspects arrested and detained at the police station. This practice spread very quickly to other bar associations, and, after a few years, all bar associations began to send lawyers to assist suspects detained at police stations.

This practice had two purposes. One was to defend a suspect in need of defense as soon as possible. The other was to expand opportunities for the lawyer to be retained as criminal defense counsel. The dispatch of a lawyer to meet a suspect was free of charge, but if the suspect wanted to see the lawyer again, the suspect had to retain the lawyer. But suspects were often indigent and could not retain lawyers. The LAA began to provide fee for suspects to retain lawyers in the 1990s. This created a precedent for a later system of public criminal defense for detained suspects.

Pre-indictment criminal defense was much needed but not possible as there were not enough lawyers to defend the accused at that stage of the matter. The JSRC recommended both to increase the lawyer population and to extend public criminal defense to suspects. The JLSC assumed responsibility for managing the whole

[75] Twenty-nine percent of all the lawyers registered in Tokyo were on the list of candidates at the bar associations in 1990. Tokyo Bar Associations assigned cases equally to all the lawyers on the list, but many of them declined to take cases, as they were allowed to choose cases in Tokyo (Murayama 1992, p. 311).

[76] Calculated from the judicial statistics (SC Jimusokyoku 1990, Tables 33–1, 33–2; 2020, Tables 23, 24).

public criminal defense system in 2006. The budget for public criminal defense that the JLSC received was 15.55 billion Yen in 2010 and 17.04 billion Yen in 2020 (JLSC 2011, p. 12; 2021, p. 12).

At first, in 2006, the JLSC provided public defense for detained indigent suspects charged with crimes whose minimum punishment was imprisonment for a year or more. When the lay judge system started in 2009, the scope of public defense for suspects was expanded to suspects who were charged with crimes whose maximum punishment was more than 3 years' imprisonment. In 2018, all suspects detained by the court became entitled to public defense. As a result, the number of suspects who were provided with public criminal defense increased dramatically.[77]

In 2010, the JLSC received 70,917 cases for suspects, 69,634 cases for defendants, and 423 cases for delinquent juveniles.[78] In 2020, it received and 76,073 cases for suspects, 50,076 cases for defendants, and 2941 cases for delinquent juveniles (JLSC 2011, p. xi; 2021, p. 13).

The number of lawyers contracted for criminal defense increased from 19,566 lawyers in 2010 to 30,897 lawyers in 2020. That for juveniles also increased from 423 lawyers in 2010 to 15,886 lawyers in 2020 (JLSC 2011, p. xi; 2021, p. 13). The JLSC improved the fee scale for public defense activities albeit not as much as lawyers desired, and the new public defense for suspects provided opportunities for an increasing number of junior lawyers.

The public defense for suspects seemed to stimulate pre-indictment defense activities and criminal defense work in general. In the last century, most criminal defense work was widely believed not to pay well. Public defense work was mostly avoided by lawyers though some might be willing to be retained for criminal defense just like civil cases. In recent years, as we saw in 1.3.3, law firms began to advertise their focused practice concerning traffic accidents in both civil and criminal matters. Some law firms also advertise their private criminal defense practice. Apparently private criminal defense work is now considered to pay enough to cover law firms' costs, although there are not many law firms specialized in criminal cases.

The need for pre-indictment criminal defense is in fact larger than it might appear. In 2020, among penal code and special penal code offenses, excluding negligent traffic and other traffic violation cases, one half of the adult suspects dealt by the prosecutors, 50% of 212,576 persons, were 'suspended' for prosecution, which means that the prosecutors did not prosecute those cases based on criminal

[77] It is to be noted that the role of a duty lawyer dispatched by a bar association remains significant after the establishment of public defense for detained suspects. In the Japanese criminal procedure, the police and the prosecutor can detain a suspect for up to 72 h. By 72 h after an arrest, the prosecutor has to decide whether to ask the court to detain the suspect (Code of Criminal Procedures Articles 203 (1), 204 (1), 205 (1) (2)). Therefore, after 72 hours from arrest, it is the court which detains a suspect. Public defense is to be provided to suspects detained by the court, but not by the police and prosecutor.

[78] All the juvenile suspects are to be sent to the family courts where judges decide whether to open the juvenile protection procedure, dismiss the matter, or send the matter back to the prosecutor for a criminal trial. The role of a lawyer for the juvenile procedure is called an attendance, not defense. Juvenile Act (Law, No.168 of 1948), Article 6 (3).

policy considerations. Similarly, in 2020, among criminal negligent traffic offenses, 83% of 293,335 adult suspects were 'suspended' for prosecution, and among the traffic law violations, 46% of 211,971 adult suspects were 'suspended' for prosecution.[79] In Japan, guilty plea negotiation does not exist, except cooperation of the accused for specific categories of crimes, such as organized crimes, tax and financial crimes, introduced in 2018 (Criminal Procedure, Article 350-2 to Article 350-15). Yet, if a negligent traffic offender pays compensation to the victim and the victim is satisfied with it, the prosecutor may suspend the prosecution of the offender. There can be always something that a defense lawyer may be able to work on to obtain a lenient decision from the prosecutor.

1.3.6.2 JLSC Staff Lawyers

As we saw, the JLSC mainly relies on the judicare model for civil legal aid and public criminal defense.[80] But the JLSC also employs private attorneys at JLSC offices. The JLSC established 50 offices at prefectural capital cities and 3 additional offices in Hokkaido as their local headquarters, 11 branch offices, 10 liaison offices, and 37 rural local offices. The JLSC appointed, in total, 194 lawyers to those various kinds of offices. The management of the JLSC organization was conducted by public officials of the MOJ, the SC and the JFBA, but the budget came from the Ministry of Justice. Therefore, the JLSC was considered as an agent of the MOJ. Directors of local headquarters were appointed from among members of local bar associations, and employed lawyers work according to the policies of the directors. If a director's policy is restrictive, an employed lawyer would not be able to work freely, making efforts not to infringe the boundaries set by the director.

The relationship between local bar association members and an employed lawyer has been often difficult at rural local offices, as JLSC lawyers are expected to take legal aid cases, and in rural areas with few lawyers, also take retained cases. The rational of the JLSC in allowing employed lawyers to take non-legal aid cases is that there are too few lawyers to satisfy the local legal need in those regions. As a result, JLSC lawyers are often alienated from local bar members.[81] JLSC lawyers conduct public criminal defense without much concern as they know local bar members would not prefer to take those cases anyway, but JLSC lawyers are careful about which civil cases they should take. This kind of problem did not exist when legal aid was managed by the local bar associations. Unless the JLSC is well accepted by local bar associations, it would not be conceivable for the JLSC and local bar associations to cooperate in expanding legal services to local people effectively.

---

[79] Calculated from the prosecutorial statistics. MOJ (2020), Tables 20-00-09, 20-00-10, 20-00-11.

[80] In the judicare model, any lawyers who are on the list of candidates can take civil legal aid cases or public criminal defense cases.

[81] Local bar members argue that the JLSC, a public agency, interferes with the private business of local lawyers.

1.3.6.3 JFBA Sunflower Fund Law Offices

The JLSC rural local offices have a precedent, which started as a kind of public office funded by the JFBA. In the 1990s when the increase of the number of lawyers was still being discussed, the JFBA was criticized that there were no lawyers in many areas where courts were located. To respond to the criticism, in 2000, the JFBA began to establish a 'sunflower fund law office' in rural areas without lawyers. Under this scheme, the JFBA funded opening a law office and guaranteed the annual income of its lawyer(s). By 2020, the JFBA helped 122 lawyers to open their sunflower fund law offices in rural areas. 83 lawyers have now retired from those offices and have settled in the same areas by opening their own law firms. In 2021, there were 36 sunflower fund law offices nationwide. In 1993, there were 50 court branch jurisdictions without a lawyer and 24 jurisdictions with just one lawyer. In contrast, by 2021, there was no court branch jurisdiction without a lawyer and only three jurisdictions with just one lawyer (JFBA 2021b, pp. 205–207).

1.3.6.4 Urban Public-Interest Law Firms

Daini Tokyo Bar Association established the first urban law firm in Tokyo in 2001 to improve the access to lawyers and to train young lawyers who would work at the JFBA Sunflower Fund law offices. The other two Tokyo Bar Associations followed that model and now, in 2023, there are five public-interest law firms employing 66 lawyers. This model spread out of Tokyo and by 2023, 6 other bar associations have established public-interest law firms employing 51 lawyers. Lawyers who had practiced for the first few years after the graduation from the LTRI at these law firms took positions at the JFBA Sunflower Fund law offices and JLSC rural local offices. After their term at the offices, they either returned to their cities or established their own law firms in rural cities. The urban public-interest law firms[82] had trained many public-interest minded lawyers and have situated themselves at the center of the national network of public-interest minded lawyers.

[82] There is one law firm in Tokyo which is not an urban public-interest law firm but performed a significant role of training competent young lawyers with a public-interest focus. The JFBA set up funds to help young lawyers to open law firms in rural local areas or work as public-interest lawyers. During the period from 2007 to 2021, lawyers received such JFBA financial assistance in 412 cases (JFBA 2021b, p. 211).

1.3.7 *From Profession to Legal Service Providers*

Article 8 of the Attorneys Ethics Code (1955) prohibited advertising by lawyers and did not allow lawyers to write their careers on their business cards or billboards, etc. except their degrees and specialization (Uetsuma 2014, p. 8). It is surprising that this Article allowed lawyers to write their specializations, which the JFBA now recommends against. In 1987, this code was changed to allow lawyers to disclose more information to the public. While prohibiting advertising of legal practice, it allowed lawyers to disclose their name, address, the name of a law firm, its location, phone number, etc. on a name card, an envelope, a greeting card, in a telephone directory, etc. In 1990 the JFBA declared that private attorneys should not make degrading advertisements (Uetsuma 2014, p. 8). Bar associations' attitudes toward advertising legal practice was still not favorable.

These prohibitive attitudes toward disclosure of lawyer's information corresponded to the pervasive way by which lawyers obtained clients. Traditionally, lawyers' main clients were small entrepreneurs and affluent individuals (Rokumoto 1988, p. 170).[83] Lawyers obtained clients by introduction through their personal networks, such as former individual clients, corporate clients and friends/acquaintances. The percentage of first clients without introduction was only 1.9% in 1990 and 1.5% in 2000, but suddenly increased to 18.2% in 2010 (JFBA Bengoshi Gyomu Kaikaku Iinkai 2002, p. 77; 2011, p. 102). The report of the 2010 survey indicates that the increased percentage was due to increased solicitation by advertisements. The 2020 survey result is unfortunately not comparable to the previous survey result as it asked through which route respondents obtain "many" clients. In the 2020 survey, 19.6% of the respondents answered that they obtained many clients through advertisements such as a homepage, and 5.6% of them answered they obtained many clients without introduction nor through advertisements (JFBA 2021a, p. 87). Therefore, in 2020, 25.5%, a quarter of the lawyers surveyed, obtained many clients without introduction.

The increase of new clients without introduction means that an increasing number of lawyers changed the way of obtaining new clients. Previously, most lawyers used to reject visitors to their offices without introduction.[84] Table 1.14 shows that competition among lawyers began to increase in the late 1990s and became stronger as the number of registered lawyers increased sharply in 2007. It would be safe to

[83] In a survey around 1960, 7% of the lawyers answered that their main clients were large companies while 72% of them had middle and small companies and individuals (Shimizu 1960, p. 47).

[84] Connection with a lawyer significantly correlates with the use of a lawyer in dealing with a legal problem (109a, 30-33). Lawyers listed three reasons why they prefer introduction: (1) It was improbable that an introduced client would lie; (2) A client sometimes asked a lawyer to do what would be legally impossible, but an introduced client would not demand a lawyer to do such a thing; (3) If there was trouble with a client, an introducer could be relied on to act as conciliator between the client and the lawyer. Therefore, both lawyers and future clients had concerns with each other, and introduction would resolve the concerns (Murayama 2009a, pp. 35–36).

Table 1.14 Exposure to competition

Year	Percentage of lawyers feeling they are exposed to competition				
	Every Day	Sometimes	Never		
1980	8.9%	38.4%	52.7%		
1990	9.6%	38.4%	51.7%		
2000	15.0%	41.4%	43.2%		
	Compared to 10 years ago, do you think competition with other lawyers has become severe?				
	I think so	I cannot say either	I do not think so	I do not know	No answer
2010	44.4%	25.4%	30.2%	–	–
2020	36.6%	20.9%	30.8%	11.0%	0.6%

Sources: JFBA (1988), p. 150; (1991), p. 98; (2002), p. 188; (2011), p. 204; (2021, b), p. 164. This table is partly taken from another table (Murayama 2020, p.761, Table 3)

conclude that increasing competition among lawyers prompted them to change their practice and accept clients without introduction.

The increase of new clients without introduction indicates that more people out of a lawyer's personal network began to seek legal services of lawyers. People who do not know lawyers typically seek free legal advice provided by a municipal government or by the legal aid agency. For instance, every ward of Tokyo provides free legal advice to residents and commuters who work in the jurisdiction. The local municipal office is a popular place to obtain free legal advice and some visitors are referred to the legal aid agency.[85] Local bar associations also open legal advice centers where lawyers give advice for 5000 Yen plus tax for 30 min.[86]

The percentage of new clients from these legal advice agencies or advice centers was only 2.2% in 1990 and 5.6% in 2000 (JFBA Bengoshi Gyomu Kaikaku Iinkai 2002, p. 77) but increased to 13.9% in 2010. In the 2020 survey, 25.9% of the lawyers answered that they accepted many clients through legal advice agencies or advice centers. This sharp increase might reflect the change of the policy which now allowed lawyers to accept such people as their clients.[87] As such a prohibition has been mostly lifted, more lawyers began to accept new clients through legal consultation.

Advertisements by lawyers undoubtedly helped people find lawyers. In 2000, the JFBA lifted the prohibition on advertising legal practice. For a few years almost nothing happened, except small advertisement plates appeared inside commuter trains. Then, a law firm began to advertise their practice for onerous debt cases and overpaid interest cases on radio and then on TV. Years later, a few other law firms

[85] In 2002, 36% of the visitors to the Legal Aid Association in Tokyo were introduced by municipal governments, while only 8% were introduced by the court (Murayama 2010, p. 407 note 17).

[86] Legal Advice Centers managed by bar associations play a significant role in providing access to lawyers for people who do not know lawyers (Murayama 2009b, pp. 184–190).

[87] As there was a common suspicion that lawyers might "make" cases without necessity, municipal governments did not even tell visitors names of lawyers for legal consultation.

followed. These advertisements on the mass media significantly changed the public image of private attorneys to legal service providers for all.

As Table 1.15 shows, younger generations of lawyers advertise more than older generations. Fourty percent of the youngest generation advertises their legal practice.

Younger generations of lawyers also have their law firm homepages on the Internet more than older generations, as is shown in Table 1.16. It is somewhat surprising that more than a quarter of the oldest generation have their law firm homepages on the Internet. Three quarters of the youngest generation have their law firm homepages on the Internet. The Internet has become an important means to provide information on legal practice.

As a homepage of a law firm on the Internet can be seen by anybody, creating a homepage of a law firm is more often than not based on a practice policy to accept new clients without introduction. As Table 1.17 shows, younger generations accept new clients without introduction more often than older generations. Yet comparing Tables 1.16 and 1.17, the percentage of lawyers who have homepages on the Internet is higher than that of those who accept new clients without introduction in every generation except the oldest. From this we can infer that some lawyers create homepages of their law firms without necessarily intending to obtain new clients through the website.

For a mass process law firm, both advertising and creating a homepage is based on the policy of obtaining new clients as many as possible.[88]

When we compare the percentage of lawyers who have homepages of their law firms according to locations of their law firms, 74% of lawyers in Tokyo and Osaka have homepages, while 65% of those in cities with a High Court have homepages and 58% of those in cities without a High Court ($p. < 0.01$). However, 76% of lawyers in Tokyo and Osaka did not advertise generally, while 63% of those in cities with a High Court and 57% of those in cities without a High Court did not advertise ($p. < 0.01$). Apparently, according to some lawyers, having a homepage does not mean advertising on the Internet.

Similarly, lawyers in Tokyo and Osaka would least accept clients without introduction. Only 46% of them accept new clients without introduction, while 68% of lawyers in cities with a High Court and 76% of those in cities without a High Court accept new clients.

The population is much larger in Tokyo and Osaka than in other areas and people in urban centers are often strangers. Therefore, one might expect that people would rely on websites to find lawyers in urban centers more than in rural cities. But this would be the case mostly for individual clients. Locations of large corporations are concentrated in Tokyo and Osaka. Large corporations have legal advisors as well as

[88] Therefore, it is important to have the name of their law firm listed at the top or near the top on the Google search. A partner of a large mass process law firm said that the cost for search engine optimization was financially a heavy burden, costing tens of millions of Yen. Interview in February 2018. A law firm specializing in over-paid interest cases went bankrupt, having spent a large amount for advertising in 2020.

Table 1.15 Do you advertise your law firm in a train /bus, on radio, on TV or others? (Career Survey 2018–2019)

	Year of LTRI graduation						
Advertisement	1950 ~ 1966	1967 ~ 1976	1977 ~ 1986	1987 ~ 1996	1997 ~ 2006	2007 ~ 2016	All generations
Yes	5.7%	10.4%	21.2%	20.7%	27.5%	40.4%	31.6%
Total of *N*	35	67	104	116	240	675	[a]1270

[a] This number is more than the total of each column, as 33 respondents did not answer the year or the term when they entered the LTRI training program

Table 1.16 Do you have homepage of your law firm on the Internet? (Career Survey 2018–2019)

Homepage	Year of LTRI graduation						All generations
	1950 ~ 1966	1967 ~ 1976	1977 ~ 1986	1987 ~ 1996	1997 ~ 2006	2007 ~ 2016	
Yes	26.5%	48.5%	50.5%	54.8%	71.7%	75.6%	67.9%
Total of *N*	34	68	103	115	240	675	[a]1268

[a] This number is more than the total of each column, as 33 respondents did not answer the year or the term when they entered the LTRI training program

Table 1.17 Do you accept a new client without introduction? (Career Survey 2018–2019)

	Year of LTRI graduation						
Client without introduction	1950 ~ 1966	1967 ~ 1976	1977 ~ 1986	1987 ~ 1996	1997 ~ 2006	2007 ~ 2016	All generations
Yes	34.3%	35.8%	35.0%	49.6%	61.1%	63.7%	57.1%
Total of *N*	35	67	103	115	239	675	[a]1267

[a] This number is more than the total of each column, as 33 respondents did not answer the year or the term when they entered the LTRI training program

law departments. They know lawyers practicing in corporate business law fields as repeat players. Therefore, law firms whose main clients are corporate business clients do not have to rely on advertisement to obtain clients.[89] They create homepages to show customers that they are respectable law firms that have competent lawyers with good educational backgrounds and experience of specialized legal practice. But they consider it different from advertising to "actively sell" their practice.

1.4 In-House Lawyers and Growth of Corporate Law Departments

1.4.1 Rapid Increase of In-House Lawyers

According to the statistics compiled by Japan In-House Lawyers Association (JILA), the number of in-house lawyers grew rapidly in the twenty-first century, from 66 lawyers in 2001, 428 in 2010, 2629 in 2020 and 3184 in 2023, or 7.1% of all the registered lawyers in Japan (JILA, 2023a). The in-house is the sector of legal practice which has grown mostly in the twenty-first century.[90]

The increase in in-house lawyers has been facilitated by the growth of legal departments in corporations. According to the Report of the 12th Survey on the Legal Departments in Japanese Corporations (hereafter, Law Departments Survey), there have been two periods when the number of law departments increased among large companies including those listed on Tokyo Stock Exchange: in the early 2000s and after 2015. In particular after 2015, not only new law departments were created but also old sections were transformed into new law departments without continuity (Yoneda 2022, p. 8).[91]

In the twentieth century, corporations employed a large number of graduates of university law faculties. Those law graduates worked as general employees and when corporations established law sections or law departments, some of those law graduates were assigned to law departments. Yet law departments could be positions where law graduates were assigned in the process of promotion to management positions inside corporations. Some of them were sent to the U.S. for studying in a Master of Laws program, and after coming back, they tended to stay in their law departments. But they were not legal professionals qualified in Japan, though they sometimes got qualified as lawyer in the U.S., passing a bar exam in the second year of their study in the U.S.

---

[89] Corporations find lawyers as they had retained or met them before, or as they are introduced by other lawyers (Yoneda 2022, pp. 283–284).

[90] According to the Law Departments Survey, the percentage of companies which employed legal professionals increased from 2.8% in 2000 to 28.3% in 2020 (Yoneda 2022, p. 209).

[91] The percentage of responding companies which had law departments or law sections increased from 52.1% in 2000 to 69.7% in 2020 (Yoneda 2022, p. 3).

Table 1.18 Career paths of in-house lawyers (Career Survey 2018–2019)

Career path[a]	Year of LTRI graduation 1977 ~ 1986	1987 ~ 1996	1997 ~ 2006	2007 ~ 2016	Total
Corporation	–	100.0%	8.3%	46.2%	42.1%
Corporation- > law firm- > corporation	–	–	–	1.1%	0.9%
Law firm- > corporation	100.0%	–	83.3%	47.3%	51.4%
Law firm- > public office- > corporation	–	–	–	4.3%	3.7%
Public office- > corporation	–	–	–	1.1%	0.9%
Public office- > law firm- > corporation	–	–	8.3%	–	0.9%
Total	100.0%	100.0%	[b]99.9%	100.0%	[b]99.9%
N	1	1	12	93	107

[a] Only the move between sectors is shown
[b] Rounding error

In the 1990s U.S. corporations in Japan began to employ Japanese private attorneys. Since then, the number of private attorneys employed by corporations grew rapidly as we saw. Table 1.18 shows this development of in-house lawyers clearly. Fourty-two percent of the in-house lawyers chose in-house position as their first career as private attorney and stayed as in-house lawyer. A larger group of in-house lawyers, 51% of them, moved from law firms to in-house positions. And some (4%) moved from a law firm via a public office to a corporation.

The increase of in-house positions began as corporations began to recruit lawyers from law firms. Corporations did not recruit many LTRI graduates in the 2000s. In our data, one lawyer who qualified as legal professional in 1984 practiced at a law firm for 12 years, then moved to a law department of a corporation in 1996. The lawyer had worked at a large law firm which had 60 lawyers when he quit. We can speculate that the lawyer practiced mainly for business corporate matters and found an in-house position which was expected to align with his experience. Among lawyers who moved from law firms to corporations, 96% of them did so in 2010 or later. Except for one lawyer who moved to a corporation after 1 year at a law firm, the lawyers practiced at least 3 years or mostly 5–10 years at law firms. Therefore, it is apparent that corporations preferred to employ experienced lawyers.[92] Recruiting many LTRI graduates is just a new phenomenon.

It is well known that the percentage of women lawyers is very high among in-house lawyers (41.6%) in comparison with that of registered lawyers (19.6%) in 2022. However, the percentage of women lawyers who chose in-house as the first position in their career is not significantly higher than men (23.0% v. 19.8%, statistically not significant). But among the lawyers who moved from their first law firms to corporations, a disproportionately higher percentage of women moved from law

[92] A senior lawyer at the JFBA said that lawyers with experience of practice at law firms were more highly evaluated by corporations (Foote et al. 2021, p. 16).

firms to in-house positions: men were 56.0% and women 44.0% ($P < 0.01$). In contrast, the percentage of women lawyers who moved from their first law firms to second law firms was 19.6%, the same as the percentage of women among all the registered lawyers.

Work-life balance is often pointed out as the main reason for moving from law firms to corporations. Whilst 68% of our respondents chose work-life balance as a main reason, which is higher than the other reasons, both men and women chose life-work balance most often and there is no gender difference (67.9% v. 68.2%). The second often chosen reason is worthwhile work, but men chose worthwhile work much more often (57.1%) than women (27.3%) as a main reason.

Large corporations have been concentrated in Tokyo. Among our respondents, all the in-house lawyers who graduated the LTRI from 1950 to 2006, except one, worked in Tokyo when they started their work at their corporations. But as the number of in-house lawyers increased, locations of their corporations began to diversify. Among in-house lawyers who graduated the LTRI from 2007 to 2016, the percentage of in-house lawyers whose workplaces located in Tokyo was 77%. In-house lawyers of this generation worked in Osaka (8%), Nagoya (1%), cities with a High Court (6%) and cities without a High Court (8%). Yet, still, the overwhelming majority of in-house lawyers work in Tokyo. For lawyers who want to live in the Tokyo metropolitan area, in-house position must be attractive in terms of office location.

1.4.2 In-House Positions: Works in Progress

Since up until 2003 lawyers had to obtain permission of the bar association in order to be employed by private companies, most lawyers who became in-house by that time did not register with the bar association. Since then, an increasing number of legal professionals have registered at the bar. There seem to be unregistered legal professionals employed by corporations, though the number is not known. Corporations tend to treat unregistered legal professionals as general employees rather than special employees. Treatment as special employees would mean paying the membership fee of the bar association, special pay for the qualification and in principle no transfer out of law departments (Yoneda 2022, pp. 249–251).

According to our survey results, when legal professionals were employed by corporations before 2007, most of them (83%) were assigned to positions which were not in law departments. Yet, from 2007, more lawyers (69%) were assigned to law departments. This increase has continued, and at the time of the survey, 73% of all in-house lawyers worked in law departments in November 2018–January 2019.

The number of lawyers in a company also increased. When legal professionals were employed by companies as their first job, 47% of them had only one legal professional, 40% had one to five legal professionals, and 14% had six or more legal professionals. At the time of our survey in 2018–19, only 30% found only one legal professional, 35% one to five, and 36% six or more legal professionals. The size of law departments in terms of the number of legal professionals has been expanding.

Although the number of in-house lawyers has been increasing, corporate law departments are still in the process of development. Most directors of law departments are not qualified as legal professionals and many members of law departments are also not qualified as legal professionals; both of them were often employed as career-track general employees after graduating from undergraduate law faculties. One criticism of law departments in corporations is that they often serve presidents of corporations, but not the corporations themselves, being unable to make rational judgments for the interests of stockholders (Karatsu 2011, pp. 195–206). If in-house lawyers are promoted together with general employees, it would be difficult for law departments to make independent legal judgments.[93] As time passes, in-house lawyers will become directors of law departments, which might make law department more independent for the interests of stockholders.

1.4.3 Income of In-House Lawyers

Most in-house lawyers were employed in the twenty-first century and it is difficult to compare the in-house lawyer's income with that of general company employees, as the data from the last century is very small. Table 1.19 shows the present income levels of in-house lawyers. The average annual income of employees at corporations listed on Tokyo Stock Exchange Market in 2018 was 6.1 million Yen (Tokyo Shoko Research 2022). Apparently two thirds of the in-house lawyers (74.6%) earned more than the average income of employees of the major corporations. In 2018, 18.9% of in-house lawyers seemed to earn an income on the same level as the employees as a whole, whereas 6.6% earned less than the average of the employees' income. But those 6.6% lawyers worked only for no more than 10 years. We can say that income of in-house lawyers is not so bad in comparison with the income of lawyers at law firms, as was shown in Table 1.10.

Changes of income during the employment of in-house lawyers are also not so large. When we calculate how many income levels in-house lawyers moved between the beginning and end[94] of their employment, just as we did for lawyers at law firms in Table 1.11, only 0.9% experienced a decrease. The majority (55.7%) stayed at the same level. 34.0% had one level up, 4.7% two levels up. 2.8% three levels up, 0.9% five levels up and another 0.9% experienced 6 levels up. As a whole, 43.4% experienced an increase in income, but the degree of increase is rather modest. There are not as large income differences among in-house lawyers as those at law firms, and their incomes are rather stable.

---

[93] In-house lawyers said that a law department of a U.S. corporation looked like a law firm inside a corporation, while a law department of a Japanese corporation is a part of the corporation (JILA 2003).

[94] If they stay in the same companies, the last time is the time of research, November 2018–January 2019.

Table 1.19 Distribution of annual income before tax from corporations (Career Survey 2018–2019)

Annual income before tax	Year of LTRI graduation				Total
	1977 ~ 1986	1987 ~ 1996	1997 ~ 2006	2007 ~ 2016	
Lesss than three million	–	–	–	–	–
3 to less than five million	–	–	–	7.9%	6.6%
5 to less than seven million	–	–	–	20.2%	18.9%
7 to less than ten million	–	–	9.1%	41.6%	35.8%
10 to less than 15 million	–	–	45.5%	24.7%	25.5%
15 to less than 20 million	–	–	9.1%	3.4%	5.7%
20 to less than 30 million	–	100.0%	27.3%	2.2%	5.7%
30 to less than 50 million	–	–	–	–	–
50 to less than 100 million	100.0%	–	9.1%	–	1.9%
Total	100.0%	100.0%	100.1%	100.0%	100.1%
N	1	1	11	89	106

1.5 Public Offices

Public offices can be classified very roughly as positions related to the court system and those in national Ministries and local governments. Graduates of law faculties in undergraduate programs have traditionally filled both positions until the new law school system was established. Graduates in law or political science took the bar exam to become legal professionals or took the national civil servant exam to become officials at national Ministries.[95] These two careers were almost independent of each other except that there have been a small number of personnel who move from the court to the Ministry of Justice and vice versa.[96]

The Japanese courts and public prosecutor's offices adopt career systems of their own and employ assistant judges and public prosecutors from among new legal professionals. As we saw at the beginning of this chapter, training processes for assistant judges, public prosecutors and private attorneys were unified after the Second World War and a certain number of LTRI graduates have chosen to become assistant judges or public prosecutors.

As is shown in Table 1.20, in the 1990s, on yearly average, among 611 LTRI graduates, 93 chose to become assistant judges, while 62 chose to become public prosecutors, 437 chose to become private attorneys and 19 chose other careers. Similarly, in the 2000s, among 1540 graduates, 107 chose to become assistant judges, while 91 chose to become public prosecutors, 1203 chose to become private attorneys and 139 chose other careers. In the 2010s, among 1848 graduates, 88

[95] Political science is a major of law faculty at national universities and students majoring political science can take courses of law; political science and law belong to different faculties at private universities.

[96] Under the pre-war French model, the courts were a branch of the Ministry of Justice and judges could become public prosecutors or other officials and vice versa at the Ministry of Justice. The post-war practice is a reminiscence of it.

Table 1.20 The average number of the LTRI graduates entering four sections per year

	1990s	2000s	2010s
Assistant judge	93	107	88
Public prosecutor	62	91	72
Private attorney	437	1203	1620
Other	19	139	68
Total	611	1540	1848

Source: JFBA (2022), p. 44

chose to become judges, 72 chose to become public prosecutors, 1620 chose to become private attorneys, and 68 chose other careers. From the 1990s, as the number of LTRI graduates increased, the percentage of graduates who chose to become assistant judges or public prosecutors decreased from 25.4% in the 1990s, to 12.8% in the 2000s and 8.7% in the 2010s. Yet, on average 150 to 200 graduates became either assistant judges or public prosecutors every year.

A small number of LTRI graduates chose other careers, which included academic careers and public officials at national Ministries. Before the establishment of new law schools, those who pursued academic careers were not required to pass the bar exam. But after the establishment of new law schools, it became preferred for academics who teach "black letter law" to have passed the new bar exam and become qualified as legal professional.

When the new law school system and bar exam started, the National Personnel Authority began to recruit bar exam passers in a separate selection procedure. But few bar exam passers chose national Ministries as their career, zero to five from 2014 to 2022 (Jinjiin 2023).[97] This indicates that a public official position is not really attractive to most bar exam passers.[98]

As we saw in Sect. 1.2, mid-career moves between public officials and private attorneys were mostly one-way that judges and prosecutors became private attorneys, but not vice versa. Yet, as we also saw, since the1990s, private attorneys began to be appointed as judges and, in this century, private attorneys began to be appointed as part-time judges for fixed term.

But what was really new is that private attorneys were employed in public office for a fixed term or permanently. Since the prohibition for a registered lawyer to be in public office was lifted in 2003, registered lawyers have been appointed to fixed term positions at national Ministries and local governments. From 2005 to 2022, the number of lawyers appointed to national Ministries for fixed terms was increasing,

---

[97] In 2010, four bar exam passers were employed by national agencies (Tanigaki 2011, p. 11, footnote 4).

[98] Twelve law school graduates were employed in major career track and seven in minor career track at national Ministries in 2020 (Jinji-in 2023). It is highly likely that these people did not pass the bar exam. National Ministry positions are still dominated by law graduates and bar exam passers may feel it difficult to envision their promotion opportunities in competition with them inside Ministries. If bar exam passers feel positions at Ministries attractive, they must have chosen such careers when they graduated from undergraduate law faculties, rather than going to law schools.

Table 1.21 Career paths from law firm to public office (Career Survey 2018–2019)

	%	*N*
Law firm→Public office	21%	7
Law firm→Public office→Law firm	58%	19
Law firm→Public office→Corporation	12%	4
Law firm→Public office→Other→Law firm	6%	2
Law firm→Public office→Law firm→Public office	3%	1
Total	100%	33

from 60 in 2005,[99] to 84 (31 women included) in 2010, 131 (34) in 2015, 123 (35) in 2010, and 145 (27) in 2022 (JFBA 2005, p. 119; 2010, p. 164; 2015, p. 151; 2020, p. 154; 2022, p. 131). In 2003, at the beginning of this practice, the percentage of women lawyers employed at national Ministries was high, but it has been decreasing gradually. For instance, in 2022, the percentage of woman lawyers at national Ministries was 18.6% while that of women lawyers among the registered lawyers was 19.6%.

Similarly, during the period from 2009 to 2022, the number of lawyers appointed to local governments for fixed terms was also increasing from 2 (0 women included) in 2009, to 56 (17) in 2015, 118 (45) in 2020, and 101 (38) in 2022 (JFBA 2009, p. 7; 2015, p. 153; 2020, p. 157; 2022, p. 133). In the case of local government positions, the percentage of women lawyers was high, for instance, 37.6% in 2022. In the case of national Ministries, personnel networks have been more or less established between law firms and Ministries. But in the case of local governments, most employers have been municipalities rather than prefectures. Among 47 prefectures only four prefectures employed lawyers for a fixed term in 2022. Among about 800 cities and Tokyo wards in Japan, 101 lawyers were employed for a fixed term in the same year. Although prefectures have larger budgets than cities, they seem to be reluctant to employ lawyers.

Table 1.21 shows the career paths of lawyers who first practiced at law firms and then moved to public offices. 24% (21% plus 3%) of them were still at the public office at the time of survey. They were all employed for fixed terms and expected to move out of their positions within a few years. Fifty eight percent of them moved back to law firms and 6% of them moved to other careers, while 12% moved to in-house positions.[100] As we saw before, there were networks between large law firms and national Ministries for personnel and such networks present a main route from law firms to public offices. It is probable that, as the business law sector grows, including the Big Five firms, the number of lawyers working at Ministries will also gradually increase.

[99] From 2005 to 2007, the number of woman lawyers were not recorded in the White Paper on Attorneys. The JFBA began to issue White paper on Attorneys in 2002. The annual White Paper has a special feature and basic statistics on the registered lawyers and their activities.

[100] A partner of a Top Ten law firm said that some lawyers who had experienced fixed amounts of salaries at national ministries were reluctant to come back to a commission-based system for income at their law firms.

Yet, just like unregistered legal professionals employed by corporations, there are unregistered legal professionals working at public offices. We saw above that the National Personnel Authority set up a special procedure to recruit bar exam passers, though the number was very small. But, in addition, there are mid-career lawyers who have been employed by national Ministries, most often after serving as a fixed term public official.[101]

The income of lawyers working in public offices is not great but not so bad. We have only six respondents in public offices and 3 of them (37.5%) earned from five to seven million Yen. Another 37.5% earned from 7 to ten million Yen, and 25% earned 10–15 million Yen. Compared to law firm positions or even in-house positions, the income from public positions is modest but very stable, since none of the lawyers who worked as public employees experienced a decrease in their annual income.

Cases

Saiko Saibansho (Sup. Ct.) November 13, 1968, Showa 41 (o) no.1281, 22 Saiko Saibansho minji hanreishu (Minshu) 144-176 (Japan).

------ November 25, 1969, Showa 44 (o) no.280, 23 Saiko Saibansho minji hanreishu (Minshu) 187-199 (Japan)

------ January 13, 2006, Heisei 16 (ju) no.1518, 60 Saiko Saibansho minji hanreishu (Minshu) 1-26 (Japan)

Statutes

Bengoshi Ho (Attorneys Act), Act No. 205 of 1949

Keiji Sosho Ho (Code of Criminal Procedure), Act No. 131 of 1948

Minji Horitsu Hujo Ho (Civil Legal Aid Act), Act No. 55 of 2000

Rinji Shihoseido Chosakai Secchi Ho (Act to Establish Provisional Justice System Investigation Council), Act No. 122 of 1962

Risoku Seigen Ho (Interest Rate Restriction Act), Act No.100 of 1954

Shonen Ho (Juvenile Act), Act No.168 of 1948

Sogo Horitsu Shien Ho (Comprehensive Legal Support Act), Act No. 74 of 2004

[101] Under the Democrats' government, the Consumer Affairs Agency was created in 2009. The first Commissioner was a lawyer of the Democratic Party, who is now the leader of Social Democratic Party. Through the professional network, lawyers at small law firms have been appointed to Consumer Affair Agencies for fixed term and some of them eventually permanently. This is a career path different from the move from the Big Five firms and other business law firms.

References

Foote D (2019), "Lawyers in Every Corner of Society: A Progress Report." In Foote D, Hamano R, Ota S, eds., Ho no Keiken Kagakuteki Shakai Kagaku no Kakuritsu ni Mukete (Toward Empirical Social Science of Law), Festschrift for Professor Masayuki Murayama, Shinzansha, Tokyo, pp. 153-174.

Foote D, Ito A, Katayama N, Sakai H, Sueyoshi W, Murakami Y, Eatanabe T (2021) Zadankai (Roundtable) - Dainibu <Bengoshi no Senmonka to Kokusaika no Genjo to Kadai> (Part 2, "The Current Situation and Problems of Specialization and Internationalization of Lawyers"), Ho no Shihai (Rule of Law), 200: 87-143.

Hamano R (2015) Kigyo Homu no Honkakuteki Tenkai: Dentoteki Kozo karano Ridatsu (Full-Fledged Development of Corporate Legal Services: Taking Off from the Traditional Structure). In: Sato I, Hamano R, eds., Henkakuki no Nihon no Bengoshi (Japanese Lawyers in the Transitional Period), Nihonhyoronsha, Tokyo.

JFBA (Japan Fdederation of Bar Associations) (Nihon Bengoshi Rengokai) (1967) Dai 18kai Teiki Sokai: Shiho Seido no Kakuritsu ni kansuru Sengen (The 18th General Meeting: Declaration on the Establishment of Justice System), May 27. https://www.nichibenren.or.jp/document/assembly_resolution/year/1967/1967_3.html. Retrieved September 18, 2023

------ (1989) Dai 32 kai Jinken Yohgo Taikai, Shinpojiumu Daiichi Bunkakai, Kicho Hokokusho Rejume, Keiji Saiban no Genjo to Mondaiten—Keisoho 40 Nen: Bengo Katsudo no Jujitsu wo Mezashite (32nd Human Rights Conference, Symposium 1st Section, Resume of Keynote Report: Current Situation of Criminal Trial and Its Problem, Toward Enhancing Defense Activities in 40th Anniversary of the Criminal Procedure), Jiyu to Seigi, 40(7): 175–215.

------ (2000) Danwa—Shiho Seido Kaikaku Shingikai 'Chukan Hokoku' no Happyo ni Atatte (Statement On the Release of 'Interim Report' of the Justice System Reform Council). Retrieved August 10, 2023.

------ (2001) Statement at the Official Announcement of the Final Opinion of the Justice System Reform Council. https://www.nichibenren.or.jp/en/document/statements/20010612.html. Retrieved September 3, 2023.

------ (2001) Shiho Seido Kaikaku Shingikai Ikensho ni tuite (On the JSRC Report). https://www.nichibenren.or.jp/document/opinion/year/2001/2001_20.html. Retrieved August 10, 2023.

------ (2001) 'Shimin no Shiho'wo mezasu Nitibenren no Torikumi no Kihon Hoshin (Basic Policies of JFBA Work toward 'Justice for Citizens'). https://www.nichibenren.or.jp/document/opinion/year/2001/2001_36.html. Retrieved August 10, 2023.

------ (2002) Dai 53 Kai Teiki Sokai: Minji Horitsu Hujo Jigyou ni taisuru Bapponteki Zaisei Sochi wo Motomeru Kinkyu Ketsugi (The 53rd General Meeting: Emergency Decision to Demand Drastic Financial Measures for Civil Legal Aid Undertaking). https://www.nichibenren.or.jp/document/assembly_resolution/year/2002/2002_2.html. Retrieved August 26, 2023.

------ (2005) Dai 56kai Teiki Sokai: Shiho Kaikaku Jikko Sengen (56th Regular General Assembly: Declaration to Carry Out Justice Reform), May 27. https://www.nichibenren.or.jp/document/assembly_resolution/year/2005/2005_2.html. Retrieved September 15, 2023.

------ (2005) Bengoshi Hakusho (White Paper on Attorneys), Nihon Bengoshi Rengokai, Tokyo.

------ (2006) Bengoshi Hakusho (White Paper on Attorneys), Nihon Bengoshi Rengokai, Tokyo.

------ (2007) Bengoshi Hakusho (White Paper on Attorneys), Nihon Bengoshi Rengokai, Tokyo.

------ (2008) Bengoshi Hakusho (White Paper on Attorneys), Nihon Bengoshi Rengokai, Tokyo.

------ (2009) Bengoshi Hakusho (White Paper on Attorneys), Nihon Bengoshi Rengokai, Tokyo.

------ (2010) Bengoshi Hakusho (White Paper on Attorneys), Nihon Bengoshi Rengokai, Tokyo.

------ (2011) Bengoshi Hakusho (White Paper on Attorneys), Nihon Bengoshi Rengokai, Tokyo.

------ (2012) Bengoshi Hakusho (White Paper on Attorneys), Nihon Bengoshi Rengokai, Tokyo.

------ (2012a) Hoso Jinko Seisaku ni kansuru Teigen (Proposal Concerning Policy on Numbers of Legal Professionals)," March 15. https://www.nichibenren.or.jp/library/ja/opinion/report/data/2012/opinion_120315.pdf. Retrieved August 29, 2023
------ (2012b) Gyomu Kokoku ni kansuru Shishin (Guidelines for Advertisement of Practice). https://www.nichibenren.or.jp/library/ja/jfba_info/rules/pdf/kaiki/kaiki_no_45-2_160620.pdf. Retrieved August 25, 2023.
------ (2013) Bengoshi Hakusho (White Paper on Attorneys), Nihon Bengoshi Rengokai, Tokyo.
------ (2014) Bengoshi Hakusho (White Paper on Attorneys), Nihon Bengoshi Rengokai, Tokyo.
------ (2015) Bengoshi Hakusho (White Paper on Attorneys), Nihon Bengoshi Rengokai, Tokyo.
------ (2016a) Shiho Shushusei, Bengoshi no Minasan, Chiho de Dokuritsu Kaigyo shite mimasenka?: Keizaiteki Gijutsuteki Shien Seido no Goannai (LTRI Graduates and Lawyers, Why Not Try Going Solo Someplace Local?: Introduction to Financial and Technical Support Program). https://www.nichibenren.or.jp/library/ja/legal_apprentice/data/2016/independent_practice_pam.pdf. Retrieved September 15, 2023.
------ (2016b) Bengoshi Hakusho (White Paper on Attorneys), Nihon Bengoshi Rengokai, Tokyo.
------ (2017) Bengoshi Hakusho (White Paper on Attorneys), Nihon Bengoshi Rengokai, Tokyo.
------ (2018) Bengoshi Hakusho (White Paper on Attorneys), Nihon Bengoshi Rengokai, Tokyo.
------ (2019) Bengoshi Hakusho (White Paper on Attorneys), Nihon Bengoshi Rengokai, Tokyo.
------ (2020) Bengoshi Hakusho (White Paper on Attorneys), Nihon Bengoshi Rengokai, Tokyo.
------ (2021a), Bengoshi Gyomu no Keizaiteki Kiban ni kansuru Jittai Chosa Hokokusho 2020 (2020 Survey Report on the Economic Basis of Legal Practice), Jiyu to Seigi, 72 (8).
------ (2021b) Bengoshi Hakusho (White Paper on Attorneys), Nihon Bengoshi Rengokai, Tokyo.
------ (2022a) Bengoshi Hakusho (White Paper on Attorneys), Nihon Bengoshi Rengokai, Tokyo.
------ (2022b) Current Direction on Policy Regarding the Number of Legal Professionals – Results of the Review for Further Reduction in the Number of Successful Bar Examinees, March 17. https://www.nichibenren.or.jp/en/document/opinionpapers/220317.html. Retrieved September 16, 2023.
------ (2022c) Kaku Bengoshikai ni okeru Sokuji/Soki Dokuritsu Kaigyo Shien wo Chusin tosita Shinki Toroku Bengoshi no Shien Taisei nado (Support Programs for Newly Registered Lawyers Focusing on Helping Going Solo Immediately or Soon at Each Bar Association)", https://www.nichibenren.or.jp/library/pdf/legal_info/legal_apprentice/dokuritsukaigyo/dokuritsu_shien.pdf. Retrieved September 9, 2023.
JFBA Bengoshi GyomuTaisaku Iinkai (JFBA Coommittee for Dealing with Lawyers' Practice), (1981) Bengoshi Gyomu no Keizaiteki Kiban ni kansuru Jittai Chosa Hokokusho (Survey Report on the Economic Basis of Legal Practice), Jiyu to Seigi: 32 (10).
------ (1991) Nihon no Horitsu Jimusho '90 – Bengoshi Gyomu no Keizaiteki Kiban ni kansuru Jittai Chosa Hokokusho – (Law Firms in Japan in 1990: Survey Report on the Economic Basis of Legal Practice), Jiyu to Seigi, 42 (13).
JFBA Bengoshi Gyomu Kaikaku Iinkai (JFBA Committee for Reforming Lawyers' Practice) (2002) Nihon no Horitsu Jimusho 2000—Bengoshi Gyomu no Keizaiteki Kiban ni kansuru Jittai Chosa Hokokusho—(Law Firms in Japan in 2000: Survey Report on the Economic Basis of Legal Practice), Jiyu to Seigi, 53 (13)
JFBA Bengoshi Rinri Iinkai JFBA Legal Ethics Committee), eds., (2017) Kaisetsu 'Bengoshi Shokumu Kihon Kitei' (Commentary on 'Basic Rules on the Duties of Practicing Attorneys'), Third Edition.
JFBA Wakate Bengoshi Support Center (JFBA Center to Support Young Lawyers) (2015) Sokugoku, Soki Dokuritsu Keikendan Shu (Collection of Experiences of Lawyers Who Went Solo On or Soon After Graduation). https://www.nichibenren.or.jp/library/ja/legal_apprentice/data/2015/dokuritsu_keikendan_201509.pdf. Retrieved September 9, 2023.
JFBA Wakate Hoso Center (JFBA Center for Young Legal Professionals) (2012) Sokudoku, Soki Dokuritsu Kaigyo Manual (Manual for Going Solo Immediately or Soon), Revised Third Edition. https://www.nichibenren.or.jp/library/ja/legal_apprentice/data/sokuji_soukidokuritu-manual.pdf. Retrieved September 9, 2023.

JILA (Japan In-House Lawyers Association) (Nihon Soshikinai Bengoshi Kyokai) (2003) In-House Lawyer Zadankai, Dai 4 Kai In-House Lawyer no Kyaria Pasu wo dou Kangaeruka (Fourth Round Table Discussion Among In-House Lawyers: How to Think About Career Paths of In-House Lawyers), July 31, 2003. https://jila.jp/wp/wp-content/themes/jila/pdf/in-house-meeting004.pdf. Retrieved September 14, 2023.

------ (2021) "Shiho Shiken Gokakusha no Zoka to Gokakuritsu no Josho wo Motomeru Rijicho Seimei (President's Announcement to Ask the Increase of Bar Exam Passers and the Rise of the Pass Rate). https://jila.jp/wp/wp-content/uploads/2021/08/seimei20210826.pdf. Retrieved August 31, 2023.

------ (2023a) Soshikinai Bengoshi Su no Suii (Changes of the Number of In-House Lawyers"). https://jila.jp/wp/wp-content/themes/jila/pdf/transition.pdf. Retrieved August 21, 2023.

------ (2023b) Kigyonai Bengshi wo Oku Kakaeru Kigyo Joi 20 Sha (2001–2023) (Top 20 Corporations Employing In-House Lawyers). https://jila.jp/wp/wp-content/themes/jila/pdf/company.pdf. Retrieved August 30, 2023.

Jinjiin (2023) Hokadaigakuinsei no Minasan e (To All Law School Students). https://www.jinji.go.jp/saiyo/syokai/houka.html. Retrieved August 25, 2023.

JLSC (Japan Legal Support Center) (Nihon Shiho Shien Center) (2011) Hoterasu Hakusho (JLSC White Paper), Nihon Shiho Shien Center, Tokyo.

------ (2021) Hoterasu Hakusho (JLSC White Paper), Nihon Shiho Shien Center, Tokyo.

JSRC (Justice System Reform Council) (Shiho Seido Kaikaku Shingikai) (2001) Recommendations of the Justice System Reform Council: For a Justice System to Support Japan in the 21st Century. https://japan.kantei.go.jp/policy/sihou/singikai/990612_e.html. Retrieved August 12, 2023.

Karatsu K (2011) 'Kigyonai Hoso' ni tsuite Ikko (Consideration of In-House Lawyers), Tokyo Daigaku Hoka Daigakuin Law Review (University of Tokyo Law School Law Review), 6: 195-206.

Keiei Ho Yukai, Shoji Homu Kenkyukai (Association of Corporate Legal Departments, Japan Institute of Business Law), (2001) Kaisha Homubu: Dai Hachiji Jittai Choua no Bunseki Hokoku (Corporate Legal Departments: Report of Analyses of Eighth Survey Findings), Bessatsu NBL 63.

Kokuritu Shakai Hosho Jinkoh Mondai Kenkyujo (National Institute of Population and Social Security Research), (2020) Jinko Tohkei Shiryo 2020 (Materials of Population Statistics 2020).

Kokuzeicho (National Tax Agency) (2021) Choki Jikeiretsu Deta (Long-Term Series Data). https://www.nta.go.jp/publication/statistics/kokuzeicho/jikeiretsu/01.htm. Retrieved September 20, 2023.

Kritzer H (1998) Legal Advocacy: Lawyers and Nonlawyers at Work, The University of Michigan Press, Ann Arbor.

MHLW (Ministry of Health, Labour and Welfare) (Kosei Rodosho) (2021), Reiwa 4 Nen no Hataraku Josei no Jokyo (The Situation of Working Women in 2021). 22-01.pdf (mhlw.go.jp). Retrieved October 15, 2023.

MOJ (Ministry of Justice) (Homusho) (2010) Kyu Shiho Shiken Dainiji Shiken Shutuganshasu/Gokakushasu nado no Suii (Annual Numbers Applicants and Passers of the Second Examination of the Old Bar Examination). https://www.moj.go.jp/content/000054973.pdf. Retrieved on August 18, 2023

------ (2011) Heisei 23 Nen Shiho Shiken Yobi Shiken (Preliminary Bar Examination in 2011). https://www.moj.go.jp/content/000080863.pdf. Retrieved September 15, 2023.

------ (2020) Kensatsu Tokei Nenpo (Annual Prosecution Statistics). https://www.e-stat.go.jp/stat-search/files?page=1&layout=datalist&toukei=00250003&tstat=000001012929&cycle=7&year=20200&month=0. Retrieved 14 September 14, 2023

------ (2021) Reiwa 3 Nen Shiho Shiken Yobi Shiken (Preliminary Bar Exam 2021). 001384104.pdf (moj.go.jp). Retrieved 25 September 25, 2023.

------ (2022a) Reiwa 4 Nen Shiho Shiken Yobi Shiken (Preliminary Bar Exam 2022). https://www.moj.go.jp/content/001384104.pdf. Retrieved September 25, 2023.

------ (2022b) Reiwa 4 Nen Shiho Shiken no Saiten Kekka (Bar Exam 2022 Results). https://www.moj.go.jp/content/001379928.pdf. Retrieved September 25, 2023.

------ (2023) Reiwa 5 Nen Shiho Shiken no Saiten Kekka (Bar Exam 2023 Results). https://www.moj.go.jp/content/001405789.pdf. Retrieved September 15, 2023.

Murayama M (1992) Keiji Kokusen Bengo no Jisshoteki Kento (Empirical Consideration on Public Criminal Defense). In: Zaidan Hojin Horitsu Hujo Kyokai (Incorporated Foundation Legal Aid Association), Rigaru Eido no Kihon Mondai (Basic Problems of Legal Aid) pp 307-338

------ (2002) The Role of the Defense Lawyer in the Japanese Criminal Justice System. In: Feeley M, Miyazawa S (eds), The Japanese Adversary System in Context: Controversies and Comparisons, Palgrave, Houndmills, Hampshire, UK, New York, N.Y., pp.42-66.

------ (2008) Mondai keiken to Mondai Shori Kodo no Kokusai Hikaku – Nichi Bei ei no Deta kara – (Internaitonal Comparison of Problem Experience and Problem Solving Behavior – From Data of Japan, U.S. and EU). In: Ito M, Omura M, Kasuga I, Kato S, Matsumoto H, Mori I (eds), Minji Shiho no Hori to Seisaku (Legal Doctorines and Policies of Civil Justice), Festschrift for Professor Takeshi Kojima, Volume 2, Shoji Homu, Tokyo, pp.1119-1149

------ (2009a) Wagakuni ni okeru Bengoshi Riyo Pattern no Tokucho – Hoka Shakai ni okeru Hunso Shori to Minji Shiho: Kokusai Hikaku wo Majiete – (Characteristics of Pattern of Using Lawyers in Our Country – Dispute Resolution and Civil Justice in the Legalized Society: With International Comparison -), Hoshakaigaku (Sociology of Law), 70: 23-46.

------ (2009b) Expanding Access to Lawyers: The Role of Legal Advice Centers. In: Sandefur R (ed), Access to Justice, Emerald, Bingley, pp.167-201

------ (2010) Rikon Mondai Tojisha no tameno Jichitai Sodan nettowaku (Municipal Consultation Network for Divorcing Spouses), Horitsu Ronso, 82 (2=3): 375-407

------ (2020) Japan: Toward Stratification, Diversification and Specialization. In: Abel R, Hammerslev O, Sommerlad H, Schultz U, Lawyers in 21st-Century Societies, Volume 1: National Reports, Hart Publishing, Oxford, New York, pp. 753-774

Nagashima Y, Nagahama T, Ejiri T, Yone M (eds) (2011) Nihon no Law Firm no Tanjo to Hatten: Wagakuni Keizai no Hukko/Seicho wo Sasaeta Business Bengosi tachi no Shogen (Birth and Development of Japanese Law Frims: Testimonies of Business Lawyers who supported Recovery and Growth of Our Country's Economy), Shoji Homu, Tokyo

Nikkei (Nihon Keizai Shinbun) (Japan Economic Newspaper) (1998) Mori Sogo Horitsu Jimusho, Kanban Bengoshi Sorezore no Michi (Mori General Law Firm, Star Lawyers Go on Their Own Ways), January 6, evening edn, 5

------ (2007) Hoka Daigakuin – Roteisuru Sekkei Misu (New Law Schools—Exposed Design Failure), November 23, p. 19, morning edn

Ohno M (1970) Shokugyo Shi toshiteno Bengoshi oyobi Bengosikai no Rekishi (History of Lawyers and Bar Associations as an Occupational History). In: Ohno M (ed), Gendai no Bengoshi (The Lawyer of the Contemporary Age), Vol.2: Bengoshi no Dantai (Assocations of Lawyers), Nihon Hyoronsha, Tokyo, pp. 1-116

'Hoso no Shitsu' Kenkyukai (Research Group on 'Quality of Legal Professionals')(2008) 'Hoso no Shitsu' no Kensho—Bengoshi ni Motomerareru Mono—(Verification of 'the Quality of Legal Professionals'—What is Required for Lawyers), Shoji Homu, Tokyo

Rinji Shiho Seido Chosakai (Provisional Justice System Investigation Council) (1964) Rinji Shiho Seido Chosakai Ikensho (Recommendations of the Provisional Justice System Investigation Council). https://www.moj.go.jp/content/000036339.pdf. Retrieved August 20, 2023

Rokumoto K (1988) The Present State of Japanese Practicing Attorneys: On the Way to Full Professionalization?. In: Abel R, Lewis P (eds), Lawyers in Society: The Civil Law World, University of California Press, Berkeley, Los Angeles, London, pp. 160-199

SC Jimusokyoku (Supreme Court General Secretariat) (1990) Shiho Tokei Nenpo (Annual Report of Judcicial Statistics) 2 Keiji Hen (Volume 2 Criminal Cases)

------ (2022) Shiho Tokei Nenpo (Annual Report of Judcicial Statistics) 2 Keiji Hen (Volume 2 Criminal Cases)

Shimizu M (1960) 'Hoso' no Ishiki Kozo to sono Henkaku (The Structure of Consciousness of 'Legal Professionals' and Its Change), Shiso, 432: 753-769

Tanigaki T (2011) Chihokokyodantai ni okeru Hoso Yushikakusha no Shokuin Toyo no Genjo to Kadai (Present Situation and Problems of Employing Qualified Legal Professionals in Local Governments), Jiyu to Seigi, 62 (11): 9-12.

Tokyo Shoko Research (Tokyo Commercial and Industrial Research) (2022) Jojo 3,213 Sha Heikin Kyuyo 605Man 5,000 Yen, 2018Nendo ni narabi Kono 10Nen de Saiko ~ 2021Nendo 'Heikin Nenkan Kyuyo' Chosa (Average Amount of Salaries at 3,213 Companies Listed on Tokyo Stock Exchange 6,055,000 Yen, Together with 2018 the Highest during These 10 Years ~ 2021 Research on 'Average Annual Amount of Salaries). https://www.tsr-net.co.jp/data/detail/1191443_1527.html. Retrieved 15 September 2023

Uetsuma E (2014) 'Bengoshi no Gyomu Kokoku ni kansuru Kitei' oyobi 'Bengoshi oyobi Bengoshi Hojin narabini Gaikoku Tokubetsu Kaiin no Gyomu Kokoku ni kansuru Shishin' no Kaisetu (Commentaries of 'Rules about Advertisements by Lawyers' and 'Guidelines about Advertisements by Lawyers, Legal Professional Corporations, and Foreign Special Members), Libra, 14 (3): 8-17

Yoneda K (ed) (2022) Kaisha Homubu: Dai12ji Jittaichosa no Bunseki Hokoku (Corporate Law Department: Report of Analyses of the 12th Survey Results), Shoji Homu, Tokyo

Masayuki Murayama is Professor Emeritus of Meiji University and Chiba University. He obtained his Ph.D. in Sociology of Law from the University of Tokyo. He studied in LL.M. Program and the Jurisprudence and Social Policy Program at the University of California, Berkeley and visited The Centre for Socio-Legal Studies, Oxford, Centre de Sociologie des Organisations, Paris, Institut fuer Rechtssoziologie, Freie Universitaet, Berlin, and Columbia Law School. He is an empirical researcher and has conducted empirical research on the police, criminal justice process, family mediation, civil disputes and access to justice, and the legal profession.

Chapter 2
Number of Lawyers and Lawyer Career Mobility in Japan

Shozo Ota

Abstract The number of lawyers has been rapidly increasing in Japan since the 1990s. This paper examines whether this increase yielded enhanced career mobility for lawyers as well. Based on our survey, we find that the answer is yes, especially after 1990s.

2.1 Introduction

The typical career for Japanese lawyers between the end of World War II and the early 1990s was simple and stable. After graduating from a university law faculty, they spend a few more years in additional preparation for the National Bar Exam before passing it in their mid- to late 20's. Upon passing, they take the two-year practical course at the Legal Training and Research Institute (LTRI) of the Supreme Court of Japan, after which they choose an occupation, from among attorney, judge, or prosecutor. On choosing to become an attorney, they first intern for about 5 years in a law office, usually a small firm with only one or two managing partner(s), to acquire practical and management skills. Thereafter, they either become a managing partner in the law office where they interned or open their own law office. In either case, the remainder of their careers are spent in general practice, which amounts to civil litigation.

Since the early 1990s, however, we have noticed changes in this trajectory. Here are some examples:

1. Mr. S.K. graduated from a graduate law school, which was established in 2004, modeled on US-style law schools, passed the National Bar Exam, worked for an international law firm (Tokyo branch: *Gaikokuho Kyodo Jigyo Horitsu Jimusho*) as an associate for some years, became in-house counsel for a Japanese interna-

S. Ota (✉)
Meiji University School of Law, Tokyo, Japan
e-mail: sota@meiji.ac.jp

M. Murayama (ed.), *The Japanese Legal Profession in Transition*, Economics, Law, and Institutions in Asia Pacific,
https://doi.org/10.1007/978-981-97-2692-9_2

tional trading company for some years thereafter, worked again for an international law firm as an associate for several more years, then became general counsel for a multinational financial services firm.
2. Mr. S.Y. graduated from a graduate law school and passed both the National Bar and National Civil Service Exams, worked in the Ministry of Economy, Trade, and Industry (METI) for a year, became an associate at a major Japanese law firm, was seconded to a securities company for 4 years, then opened his own firm.
3. Mr. M.O., after receiving qualification as a lawyer, worked for a railroad company for 6 years, practiced law for 10 years, served in a government ministry for 3 years, worked as a district court judge for 10 years, and eventually became a director of a railroad company.

This chapter examines whether our sense of change in lawyer's career patterns is in fact happening.

2.2 Post-1990 Increase in Lawyers

The pass rate for Japan's National Bar Exam has historically been notoriously low, on the order of 2.5% between 1961 and 1995, or in numerical terms, an annual average on the order of 490 successful applicants between 1961 and 1990. This total began rising to 605 in 1991, 712 in 1993, and 812 in 1998. Prior to 1998, as mentioned above, those who passed the National Bar Exam also had to attend the LTRI for 2 years, resulting in a typical three-year interval between passing the bar exam and being registered with the bar.[1] In 1999, the LTRI course was shortened to 18 months until 2005, when it was further shortened to 16 months for applicants who passed the old pre-2011 National Bar Exam. Since 2006, the required LTRI course has been one year for graduates of the aforementioned newly established graduate law schools.

Although the number of successful applicants rose beginning in 1991, as mentioned above, the annual average number of new lawyers still remained below 300, with more judges and prosecutors accounting for the difference. Figure 2.1 clearly shows the per capita shortage of lawyers in Japan, from 6.9 per 100,000 in 1950, 8.1 in 1970, 9.0 in 1975, 10.0 in 1982, 11.2 in 1990, 11.3 in 1991, 11.5 in 1992, 11.7 in 1993, 11.8 in 1994, and 12.0 in 1995. Even in 2022, the number was only 35.3.[2]

While the aforementioned new graduate law school scheme was intended to produce more lawyers, the increase in lawyers predates its adoption. In 1996, new lawyers surpassed 400 to 410, rising further to 595 in 2001 and 716 in 2003. With the new law school graduates, the number of new lawyers surpassed 1000 to 1098,

[1] In Japan, a lawyer must register with a bar association to practice law.

[2] Figure 2.1 is based upon data from Japan Federation of Bar Associations (JFBA 2022, p. 24), and Ministry of Internal Affairs and Communications (2023).

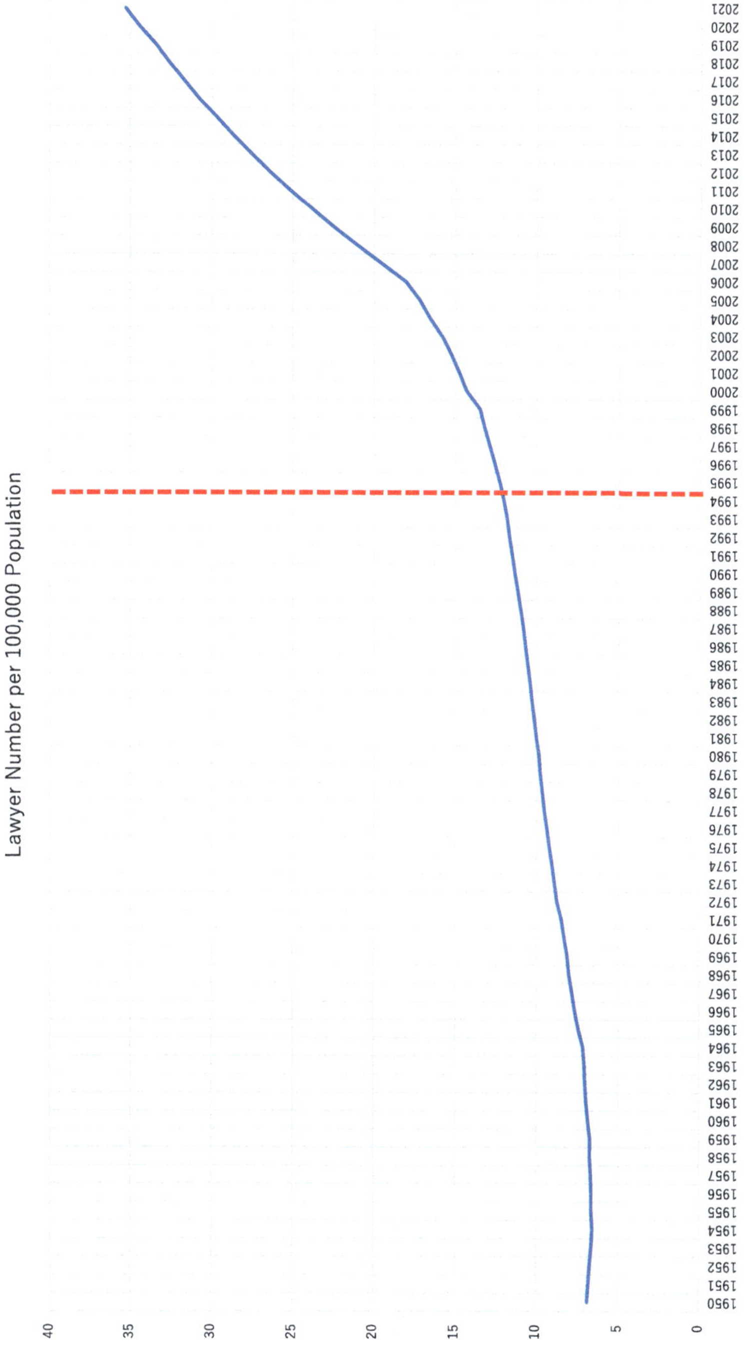

Fig. 2.1 Lawyers per 100,000 Population

1922 in 2007, then decreasing almost monotonically thereafter to 1889 in 2008, 1421 in 2013, 1052 in 2018, and 895 in 2021.

Figure 2.2 shows that although the number of new lawyers fluctuated, lawyers per capita[3] has constantly increased since 1960, on the order of 0.15 annually through 1993, rising to more than 0.2 increase in 1994, 0.24 in 1995, 0.84 in 2000, 0.64 in 2005, 1.37 in 2010, 1.03 in 2015, and 1.00 in 2020.[4] Accordingly, we compare lawyer mobility through 1993 and after 1994, meaning those who passed the National Bar Exam through 1991 and after 1992. This gives parameters for the question for this chapter: Whether the increase of lawyers since 1994, when more than 0.2 new lawyers per 100,000 annually enter the legal service market, leads to changes in lawyers' careers.

2.3 Self-reported Moves per Year

To this end, respondents were asked the following questions:

F.8. The year in which you passed the bar exam or became recognized by Article 5/6 (of the Attorneys Act)? ( )[Please fill in the year]

F.14. How many times have you moved jobs? (Here, move means move between different sectors or move between law firms, but not move inside a single law firm. In the case of break-up, acquisition, or merger, please consider it as a move if the name of your law firm changed.)

1. I have not moved. 2. I moved: In total ( ) time.

We used responses to these questions to examine changes in rate of job changes for lawyers who pass the National Bar Exam before 1991 versus those who passed it after 1992.[5] Responses of "I have not moved" were marked as zero in our tabulation. We further define career length as from Year of Qualification to 2018, the year the survey was conducted. We excluded data from respondents who registered with the bar after 2008, i.e., less than 10 years as of when the survey was conducted, as being too short.[6] Based on these, we define number of moves per year as follows:

$$\text{Number of Moves per Year} = \frac{\text{Number of Moves}}{\text{2018 minus Year of Qualification}}$$

The Year of Qualification is the year the National Bar Exam is passed, except for those few who were qualified by the special law (without taking the National Bar Exam).

[3] Lawyers per 100,000 population.

[4] Figure 2.2 is calculated from data shown in Fig. 2.1.

[5] Most applicants who passed the National Bar Exam in 1992 registered with the bar in 1995 after the then-requisite two-year LTRI course.

[6] Those who pass the New post-2006 National Bar Exam need only attend LTRI for 1 year.

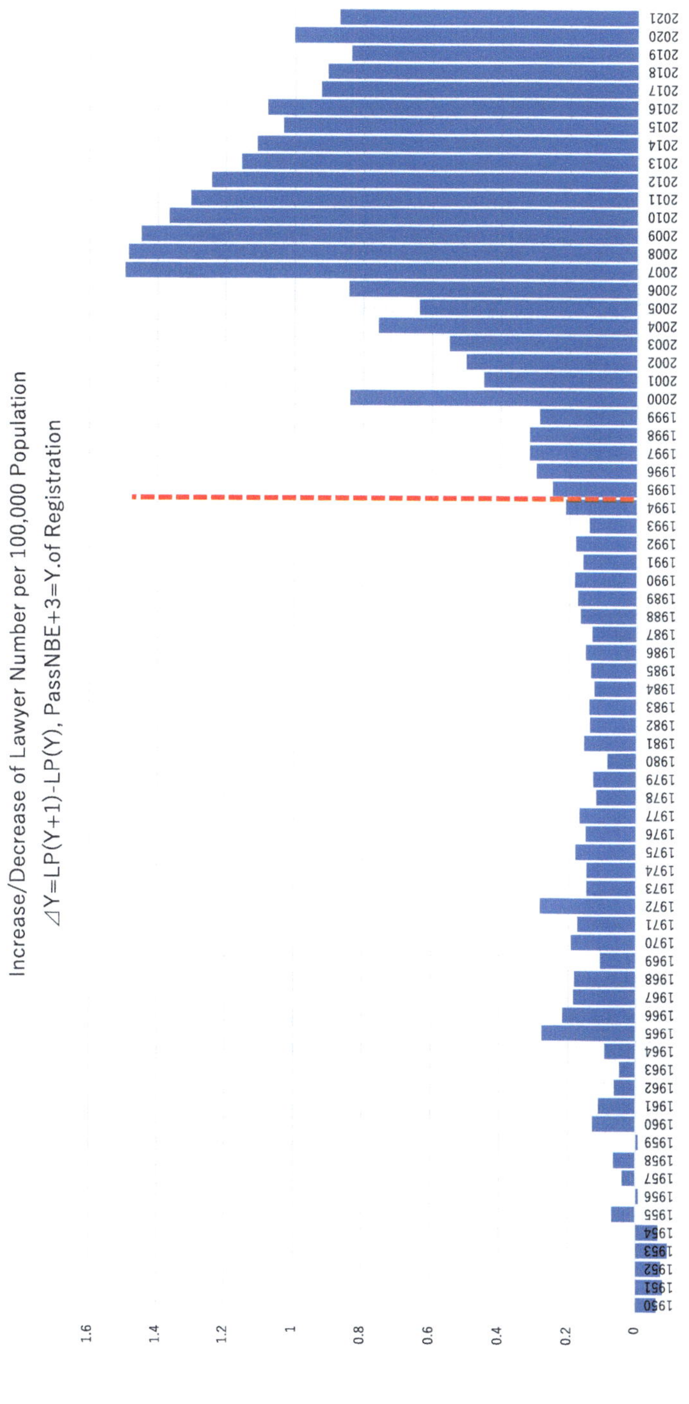

Fig. 2.2 Change in Lawyers per 100,000 Population

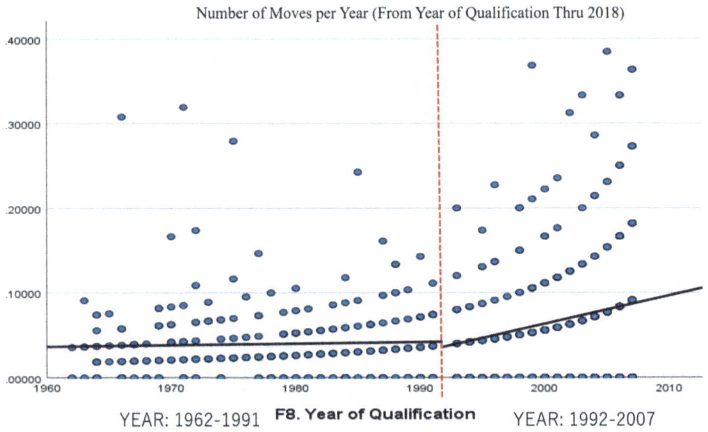

Number of Moves p<0.000			
	1. 1962-1991	289	0.04
	2. 1992-2007	466	0.07
	Total	755	0.06

Year of Qualification 1963-1991							Year of Qualification 1992-2007						
R2	F	df-1	df-2	p	Const.	b1	R2	F	df-1	df-2	p	Const.	b1
0.001	0.326	1	287	0.569	-0.309	0.000	0.030	14.587	1	464	0.000	-5.595	0.003

Fig. 2.3 Number of Job Changes per Year

We made scatter plots with linear regression lines, one for 1962–1991 and the other for 1992–2007, and combined them. Figure 2.3 shows the result.

The value of b1 (in the table of Fig. 2.3) and the average number of job changes per year in 1992–2007 are 0.003 and 0.07 respectively, versus 0.000 and 0.04 in 1963–1991. The acceleration in speed of changes for 1962–1991 was zero, and the average number of job changes per year was nearly flat as well, at 0.04. The speed of changes accordingly accelerated for the first time since World War II in 1992–2007 when b1 is 0.003. The only factor that leaps to mind, absent unidentified confounding variables, is increases in the number of lawyers.

The left–hand side shows few increases for 1963–1993, a period in which Japan experienced dramatic economic and societal change, including rapid economic growth in 1955–1973, the US dollar being taken off the gold standard in 1971 (Nixon Shock), the 1970s oil crises, the 1986–1991 real estate bubble, and the ensuing post-bubble years of the 1990s when Japan suffered slow, even negative, growth and deflation. As mentioned above, the annual increase in lawyers remained nearly constant, at some 300.[7]

The right-hand side shows significantly larger, more consistent increases for 1991–2007, Japan's so-called lost decades following the aforementioned real estate bubble burst. These finding show that career mobility in the Japanese legal profession has been substantially insulated from socioeconomic change in Japanese society as a whole.

[7] The capacity of the LTRI building was about 1000 (500 each year), which set the limit of number who passed the National Bar Exam.

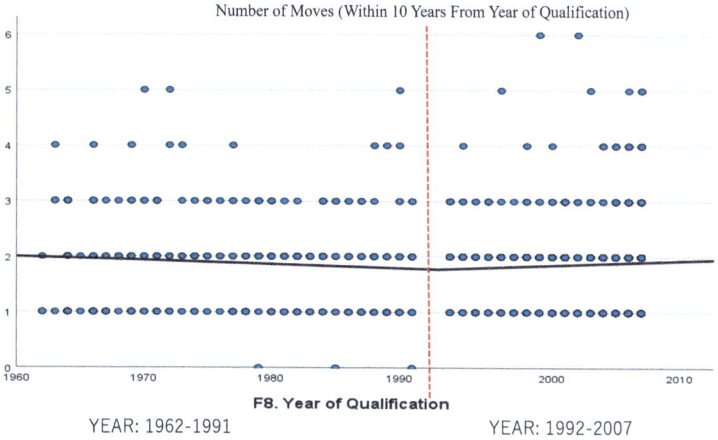

Number of Moves p=.79	1. 1962-1991	291	1.88
	2. 1992-2007	467	1.86
	Total	758	1.87

Year of Qualification 1962-1991							Year of Qualification 1992-2007						
R2	F	df-1	df-2	p	Const.	b1	R2	F	df-1	df-2	p	Const.	b1
0.005	1.342	1	289	0.248	15.750	-0.007	0.002	0.827	1	465	0.364	-14.910	0.008

Fig. 2.4 Number of job changes within 10 years of accreditation

2.4 Career Changes Based on Career History

We asked respondents for time, location, job status, income, etc., of their first through seventh jobs.[8] Categories included law firms, corporations, and public office, including prosecutor's offices and courts, and the other jobs, after respondents were qualified as legal professionals, i.e., passing the National Bar Exam. We call it Year of Qualification again.

Based on this data, we calculated the number of job changes within 10 years after Year of Qualification. As above, we excluded data from respondents qualified after 2008, and made a combined scattered plot with linear regression lines, with results as shown in Fig. 2.4.

Although the average numbers of job changes on the left and right sides of Fig. 2.4 are almost the same, at 1.88 and 1.86 respectively, the speed of career change, i.e., $\beta 1$, shifts from negative in 1962–1991 to positive in 1992–2007, suggesting that the pattern of career change has changed after 1992 with the increase of lawyers. Whereas during 1962–1991, the number of job changes within 10 years after Year of Qualification constantly decreases, albeit slightly, at $\beta 1 = -0.007$, the same value during 1992–2007 has instead been constantly increasing, again, albeit slightly, at $\beta 1 = 0.008$. Thus, the increase of lawyers after 1992 did have an impact on lawyers' career moves.

[8] We included first jobs after LTRI graduation, despite these not strictly representing job changes.

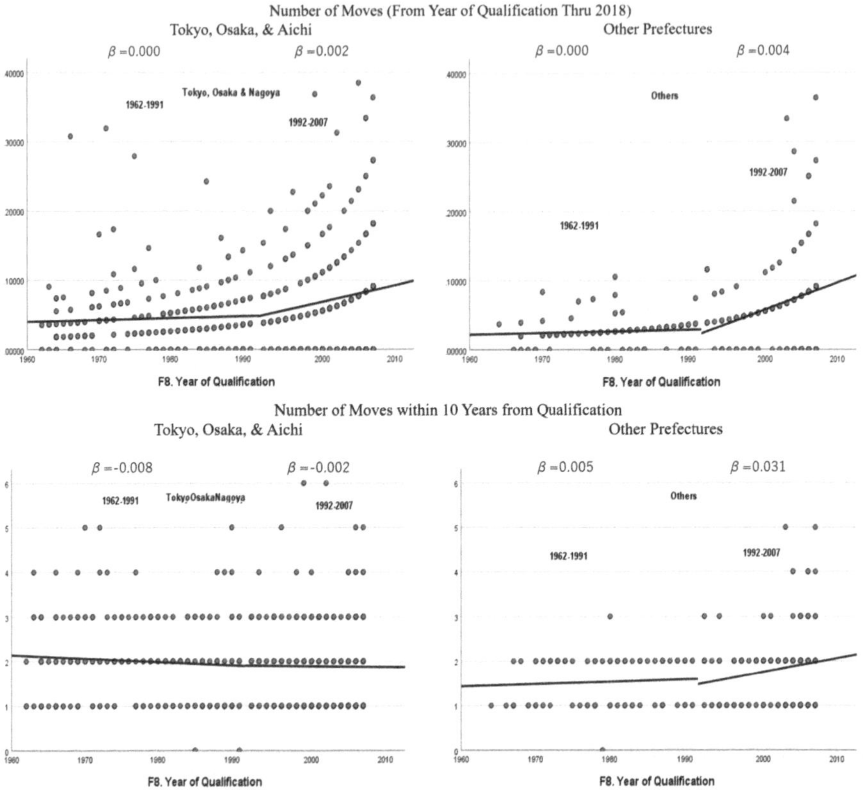

Fig. 2.5 (**a**) Number of Job Changes per Year. (**b**) Number of Job Changes within 10 Years of Qualification

2.5 Career Change Differences Between Urban and Rural Lawyers

We also asked in which prefectures respondents' first through seventh workplaces were located, offering choices of Tokyo, Osaka, Aichi, and other regions either with or without high courts,[9] because Tokyo, Osaka, and Aichi are prefectures with large metropolitan areas, Metropolitan Tokyo, Osaka City, and Nagoya City respectively. We used data thus obtained to find differences in impact of increases in numbers of lawyer after 1992, using the same methods as above. The resulting combined scattered plots are shown in Figs. 2.5a, b.

[9] Japan has eight high courts, Tokyo, Osaka, Nagoya, Sapporo (Hokkaido), Sendai (Miyagi Prefecture), Hiroshima, Takamatsu (Ehime Prefecture), and Fukuoka.

Figure 2.5 shows that average numbers of job changes are virtually flat in 1962–1991, at 0.045 for Tokyo, Osaka, and Aichi, and 0.025 for other prefectures. Neither urban nor rural areas showed any change over time. The difference (0.045 and 0.025) suggests that urban lawyers were already changing jobs more frequently in this period than those in other, mostly rural, prefectures. It also shows increasing average numbers of job changes in 1992–2007, and that the rate of increase is higher in other prefectures, at $\beta = 0.004$, than in metropolitan areas, at $\beta = 0.002$. Average numbers of job changes in 2007 are almost the same for rural and urban lawyers alike, signifying that increasing numbers of lawyers in rural area helped rural lawyers' job changes catch up with that of urban lawyers.

Despite some discrepancies, trends are similar between Fig. 2.5a, b. In Fig. 2.5b, the number of moves within 10 years of qualification is almost flat for urban lawyers in 1962–2007, at approximately 2.0, while that for rural lawyers is increasing, at $\beta = 0.005$ in 1962–1991 and $\beta = 0.031$ in 1992–2007). Thus, the increasing numbers of lawyers after 1992 accelerated the speed of increase only for rural lawyers, i.e., β increases from 0.005 to 0.031, catching up with that of urban lawyers by 2007, i.e., at approximately 2.0 in 2007 for both urban and rural lawyers.

2.6 Discussion

According to analyses by Tsutomu Watanabe (2018), turnover rates for male and female workers are shown in Figs. 2.6a, b respectively.

These figures show that turnover is higher for both male and female workers in their 20 s, declining as they age. The longitudinal change between the 1960s and

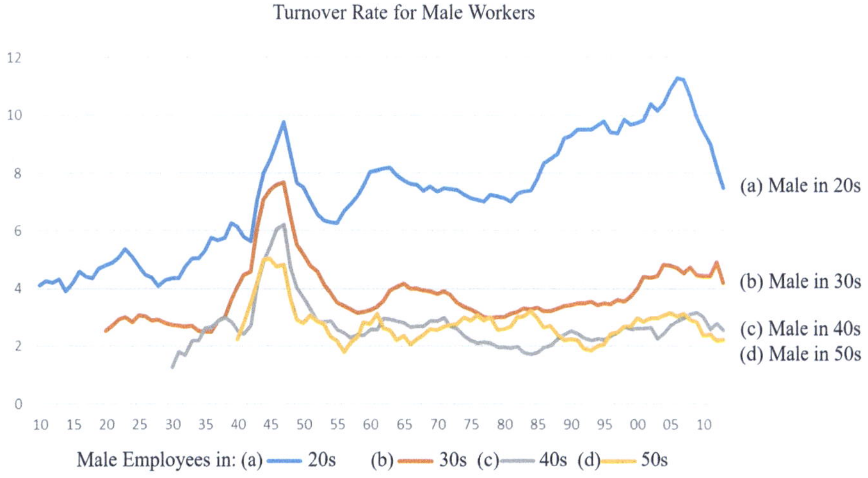

Fig. 2.6 (**a**) Turnover rates for male workers by age cohort. (**b**) Turnover rates for female workers by age cohort

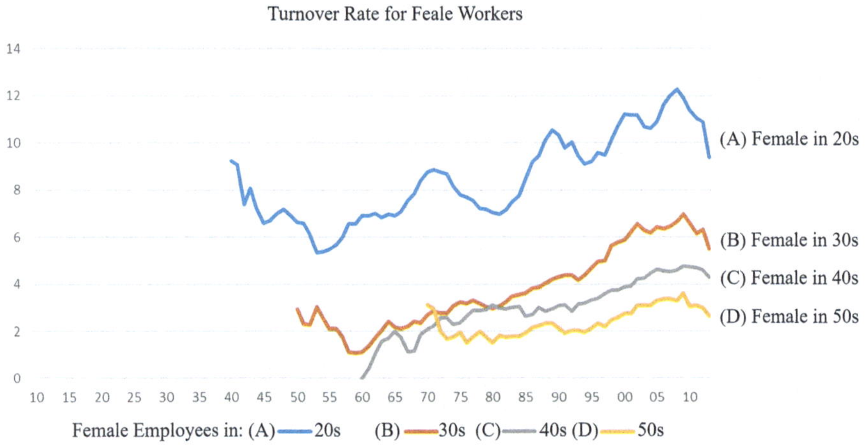

Fig. 2.6 (continued)

2010 is accounted for by the turnover rates of male and female workers essentially increasing virtually monotonically with some degree of fluctuation until around 2008, falling precipitately thereafter.

As shown above, lawyers constantly made few or no job changes until around 1991, after which the rate increased substantially, showing that lawyers' job changes and general labor turnover rates are changing in independent to opposite directions. It is therefore safe to conclude that changes in lawyers' careers have been caused by the increases in numbers of lawyers beginning in 1992.

References

JFBA (2022) *Bengoshi Hakusho* (White Paper on Attorneys), Nihon Bengoshi Rengokai, Tokyo.

Ministry of Internal Affairs and Communications (Somusho)(2023) *Nihon Tokei Nenkan* (Japan Statistical Yearbook), Nihon Tokei Kyokai, Tokyo,

Watanabe T (2018) *Kin Gendai Nihon no Shokugyo Keireki no Jidaiteki Henka* (Careers in Modern Japan: 1910s–2010s). https://www.l.u-tokyo.ac.jp/2015SSM-PJ/06_15.pdf. Retrieved November 19, 2023.

Shozo Ota is Professor Emeritus of The University of Tokyo, Professor of Law at Meiji University School of Law, and a practicing attorney at Fairness Law Office. His fields of teaching and research include Law & Social Science, Law & Economics, Negotiation and Dispute Resolution, AI and Law, and NeuroLaw. He is president of the Japan Law and Economics Association and the Japan Access to Justice Association, Chairman of the Board of the Foundation for Research in Civil Dispute Resolution, and a member of the Japan Association of Sociology of Law, LSA, and RCSL.

Chapter 3
Work History Factors Affecting Lawyers' Incomes: Firm Size, Clientele, and Legal Apprenticeship Cohort

Isamu Sugino

Abstract Most of the previous surveys have been cross-sectional and did not track the same individuals. We accordingly conducted this survey of lawyers' occupational careers to obtain retrospective work history data from a wide range of lawyers. The cross-sectional analysis of our survey data reveals that factors such as firm size and clientele relate to lawyers' income. Analyses of longitudinal panel data show differences in how annual earnings vary by length of employment at a given office and legal apprenticeship cohort, while confirming the effects of gender, practice settings, and law school categories. The larger the firm, the greater the effect of seniority on income, albeit more for men than women. This gender impact also emerges in earnings growth per job change. More recently accredited lawyers also tend to earn less than lawyers in older legal apprenticeship cohorts regardless of experience and service. We must thus pay continuous attention to both gender and cohort differences, as well as the "Two Hemispheres" hypothesis of *Chicago Lawyers* with respect to existing income disparities among Japanese lawyers.

3.1 Introduction

In Japan, lawyers have long been seen as members of an elite, enjoying high social status and substantial income. However, judicial system reforms, including the establishment of law schools, with the goal of increasing the number of lawyers, have transformed the way lawyers work and the nature of their jobs, affecting this perceived social status to varying degrees. In this chapter, we analyze career data to explore what factors contribute to differences in income, a key indicator of social stratification, and how these factors change over time.

I. Sugino (✉)
Ochanomizu University, Tokyo, Japan
e-mail: sugino.isamu@ocha.ac.jp

M. Murayama (ed.), *The Japanese Legal Profession in Transition*, Economics, Law, and Institutions in Asia Pacific,
https://doi.org/10.1007/978-981-97-2692-9_3

3.2 Previous Surveys and Lawyer Income Statistics

The average annual income of legal workers, including judges, prosecutors, lawyers, patent attorneys, and judicial scriveners, of approximately 11 years' average experience in workplaces with 10 or more regular employees is JPY9,710,000 (MHLW 2023). In the Basic Survey of Wage Structure, wherein lawyers were treated as an independent category prior to 2019, in 2018, lawyers' average annual income, again, in workplaces with 10 or more regular employees, was JPY7.7 million for men and JPY7.6 million for women. The survey of necessity excludes small firms and solo practitioners, which account for a significant share of law firms, and thus likely biases Japanese lawyers' earnings estimates.

The Japan Federation of Bar Associations (JFBA) has conducted decadal "Fact-finding Survey on Economic Base of Attorneys'Practices" since 1980, as its roster of all accredited lawyers yields an ideal sampling frame. And it accordingly gives superior population coverage. The questionnaire's complexity contributes to low response rates, however, with 17.0% in 2000, 17.95% in 2010, and 18.3% in 2020 (JFBA 2021), raising risks of measurement error and non-response bias. According to these surveys, the respondents' average incomes were JPY15.44 million in 1990, 17.01 million in 2000, and 15.71 million in 2010, with median incomes of JPY11.03 million in 1990, 13 million in 2000, and 9.93 million in 2010.

The JFBA also carries out biennial surveys on the actual circumstances of Japanese attorneys, named the Census of Attorneys. The response rate for the 2018 survey was 7.15%, lower even than the Economic Base surveys (JFBA 2018). Based on these Censuses of Attorneys, lawyers' median annual incomes in 2006, 2008, 2014, and 2018 were JPY12 million, 11 million, six million, and 6.5 million respectively. Figure 3.1 shows that averages were approximately 1.5 times these medians.

In recent times, more Japanese lawyers are taking in-house jobs, especially female lawyers. The Japan In-House Lawyers Association (JILA) has conducted an annual 'Survey on Corporate In-House Lawyers'since 2013, and publishing respondents' income distributions (JILA 2023). I calculated means and medians for each survey year myself from the JILA frequency distribution tables, with results suggest that lawyers' average income has declined significantly since the mid-2000s, as shown in Fig. 3.2.

As previously mentioned, however, these survey have low response rates, probably partly due to questionnaire complexity, leaving multivariate or otherwise detailed analyses yet to be carried out. It might be inferred that in-house lawyers' income began to rise around 2020, but the target population of these surveys is limited to a small and somewhat specific portion of all the lawyers. Thus, this tendency, if any, is not able to be generalized to the entire attorney community.

Moreover, all of these surveys are cross-sectional and hence there are no panel data tracking individuals over time. Although a group of researchers has been conducting just such a longitudinal survey of lawyers in two particular terms (Fujimoto

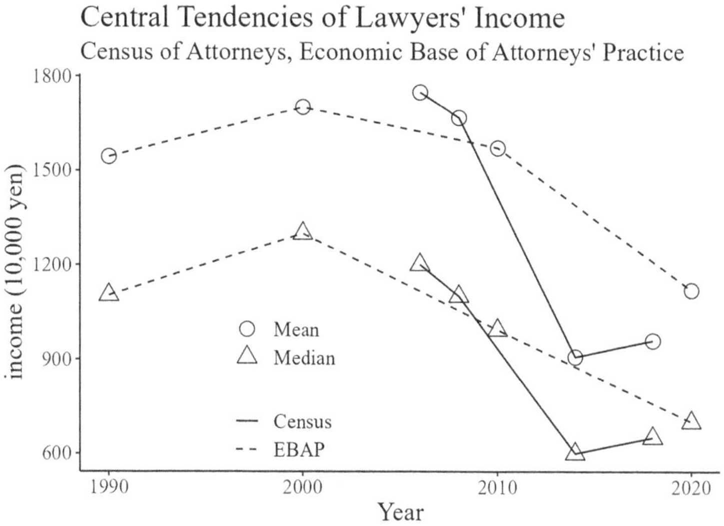

Fig. 3.1 Lawyers' income from surveys by JFBA. *Source*: Japan Federation of Bar Associations

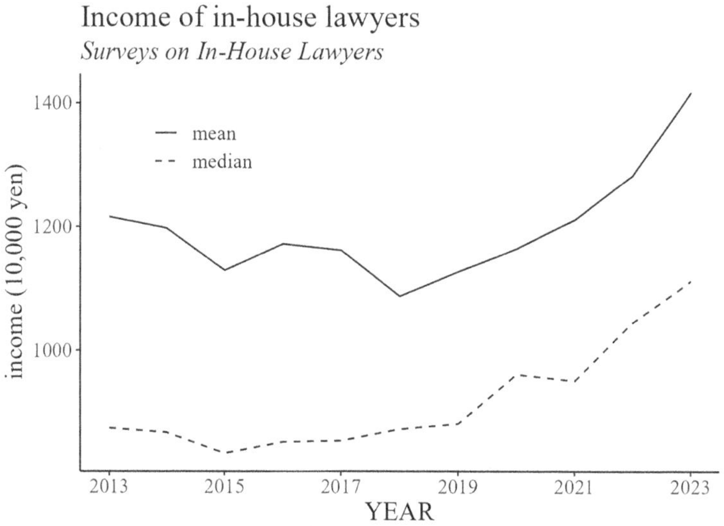

Fig. 3.2 In-house Lawyers' income. *Source*: Japan In-House Lawyers Association

et al. 2020), they target the 62nd and 67th legal apprentice cohorts[1] then the generalizability is naturally limited.

We therefore conducted our own survey of lawyers' occupational careers to obtain retrospective work history data from a wide range of lawyers. See Appendices A and B for details.

[1] See Sect. 4.2.2 for a definition of "legal apprenticeship."

3.3 Analysis 1: Cross-Sectional at Time of Survey

We began by analyzing lawyers' income at time of survey. This equivalent to an typical cross-sectional survey analysis.

3.3.1 Independent Variables

3.3.1.1 Practice Settings

We originally asked questions in the survey questionnaire to distinguish between law firms, corporations, public agencies, and other settings, but further classified law firms into small, medium, and large by number of lawyers.

It is, of course, a difficult decision to determine how many lawyers are part of a law firm that can be considered "small". Here, "Small" means fewer than ten lawyers, or 80% of the sample, "medium" 10–29 lawyers, and "large" 30 or more lawyers, each accounting for 11% respectively.[2]

3.3.1.2 Clientele

With reference to the well-known Two Hemispheres thesis argued in "Chicago Lawyers" (Heinz and Laumann 1982) and "Urban Lawyers" (Heinz et al. 2005), we attempted to sort lawyers by clientele, corporate or individual. Since we did not ask directly about the respondents' customers, so we will sort the respondents according to their specializing fields of law.

We have asked the respondents in our questionnaire about the fields of law, the income from which accounts for one third or more of his/her total income. Because our questionnaire on work career had a complicated multi-part structure and already contained numerous questions about respondent's work history, we did not include questions about time spent in given fields, nor questions directly asking who the clients were.

We conducted a hierarchical cluster analysis regarding co-practice. As the measure of distance among respondents, following Heinz and Laumann (1982), we used the average conditional probabilities of co-practice of the pairs of fields of law, on condition that any one of the fields account for at least one third of each lawyer's total income.

From the results shown in Fig. 3.3, we included intellectual property, M&A, finance, tax law, and international transactions in the corporate client category.

---

[2]The phenomenon of large proportions of small law firms is by no means unique to Japan. Abel (2020, p. 899) says, "But it [solo practice] remained significant or even dominant in many other countries," after pointing out its dramatic decline in Brazil and the Netherlands.

Conversely, fields such as traffic accidents, family, real property, consumer loans, personal bankruptcy, and criminal cases were coded as personal clients. While we recognize that there is room for doubt whether tax law should be included in the former, as Heinz and Laumann (2005) realized that there are personal and corporate or organizational clients alike in such fields as tax law, labor law, medical malpractice, and traffic accidents, our clustering results suggest to us that this classification is indeed preferable.

Let us examine the relationship between firm size and clientele. Fewer than 8% of lawyers in small firms are coded as having corporate clients, versus 25% for medium firms and nearly 49% for large firms. This translates into odds of 0.085, 0.333, and 0.944, respectively, giving an odds ratio of medium firms to small firms of 3.92, of large firms to medium firms of 2.83, and of large firms to small firms greater than 11. These relationships are said to be very obvious. Conversely, the smaller the firm, the more personal clients they take on.

3.3.1.3 Management Structures

We also asked lawyers in law firms about their management structures, having pre-coded them into solo practice, cost-sharing, income-sharing, legal professional corporation, and other, with multiple choices possible. In this chapter,

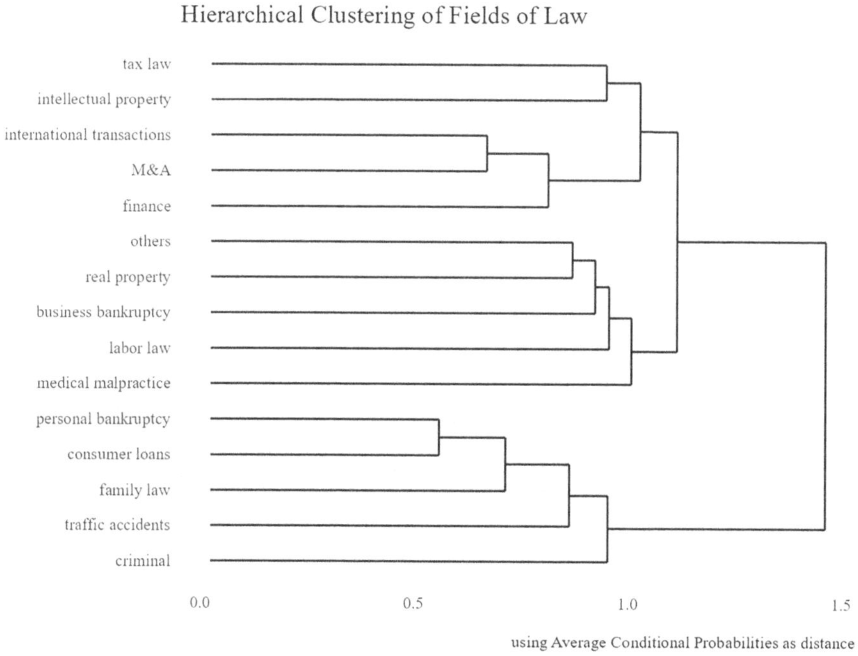

Fig. 3.3 Clusters of focused fields of law

these categories are reclassified into shared, i.e., either cost- or income-sharing, and ordinary, i.e., everything else. While fewer than 8% of the latter work in corporate client sectors, more than 25% of the former do. Both types of firms indicate almost the same degree of work in personal client sectors, however, at approximately 29% each. Hence, there does not appear to be as strong a relationship between management structure and clientele than to firm size and clientele.

3.3.1.4 Law School Categories

The Japanese law school system started in 2004, with its first graduating class in 2006. Out of 74 law schools operating in 2005, only 34 remain as of this writing. In "Chicago Lawyers," law schools were classified as elite, prestige, regional, and local. Given that Japanese law schools are, as indicated, few in number and of such recent origin, we will instead classify them only as prestige and others. Many currently practicing lawyers in Japan who started before 2004 are designated as "non-law school." The prestige law schools are Kyoto, Keio, Chuo, Tokyo, Hitotsubashi, and Waseda, so designated because more than 50 students pass the bar exam from each school on an almost annual basis, i.e., more than 15 times in 17 years.

3.3.1.5 Reasons for Changing Jobs

The questionnaire runs to seven pages for each of four practice settings. As each page corresponds to one workplace, each respondent might report six job changes at most. Under possible reasons for changing jobs, respondents could choose from "for better income", "for worthwhile work", "by reason of human relations", "for Work-Life balance", and "to have my own law firm"(this category was shown only in Law Firm page in the questionnaire).

3.3.1.6 Legal Practice Experience

We next asked when respondents were accredited, from which we calculated how long they had worked as lawyers. We also asked when they completed their legal apprenticeships. These variables can be regarded as proxies for legal practice experience.

Table 3.1 Median and mean income by gender and practice settings (JPY10,000)

Practice Settings	Gender	*n*	Median	Mean
Small firm	Male	663	1229	1379
	Female	149	590	861
Medium firm	Male	88	1229	1782
	Female	24	1032	1272
Large firm	Male	82	1721	2916
	Female	21	1229	2423
Corporation	Male	68	836	1275
	Female	33	836	888
Public agency	Male	5	836	944
	Female	3	590	672
Others	Male	4	713	811
	Female	0		

3.3.2 *Preliminary Investigations*

Distinct variations across firms of different sizes and genders are observed, per Table 3.1. Men working in large firms earn on average more than twice what their counterparts in small firms earn, and over 60% more than those in medium-sized firms. The difference is starker for women, who earn more than 2.8 times on average in large firms than in small firms, and 1.9 times more than in medium-sized firms.

While there are clear gender-based income discrepancies within small law firms, these appear less pronounced in medium or large firms, with ratios of average female income to male income of 0.62 in small firms, 0.71 of medium firms, and 0.83 of large firms. This ratio hovers around 0.7, in corporations and public agencies. Ratios of medians are 0.48, 0.84, 0.71, and 1.0 for small, medium, large firms, and corporations respectively.

Average incomes in the corporate client sector are roughly twice those in the non-corporate client sector, except for women in small firms and men in large firms. Conversely, law school does not appear to have much impact. A comparison of average incomes between graduates from prestigious law schools and those from other law schools by gender, restricted to those aged 20–49, revealed that the difference was only around 1.2 times for both men and women. On the other hand, gender differences within law school categories were such that women's incomes were approximately three-fourth that of men's.

3.3.3 *OLS Regression*

We next conducted multiple regression analyses to simultaneously examine associations between many variables and annual income, with results per Table 3.2. Average income traces an upward convex parabolic relationship with respect to age

Table 3.2 OLS results at time of survey

	coefficient	*p*-value	
Age	0.053	0.017	*
Age squared	−0.001	0.002	**
Years since accreditation	0.051	0.000	**
Years since accreditation squared	−0.001	0.019	*
Female (vs. male)	−0.109	0.340	
Ordinary law school (vs. prestigious law school)	−0.087	0.144	
Non-law school	−0.087	0.288	
Previous work experience	0.117	0.040	*
Study abroad	0.119	0.156	
Law firm 10 or more lawyers (vs small firm)	0.156	0.169	
Law firm 30 or more lawyers	0.085	0.489	
Corporation	0.031	0.837	
Public agency	0.455	0.318	
Others	−0.533	0.579	
Duration of employment	0.012	0.003	**
Tokyo	0.121	0.028	*
Osaka	0.056	0.470	
Aichi	−0.012	0.896	
Shared management structure	0.053	0.286	
Partner position in law firm	0.033	0.605	
Corporate clients	0.451	0.000	**
Personal clients	0.075	0.145	
Job-change for higher income	0.232	0.011	*
For worthwhile work	−0.012	0.872	
Because of human relations	0.069	0.325	
For work-life balance	−0.101	0.200	
For having own law firm	0.080	0.244	
Duration of employment * law firm 10+	0.007	0.427	
… * law firm 30+	0.029	0.000	**
… * corporation	0.025	0.288	
… * public agency	−0.073	0.299	
… * others	0.090	0.550	
Female * Tokyo	−0.289	0.020	*
… * Osaka	−0.393	0.015	*
Female * law firm 10+	0.089	0.622	
… * law firm 30+	0.400	0.037	*
… * corporation	0.109	0.533	
… * public agency	−0.782	0.147	
… * others	NA	NA	
Female * corporate clients	−0.255	0.128	
… * personal clients	−0.391	0.001	**
Female * for higher income	−0.042	0.858	
… * for worthwhile work	0.483	0.008	**

Table 3.2 (continued)

	coefficient	*p*-value	
... * because of human relations	−0.289	0.060	
... * for work-life balance	0.097	0.510	
... * for having own law firm	0.278	0.047	*
Multiple R-squared	0.3598		
Adjusted R-squared	0.3316		

and years since accreditation, with average income reaching its peak at approximately age 38 (=0.0531787/2/.0007063), other variables being equal, and 47 years (=0.0513683/2/.0005454) from accreditation, *ceteris paribus*. As these variables are highly correlated, however, it might instead be best to treat them solely as control variables.

Neither law school category, nor study abroad, nor management structures, nor partner status had any significant relationship to income. On the contrary, working for corporate clients and workplace seniority have evidently significant effects. Lawyers working for corporations earn 57% more on average than those who do not (exp (0.4509735) = 1.5698), and each year of workplace seniority results in 1.2% more income. In other words, 10 years on the job means nearly 13% (1.012^{10}) higher wages. Moreover, each year worked in a large law firm means an additional 2.9% in earnings. In short, each year in a large firm generates 4.1% more income.

It is surprising that the main effects of gender and practice settings were not significant, but large firms may have an advantage for women. Instead, women may find working in Tokyo or Osaka detrimental to their earnings. It might be possible to conclude that women working at small firms in urban areas are at an earnings disadvantage. Working for personal, individual clients is another disadvantage for female lawyers. This kind of disadvantage is not seen in men.[3]

Turning to reasons for changing jobs, while higher income seems to benefit both men and women, but for women, changing jobs for a more worthwhile job also has the effect of increasing income, and quite a large effect (60% more than otherwise). For women lawyers, a worthwhile job may also be highly rewarding, although it is often thought that changing to a more worthwhile job is a different reason than money or prestige.

As more than one-third of total variance of logged income is explained by this model, it has moderately high explanatory power. Figure 3.4 illustrates the relationship between four independent variables and income.[4] Male lawyers tend to have higher incomes as they get older across all practice settings, but this isn't

[3]Choroszewicz and Kay (2022) review the various heterogeneities between men and women, as well as among women, across many countries. For instance, they argue the positive impact on women lawyers of the emergence of global law firms or the expansion of corporate law firms, but also discuss the gender inequalities in financially rewarding positions in law firms.

[4]This graph is rendered by Locally Estimated Scatterplot Smoothing (LOESS). Individual points are omitted from this figure for clarity. Figs. 3.7 and 3.8 are rendered in like manner.

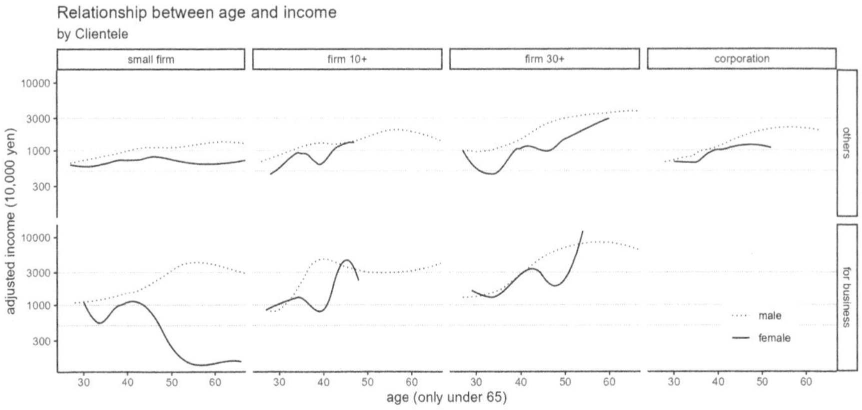

Fig. 3.4 Age, clients, practice settings, and income

necessarily the case for women. This trend is observed for women only in medium or large firms. Corporate in-house lawyers are similar to those in medium-sized law firms. Differences by firm size and clientele are also apparent.

3.4 Analysis 2: Longitudinal

3.4.1 Dependent Variable

Most of the information contained herein represents the state of affairs in 2018, the year the survey was conducted. The last question about work history asks respondents their annual income at that time. However, in some cases, older respondents supplied annual income from earlier times, the oldest dating to 1952, precluding direct comparison. Thus, I adjusted the annual income variable using the Consumer Price Index (CPI), which has not changed significantly since 1990, per Fig. 3.5, albeit decreasing significantly before 1980 (Somusho Tokeikyoku 2023). Hence, as earlier annual income values tend lower, adjustments tend to increase these significantly. The multiple regression analysis on data from 2018 is noticeably similar to that of the entire work history data, possibly due to the large amount of data from 2018.

3.4.2 Multilevel Model for Nested Data, Longitudinal Values Nested in Persons

In the work history data, income values at level 1 are nested within a single person at level 2. As the income variable has an unobserved heterogeneity among respondents, we use a multilevel modelling that contains income measurements as level 1 and respondents as level 2. The dependent variable is the logged value post-CPI

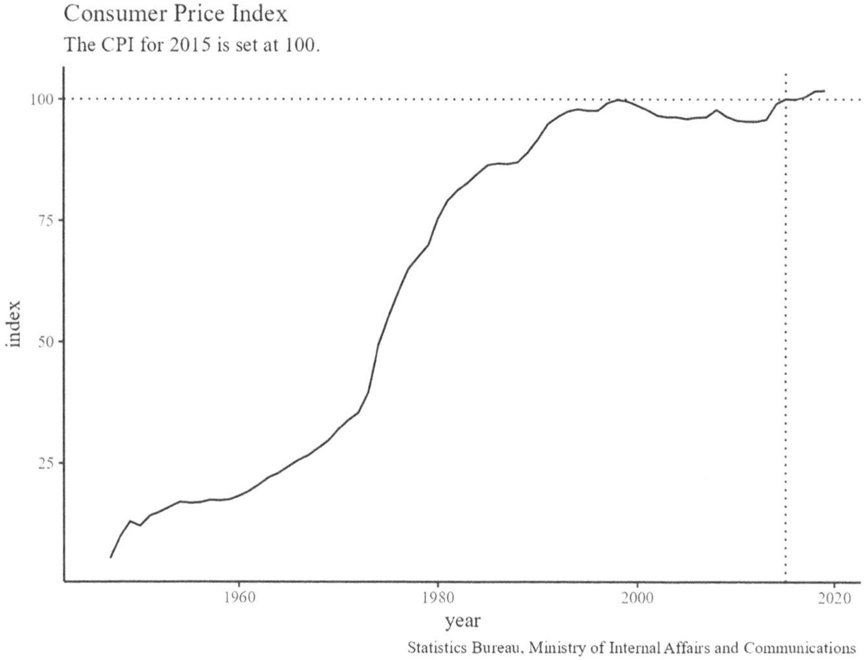

Fig. 3.5 Longitudinal change in CPI

adjustment. We begin by obtaining the Intraclass Correlation Coefficient (ICC) for this multilevel model, then confirm the necessity for multilevel analysis. In this two-level hierarchy, income values at different time points are nested within a given person. Therefore, the ICC indicates the proportion of the total variance in the dependent variable attributable to differences among respondents. The ICC calculated in this analysis is $0.44861^2/(0.44861^2 + 0.55246^2) = 0.397$, which is large enough to make multilevel model appropriate.

We then conduct a multilevel analysis of all settings in which we include such individual-level variables as age, gender, category of law school attended, study abroad, and legal apprenticeship cohort, with such level 1 variables as length of service with the same workplace, number of job changes, reasons for changing jobs (for better income or not), law firm management structures, partnerships, and clientele. As these independent variables include those specific to law firms, we also examined a model with all settings excluding these firm-specific variables, and another model only with law firms including these variables. But the results were almost the same. The result is shown in Table 3.3.

The association with clientele is consistent with the results of the OLS regression of the cross-sectional data. Income is almost 40% (exp (0.3249) = 1.384) higher when working for corporate clients. We also see here the relationship to duration of employment. Just like in the previous OLS regression above, the larger the firm one works for, the more money one is likely to earn as well.

Table 3.3 Multilevel regression estimates

Level 1		
Age at that time (centered)	−0.010	**
Age squared	−0.001	**
Period (vs. 1950s) 1960s	−0.341	**
1970s	−0.592	**
1980s	−0.560	**
1990s	−0.267	
2000s	0.020	
2010s	−0.134	
Law firm 10 or more lawyers (vs. small firm)	0.087	**
Law firm 30 or more lawyers	0.240	**
Corporation	0.205	**
Public agency	0.177	**
Others	0.389	**
Duration of employment	0.028	**
Corporate clients	0.325	**
Shared management	0.049	**
Partnership	0.151	**
Job-change for higher income	0.254	**
Number of job changes	0.125	**
Level 1 interaction		
Duration of employment * law firm 10+	0.007	
… * law firm 30+	0.023	**
… * corporation	0.008	
… * public agency	0.000	
… * others	−0.024	**
Level 2 time-constant		
Legal apprenticeship cohort	−0.008	**
Female (vs. male)	−0.113	**
Ordinary law school (vs. prestigious law school)	−0.163	**
Non-law school	0.019	
Study abroad	0.143	**
Level 1 * level 2 interaction		
Female * number of job changes	−0.126	**
Female * duration of employment	−0.009	**

By contrast, unlike the cross-sectional OLS results, in this analysis, gender and law firm size does indeed affect income. Female lawyers earn approximately 10% (exp (−0.1134) = 0.893) less on average than their male counterparts.[5] Medium firms yield more than 9% (exp (.08744) = 1.091) more income, and large firms and corporations approximately 27% (exp (.2397) = 1.271) more income, than small

[5] Twenty years earlier, Ulrike Schultz (2003, p. xliv) noted that average gender-based income differentials in various countries tend to range between 10% and 35%. The difference shown here might be considered relatively modest by comparison.

firms. Additionally, the results of alternative models containing interaction terms between gender and firm size (not shown) indicate an even greater premium for women within large law firms.

The differences among law schools, the effects of sharing-type of management, partner position, and the experience of studying abroad are also shown. Although there is no difference between prestigious law school graduates and pre-law school generations, the average income of non-prestigious law school graduates is 15% (exp (−0.1633) = 0.849) lower than that of prestigious law school graduates. The premium of study abroad and partnerships are almost identical, at 15–16%.

The data also covers respondents' jobs throughout their careers, showing as indicated above that only men's earnings benefit from moving from one workplace to another. When the interaction term is included in the model, changing jobs does not significantly improve women's earnings, as seen in Fig. 3.6.

Legal apprenticeship cohorts also significant relationship to income, even after controlling for age and when income is earned. Figure 3.7 shows how the relationship between years since accreditation, and Fig. 3.8 that between duration of employment, and income, changes legal apprentice cohorts, grouped by gender and practice settings.

As mentioned above, the vast majority of Japanese lawyers work either as solo practitioners or in small firms. Figure 3.7 further shows that time since accreditation has a smaller effect on income in these small firms than in large firms or corporations. It also shows that lawyers in the 60th or later cohorts likely to earn less than those in the 59th or earlier cohorts, for an equal number of years after accreditation. While the trend of gradually increasing income by seniority is barely noticeable for small or medium-sized firms, the rate of increase is still thought to correspond to firm size, per Fig. 3.8. However, it should be noted that women tend to demonstrate greater variability than men in this regard, as well as that lawyers from the 60th cohort onwards, especially from the 66th cohort, are likely to earn less than earlier cohorts, other factors being equal and regardless of gender.

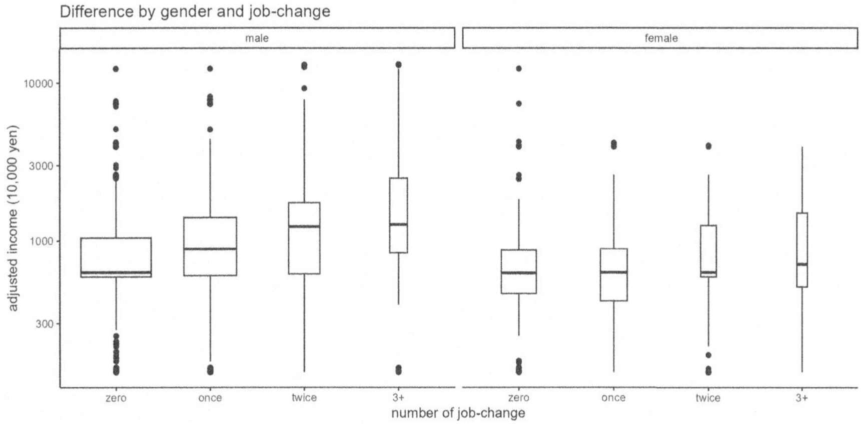

Fig. 3.6 Job changes by Gender

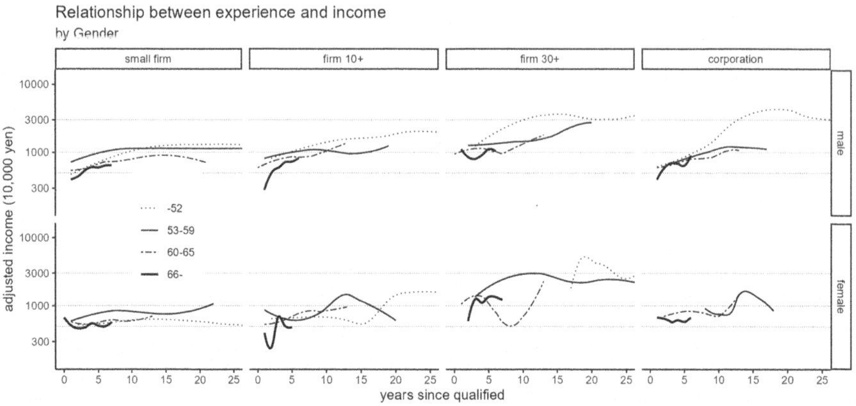

Fig. 3.7 Experience, gender, practice settings, and income

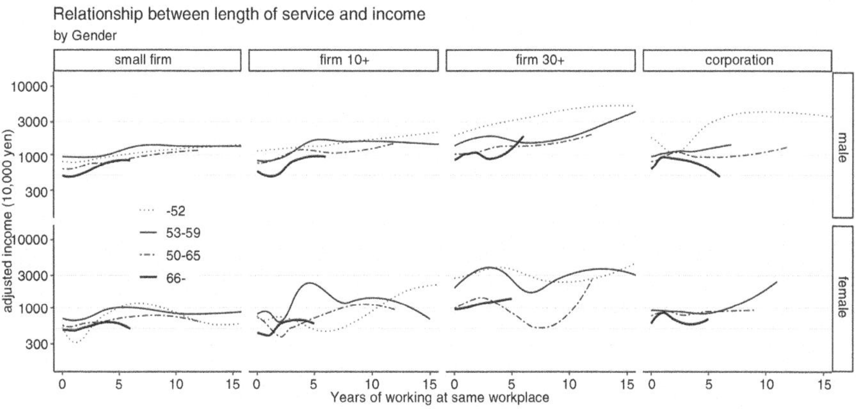

Fig. 3.8 Seniority, gender, practice setting, and income

3.5 Conclusion

Cross-sectional analysis reveals that such factors as firm size and clientele relate to lawyers' income, similar to Heinz et al.'s previous study. As our survey retrospectively traces respondents' career histories, we further analyzed longitudinal panel data. We found variations in annual earnings by duration of employment and legal apprenticeship cohort, while at the same time confirming effects of gender, practice settings, and law school category, which were not seen in the cross-sectional analysis. The larger the firm, the greater the effect of duration of employment on income, albeit to a lesser degree for women. Men's incomes also tend to increase steadily with each job change, whereas women's incomes tend not to improve nearly as much. Finally, a generational difference among lawyers emerged in changes in income based on legal apprenticeship cohorts, with more recently accredited lawyers tending to earn less than older lawyers did when the latter were starting out, even with equal experience and seniority. The results of surveys by the JFBAs and the JILA may indicate that the income of lawyers may have entered an upward phase again, therefore further research should be done in the future. Regarding the present income disparity among Japanese lawyers, it is necessary to pay attention to both gender and legal apprenticeship cohort differences, concurrently with the aforementioned Two Hemispheres thesis.

References

Abel R (2020) Comparative Sociology of Lawyers, 1988–2018: The Professional Project. In Abel RL, Sommerlad H, Hammerslev O and Schulz U, eds., Lawyers in 21st-Century Societies: Volume 1: National Reports, Hart, Oxford, pp.879–915.

Choroszewicz M, Kay F (2022) Understanding Gender Inequality in the Legal Profession. In Abel RL, Hammerslev O, Sommerlad H, Schulz U, eds., Lawyers in 21st-Century Societies: Vol. 2: Comparisons and Theories, Hart, Oxford, pp.127–149.

Fujimoto A, Ishida K, Bushimata A, Ageishi K, Miyazawa S (2020), 62 Ki Bengoshi Dai 3 Kai/ 67 Ki Bengoshi Dai 2 Kai Web Chosa: Kijutu Tokei ni yoru Bunseki (The Second Report of the 2019 Web Questionnaire Survey of the 62nd and 67th Cohort Attorneys: Analysis based on Descriptive Statistics), Journal of Law and Politics, Graduate School of Law, Nagoya University, 285: 1–58.

Heinz J, Laumann E ((1982) 1994) Chicago Lawyers: The Social Structure of the Bar, Revised Ed. Northwestern University Press, Evanston.

Heinz J, Nelson R, Sandefur R, Laumann E (2005) Urban Lawyers: The New Social Structure of the Bar. The University of Chicago Press, Chicago.

JFBA (Japan Federation of Bar Associations) (Nihon Bengoshi Rengokai) (2018) Bengoshi Hakusho 2018 (White Paper on Attorneys 2018). https://www.nichibenren.or.jp/en/about/publications/whitepaper_2018.html. Retrieved 22 August 2023.

------ (2021) Bengoshi Hakusho 2021 (White Paper on Attorneys 2021). https://www.nichibenren.or.jp/en/about/publications/whitepaper2021.html. Retrieved August 22, 2023.

JILA (Japan In-House Lawyers Association) (Nihon Sosikinai Bengoshi Kyokai) (2023) Kigyonai Bengosi ni kasuru Anketo Chosa Kekka [Questionnaire Survey Results on In-House Lawyers]. https://jila.jp/material/. Retrieved August 22, 2023.

MHLW (Ministry of Health, Labour and Welfare) (Kosei Rodo Sho) (2023) Chingin Kozo Kihon Tokei Chosa (Basic Survey on Wage Structure). https://www.mhlw.go.jp/toukei/list/chinginkouzou.html. Retrieved August 22, 2023.

Schultz U (2003) Introduction: Women in the World's Legal Professions: Overview and Synthesis. In: Schultz U, Shaw G, eds., Women in the World's Legal Professions. Hart Publishing, Oxford and Portland, pp.xxv–lxii.

Somusho Tokeikyoku (Ministry of Internal Affairs and Communications, Statistics Bureau) (2023) Shohisha Bukka Shisu (Consumer Price Index). https://www.e-stat.go.jp/stat-search/files?page=1&toukei=00200573&tstat=000001084976). Retrieved August 22, 2023.

Isamu Sugino is Professor of Sociology at Ochanomizu University, Japan. His principal research interest is social survey methodology, especially inquiry into web survey methods. He has conducted research projects into mixed-mode surveys and probability-based online panels. His most recent publication is *The Challenge of Random Sampling Web Surveys*.

Chapter 4
Japanese Lawyers' Careers Through the Lens of Gender

Kyoko Ishida

Abstract This chapter examines lawyers' careers through a gender lens. There is a significant numerical gender disparity in within the Japanese legal community. Fewer than 20% of Japanese lawyers were women when this survey was conducted. A gender analysis of career paths from first through third jobs reveals that for older generations, up to the 59th legal apprenticeship cohort, the income gap between men and women tends to widen between first and third jobs. For younger generations, after the 60th legal apprenticeship cohort, income disparities also tended to widen throughout affiliation between first and second law firm jobs, although less significantly than for their predecessors. Additionally, no such gender disparity in earnings was found on the part of in-house lawyers. These analyses suggest that going forward, many women lawyers will take in-house jobs, even as the gender gap at law firms slowly shrinks, and that law firms are expected to try to create more attractive work environments in response, albeit likely only gradually.

4.1 Introduction

The participation of Japanese women in the legal professional community dates to 1940, when three women registered as lawyers for the first time.[1] The first Attorneys Act (Bengoshiho) of 1889 barred women from becoming lawyers by stipulating that candidates be "Japanese adults with legal capacity and male."[2] Although the revised Attorneys Act of 1933 removed the latter requirement, the first women lawyers were still not accredited for another 7 years, as per the foregoing.

[1] For a general history of Japanese female legal professionals, see Mibuchi et al. (1983).

[2] Bengoshiho (Attorney Act) of 1889, Article 2(1).

K. Ishida (✉)
Waseda Law School, Tokyo, Japan
e-mail: kyo@waseda.jp

M. Murayama (ed.), *The Japanese Legal Profession in Transition*, Economics, Law, and Institutions in Asia Pacific,
https://doi.org/10.1007/978-981-97-2692-9_4

After World War II, Japan adopted its New Constitution, which decreed equality between the sexes. No did the new Attorneys Act of 1949 discriminate against women for purposes of admission to the bar. Female participation in the legal community was not uniformly encouraged, however. The ratio of women lawyers grew very slowly, especially before 2000. In 1970, more than 20 years after the new Constitution's adoption, only 180 of 8478 of lawyers were women, or 2.1%. These numbers have increased only slightly, to 766 of 13,800, 5.6%, in 1990, 1530 of 17,126, 8.9%, in 2000, 4660 of 28,789. 16.2%, in 2010. As of this writing, this share peaked in 2022 at 19.6% of lawyers, 26.4% of prosecutors, and 28.2% of judges (JFBA 2022).

In the twentieth Century, Japanese corporate clients were said to be reluctant to have women lawyers represent them, due to a perception that women would be "weak" negotiators. While such views are gradually fading as more women assume management positions, statistics show that women lawyers and women in management positions are still a minority in Japan.[3]

While the gender gap in the legal profession is not unique to Japan, many other jurisdictions appear to be surmounting the gap in the actual numbers of male and female lawyers.[4] As stated above, however, the situation in Japan remains dire, as women do not constitute 20% of the legal profession. Past empirical surveys have also found significant gender gaps in actual working conditions, including income, specialization, and career advancement (Nakamura 2015; Ishida 2016). As I pointed out in 2016, gender gaps that exist at time of entry into the profession only expand over time. When changing jobs, male lawyers tend to earn more, whereas female lawyers tend to earn less (Ishida 2015). This chapter examines lawyers' careers through a gender lens to determine whether things have since improved. It begins with an overview of the respondents, followed by an analysis of the data for differences between men and women in career terms.

4.2 Overview

4.2.1 Survey Respondents Vs. Total Number of Practicing Lawyers

Following is an overview of survey respondents, who are sorted by registered gender and age. As shown in Table 4.1, respondents correspond closely to the total number of practicing lawyers by age brackets, with women ($N = 285$) skewing younger than men ($N = 1179$). Note also that men averaged 16.26 years of experience vs. 11.85 years average for women. (Independent Samples Test, $p < 0.01$).

[3]The share of women in corporate management in Japan was only 13.3% in 2020 (Naikakuhu, Danjo Kyodo Sankaku Kyoku 2023, Fig. 1.14).

[4]For example, as of 2021, 37% of lawyers in the United States will be women (American Bar Association 2021). For a historical view of the situation of women in the US legal profession, see Epstein (1981).

Table 4.1 Male/Female by age: comparison with the total population

		Survey respondents				Whole lawyer population			
		Under 39	Age 40–59	Over 60	Total	Under 39	Age 40–59	Over 60	Total
Men	N	438	436	310	1184	12313	10639	8849	31801
	%	37.0%	36.8%	26.2%	100.0%	38.7%	33.5%	27.8%	100.0%
Women	N	138	121	24	283	3653	2879	647	7179
	%	48.8%	42.8%	8.5%	100.0%	50.9%	40.1%	9.0%	100.0%
Total	N	576	557	334	1467	15966	13518	9496	38980
	%	39.3%	38.0%	22.8%	100.0%	41.0%	34.7%	24.4%	100.0%

(Chi-Squre Test, $p < 0.01$)

Table 4.2 Apprenticeship Cohort vs. Gender

		Cohort 2–29	Cohort 30–39	Cohort 40–49	Cohort 50–59	Cohort 60–69	
Men	N	132	109	110	192	611	1154
	%	11.4%	9.4%	9.5%	16.6%	52.9%	100.0%
Women	N	10	9	17	66	178	280
	%	3.6%	3.2%	6.1%	23.6%	63.6%	100.0%
Total	N	142	118	127	258	789	1434
	%	9.9%	8.2%	8.9%	18.0%	55.0%	100.0%

(Chi-Squre Test, $p < 0.01$)

4.2.2 Apprenticeship Cohorts Vs. Gender

In Japan, legal careers are demarcated by "cohort (*ki*)" of legal apprenticeship. The 60th cohort, comprising attorneys who served their apprenticeships in 2006, was the first after Japanese graduate law schools were established. Table 4.2 cross-references gender with apprenticeship cohort, showing that men dominate the second through the 29th cohorts and the 30th–39th cohorts. Due to the rapid increase in legal professionals following the judicial reforms of the 2000s,[5] most survey respondents, male and female alike, are in the so-called post-reform period, comprising the 60th and later cohorts. In particular, more than 60% of women lawyers are part of these cohorts.

4.2.3 Current Job Vs. Gender

The questionnaire also asks about respondents' current jobs. Women are more likely to be employed in law firms or in-house counsel, encompassing both corporate legal departments and other positions. By contrast, men are more likely to be managing

[5] See Chap. 1 of this book and Miyazawa (2001) for an overview of Japanese judicial reforms in the early 2000s.

partners at law firm. Other clear differences include women being younger, having fewer years of professional experience, and being more likely to be associates than men. Interestingly, however, there are no gender differences in changing law firm jobs or number of job changes. 710 men, 59.8%, and 181 women, 63.5%, reported having changed jobs at least once, with men and women averaging 1.67 and 1.69 job changes respectively.

4.2.4 *Analysis Criteria*

For present purposes, the following analysis of gender differences at work excludes respondents whose first occupations after obtaining their licenses were other than lawyers, i.e., judges (N = 37), prosecutors (N = 34), or other (N = 17). It also focuses on those whose first jobs were in law firms after qualification, which remains the most common career trajectory for lawyers in Japan as of this writing. This yields 1108 male and 278 female respondents, of whom 1062 men, or 96.3%, and 263 women, or 95.9%, had their first jobs in law firms, for a total sample for analysis of 1325 respondents.[6]

4.3 Career Comparisons by Gender

The questionnaire allows respondents to report up to seven jobs apiece.[7] As mentioned above, however, women make up less than 20% of lawyers in Japan, constraining statistical gender analysis. Table 4.3 shows careers by gender up to respondents' fifth and sixth jobs. Only six women in the 60th–69th cohorts and who have changed jobs four times are working in law firms. The following discussion accordingly deals with up to the first three jobs in a given career.

4.3.1 *First Law Firm Jobs*

4.3.1.1 First Jobs by Firm Sizes

This section analyzes sample respondents' first jobs after qualification by gender, including firms' size and respondents' income. Firm sizes were compared based on average numbers of associates. In the 1950s cohorts, who served their

[6] Remaining respondents were as follows. Men: Corporations, 3.2% (*N* = 35); Government, 0.5% (*N* = 5), Other, 0.3% (*N* = 1); and Women: Corporations, 5.0% (*N* = 14), Government, 0.4% (*N* = 1), Other, 0% (*N* = 0).

[7] See the Introduction of this book for more information about survey design.

Table 4.3 Careers for those whose first jobs were in law firms

		First workplace	Second workplace				Third workplace				Fourth workplace				Fifth workplace				Sixth workplace			
		Law firm	Law firm	In-house	Public official	Others	Law firm	In-house	Public official	Others	Law firm	In-house	Public official	Others	Law firm	In-house	Government	Others	Law firm	In-house	Government	Others
Cohort 2-59	Men	468	296	5	7	1	114	5	0	1	35	6	2	0	15	3	2	0	6	0	0	1
	Women	98	70	4	1	0	33	1	2	1	17	0	0	0	4	0	0	0	2	0	0	0
Cohort 60-69	Men	568	226	22	11	4	65	10	3	1	12	3	0	0	3	0	1	0	0	0	0	0
	Women	161	59	18	5	1	14	5	1	0	6	1	0	0	1	0	0	0	0	0	0	0

apprenticeships in 1996–2005, men were employed by larger firms than women. Male lawyers started their careers with in firms averaging 11.02 associates, vs. 4.49 average. Firms began increasing in size at this time,[8] with relatively large firms probably employing more male lawyers as they expanded. While firms gradually increased in size as the generation went up, gender bias was found only in these selfsame 50s cohorts. In the subsequent 60s cohorts, by contrast, male lawyers started their careers at firms averaging 19.87 associates, vs. 26.20 for female lawyers' first law firm jobs, i.e., no statistically significant gender bias.

4.3.1.2 Income at Start and End of Affiliation

The lack of women in earlier cohorts necessitates comparing cohorts grouped into the second through the 59th cohorts, comprising 566 respondents, 468 male and 98 female, and the 60th–69th cohorts, following the Justice System Reform as mentioned elsewhere, comprising 729 respondents, 568 male and 161 female. Table 4.4 shows analysis by gender of annual starting and ending pre-tax incomes for affiliation at law firms, with highlighted cells signifying statistically significant differences.

In the second through 59th cohorts, 505 respondents, or 89.4%, started their careers at law firms, with no significant gender bias in position. The same is true for 662 respondents, or 90.8%, in the 60th–69th cohorts. Nonetheless, gender differences in income are evident from the first year at the first law firm for the second through 59th cohorts, with 37.4% of men and 22.9% of women earning less than JPY5 million annually ($p < 0.01$), possibly because the consumer price index (CPI) was not adjusted for the earliest cohorts, which comprised almost exclusively male lawyers. Instead, it is noteworthy that 12.7% of male lawyers in these cohorts had annual incomes of JPY10 million or more immediately after starting their careers, versus 5.2% of female lawyers, after accounting for including substantial numbers of male lawyers from the 1960s and 1970s. On the other hand, 22.9% of female lawyers who entered the job market in later cohorts earned less annually than JPY5 million, and 47.9% JPY5–seven million, versus 29.4% of men. This shows that women and men have been treated differently throughout their legal careers, at least until the early 2000s.

The questionnaire asks about income on a 10-point scale, from "less than JPY3 million" to "over JPY100 million." The median in each category is then treated as estimated income. Comparing between men and women, it is found that in the first year at a law firm job, average income was JPY6.4 million for men and JPY6.2 million for women, which is statistically insignificant.

By contrast, no such statistically significant income disparity was found in the 60th–69th cohorts. As Table 4.4 shows, approximately 10% of respondents, regardless of gender, earned more than JPY10 million at the start of their careers, while approximately 30% earned less than JPY5 million. Again, average estimated income

[8] See Sect. 1.3 for a discussion of expansion by Japanese law firms.

Table 4.4 Gender Differences in Income at start and end of Affiliation

Cohort of Judicial Apprenticeship			Income Immediate of the First Year: Less than 5 million yen	5–7 million yen	7–10 million yen	Over 10 million yen	Total	Income of the Last Year: Less than 5 million yen	5–7 million yen	7–10 million yen	10–15 million yen	Over 15 million yen	Total
Cohort 2-59	Male	N	*173*	*136*	95	*59*	463	92	*65*	97	92	108	454
		%	*37.3%*	*29.5%*	20.5%	*12.7%*	100.0%	20.2%	*14.5%*	21.3%	20.2%	23.7%	100.0%
	Female	N	22	*46*	23	*5*	96	18	*26*	25	12	14	95
		%	22.9%	*47.9%*	24.0%	*5.2%*	100.0%	18.9%	*27.4%*	26.3%	12.6%	14.7%	100.0%
Cohort 60-69	Male	N	169	245	100	54	568	*88*	147	*148*	114	59	556
		%	29.8%	43.1%	17.6%	9.5%	100.0%	*15.8%*	26.4%	*26.6%*	20.5%	10.6%	100.0%
	Female	N	58	56	31	16	161	*44*	47	*30*	25	13	159
		%	36.0%	34.8%	19.3%	9.9%	100.0%	*27.7%*	29.6%	*18.9%*	15.7%	8.2%	100.0%

for men and women is JPY6.5 million and JPY6.3 million respectively, which is still statistically insignificant.

Next is a comparison of incomes at end of affiliation in these first jobs, which reveals gender disparities in the second through 59th and the 60th–69th cohorts alike. For starters, average duration of affiliation at first law firm jobs was significantly longer for men in the second through 59th cohorts, at 9.6 years, versus 7.8 years for women in the same cohorts (Independent Samples Test, $p < 0.05$). Significant differences also emerge in income. Females, at 27.4%, were the most frequent, and males least frequent, in the "JPY5–seven million" category. Conversely, men most frequently responded "More than JPY15 million," at 23.7%. It can thus be seen that men are more skewed toward the higher income brackets than women, possibly due to the aforementioned gender gap in duration of affiliation.

Average estimated annual income for men in the second through 59th cohorts is JPY13.6 million vs. JPY11 million for women, although the difference is again statistically insignificant. Average increase in income during duration of affiliation at first job, derived from estimated first- and last-year annual incomes, was USD7.2 million for men and JPY4.8 million for women. While statistically significant differences were not found between these values, it seems probable that men's annual income increased more than that for women over the course of these first jobs.

On the other hand, comparing incomes for the 60th–69th cohorts shows significant differences in the "less than JPY5 million" and "JPY7–ten million" categories. In the final year of their first jobs, 27.7% of women earned less than JPY5 million, and 29.6% JPY5-seven million. By contrast, men were most likely to be in the "JPY7–ten million" range, followed by the "JPY5–seven million" range, at 26.4%, indicating that women in these cohorts are disproportionately in lower income brackets than men. Also, while there were no gender differences in average duration of affiliation at first law firm jobs, at 4.3 years for men and 4.2 years for women, income differences not seen at start of said affiliation were found at end of said affiliation. In fact, average estimated annual income in these cohorts was JPY9.2 million for men and JPY8 million for women, which was lower for both men and women than in the second through 59th cohorts, which is statistically significant (Independent Samples Test, $p < 0.05$). Finally, average increase during duration of affiliation at first job, derived as described above, was JPY2.7 million for men and JPY1.7 million for women, again yielding a statistically significant JPY1 million difference (Independent Samples Test, $p < 0.05$).

4.3.1.3 Fields of Practice

Respondents were also asked about fields of practice accounting for more than one-third of income. They were offered up to three choices from labor law, malpractice, accidents, family law, real estate, multiple sectors, personal bankruptcy, criminal law, intellectual property, finance, M&A, corporate bankruptcy, international business, and tax law. Data was again analyzed by gender and legal apprenticeship cohort category.

Only Family Law showed a gender difference in the second through 59th cohorts, at 29.2% of women versus 9.8% of men (Chi-Square, $p < 0.01$).[9] The next nearest in terms of potential statistical significance was Personal Bankruptcy, at 9.4% of women versus 4.6% of men ($p = 0.058$).

Accidents and Family Law, by contrast, showed gender differences in the 60th–69th cohorts, with 19.1% of men and 11.4% of women choosing the former ($p < 0.05$), whereas 24.7% of women and 9.6% of men the latter ($p < 0.01$). Personal Bankruptcy again just missed statistical significance in gender differences, at 8.9% of women versus 4.8% of men ($p = 0.053$).

These results show that women are more likely than men to have family law and personal bankruptcy account for more than one-third of their income from the outset of their careers, regardless of apprenticeship cohort. This tendency for female lawyers to concentrate on such fields is often found in other empirical reports as well.[10]

4.3.1.4 Summary

In summary, the second through 59th cohorts showed gender differences in income from the outset in their first law firm jobs, with men tending to have higher incomes than women. Additionally, significantly more women than men in the second through 59th and 60th–69th cohorts of respondents alike indicated family law and personal bankruptcy as accounting for more than one-third of their incomes. The difference is particularly pronounced in family law, suggesting that female lawyers, who are underrepresented to begin with, bear more of the burden in such matters as divorce and child support.

There were also significant gender differences in income in both cohort categories in last-year income at these jobs, with men in the second through 59th cohorts disproportionately in higher income brackets and women in the 60th–69th cohorts disproportionately in lower income brackets, despite having passed the same exam, taken identical apprenticeships, and obtaining identical qualification. The 60th–69th cohorts showed no gender-based gaps in income at the start of first law firm jobs, however, suggesting that such gaps are narrowing post-Judicial Reform. Nor are gender differences found in average duration of first affiliation for these cohorts, at 4.3 years. As the survey does not inquire into such personal matters as marriage or childcaring, these gender disparities will be discussed by comparing second and subsequent jobs to investigate whether these factors affect gender disparities in earnings in the last year of a given job.

---

[9] Statistical tests hereinafter are Chi-squared unless otherwise noted.

[10] See for example 2010 JFBA Economic Surveys (Ishida 2011).

4.3.2 *First Job Changes*

This section examines the 730 respondents, 572 men and 158 women, who changed jobs after first jobs at law firms. In the 60th–69th cohorts, women are significantly more likely to move to in-house positions than men, with 18 women, or 24.1%, doing so versus 22 men, or 9.5% (Fishers' Exact Test $p < 0.05$). Conversely, most lawyers in the second through 59th cohorts move to other law firms, with 296 men, or 95.8%, and 70 women, or 93.3% doing so. Following are analyses by gender of both groups of respondents, including incomes and reasons for changing jobs.

4.3.2.1 Changing Law Firms

Reasons

The questionnaire asked respondents to choose as many as apply from the following reasons for changing law firms after their first law firm jobs: Higher Income, Job Satisfaction, Workplace Relations, Work-Life Balance, Open Own Firm, and Other. While both men and women in the second through 59th cohorts both chose Open Own Firm most, significantly more men, 58.6%, chose this option than women, 38.6% ($p < 0.01$)). Women chose Work-Life Balance second, at 21.4%, and significantly than men, at 7.8% ($p < 0.01$). Men chose Workplace Relations second, at 19.1%, and women third, at 17.1% showing no significant gender difference.

On the other hand, the 60th–69th cohorts shows gender differences across the board. Men's top choice was Open Own Firm, at 43.8% versus 20.3% for women, while women chose Workplace Relations most often, at 40.7%, versus 27.0% for men ($p < 0.05$). More women chose Work-Life Balance, at 33.9%, versus 14.6% for men ($p < 0.01$), while Job Satisfaction was cited more by men, at 26.1%, versus 11.9% for women ($p < 0.01$). Men were also more likely to cite Higher Income, at 21.7%, versus 11.9% for women ($p = 0.09$).

Firm Size and Position

No gender differences are seen in sizes of law firms that the second through 59th cohorts switched to. While average number of associates at new firms was 27.7 for men and 4.1 for women, the standard deviation for men was vast, at 237.9, versus 9.4 for women, and hence statistically insignificant. What did differ, however, was their position in the new firm, with 76.1% of men and 60% of women being partners ($p < 0.01$), showing women are more likely to be associates, men more likely to be partners.

By contrast, average numbers of associates in new firms for the 60th–69th cohorts was 13.0 for men and 5.0 for women, almost reaching statistical significance (Independent Samples Test, $p = 0.07$). Also, 62.0% of men were partners in their new firms, whereas 57.1% of women changing jobs were associates, achieving statistical significance ($p < 0.05$). These data show parallels with the abovementioned differences by gender in reasons cited for changing jobs.

Income

Gender differences in earnings are more apparent after leaving a first job for a second job. In the second through 59th cohorts, in changing jobs men gain JPY1.7 million whereas women lose JPY95,588 (JPY0.1 million) on average, a significant gender-based difference (Independent Samples Test, $p < 0.05$). Estimated average first-year income at the new job was JPY12.0 million for men versus JPY8.5 million for women, again statistically significant (Independent Samples Test, $p < 0.01$). Breakdown by income bracket was 16.8% of men and 35.3% of women earning less than JPY5 million, 16.5% of men and 23.5% of women earning JPY5–seven million, 22.3% of men and 10.3% of women earning JPY10–15 million, and 24.4.% of men and 11.8% of women earning more than JPY15 million. In other words, 47.7% of lawyers earning JPY10 million or more are men, while 58.8% earning less than JPY7 million are women.

Differences were even starker for estimated average last-year income at the new job, at JPY18.9 million for men versus JPY10.4 million for women (Independent Samples Test, $p < 0.01$). Estimated difference income between first- and last-year income was also statistically significant, at JPY6.8 million for men versus JPY1.5 million for women (Independent Samples Test, $p < 0.01$). Breakdown by income bracket was 11.6% of men and 25.0% of women earning less than JPY5 million, 14.2% of men and 25.0% of women earning JPY7–ten million, and 43.3% of men and 17.2% of women earning JPY15 million (Men: 43.3%, Women: 17.2%). Hence, 67.2% of women earned less than JPY10 million in the last year of their second jobs, compared with 64.6% of men earning more than JPY10 million, despite men and women alike seeing incomes increase across duration of affiliation therein. This suggests that the income gap between men and women widens at these jobs, and a comparison of duration of affiliation at such jobs also shows that as at first jobs, men had more seniority than women, averaging 12.9 and 8.8 years (Independent Samples Test, $p < 0.01$), which may explain these earnings gaps at least partially. In this manner, in the cohort 2-59 group, gender differences were identified in all of the following areas: starting with the difference in income from the first law firm, income in the first year of the move, income in the final year of the move, and the amount of increase in income.

In the 60th–69th cohorts, by contrast, average estimated change in income due to changing jobs was JPY1.2 million for men and JPY0.2 million for women, albeit statistically insignificant, with a standard deviation for men of 7.1 million. On the other hand, average estimated first-year income at such jobs was JPY8.6 million for men and JPY6.1 million for women, achieving statistical significance (Independent Samples Test, $p < 0.01$). The most notable gender differences by income bracket were 28.8% of men and 43.1% of women earning less than JPY5 million, and 8.8%

of men and zero% of women earning more than JPY15 million (Exact Test, $p < 0.01$). While both men and women in these cohorts are earning less than the second through 59th cohorts, women are still skewing lower than men.

Average estimated last-year earnings at second jobs for these cohorts are JPY11.6 million for men and JPY7.3 million for women, a statistically significant gender difference (Independent Samples Test, $p < 0.01$). Additionally, average differences in estimated first- and last-year earnings at such jobs is JPY3.2 million for men and JPY1.2 million for women, also statistically significant (Independent Samples Test, $p < 0.01$). Breakdown by income bracket was 16.4% of me and 38.9% of women earning less than JPY5 million, 25.3% of men and 11.1% of women earning JPY10–15 million, and 20.3% of men and 3.7% of women earning more than JPY15 million (Exact Test, $p < 0.01$). Women thus comprise 59.3% of respondents earning less than JPY7 million, while men comprise 45.6% earning more than JPY10 million. Average duration of affiliation in such jobs, however, is 3.3 years for men and 2.9 years for women, signifying that the 60th–69th cohorts showed differences in increases in incomes during these jobs, despite lack of gender difference in duration of affiliation.

Fields of Practice

As with first jobs, the questionnaire asks respondents for fields of practice that account for more than one-third of income at their second jobs, which do not show much difference from those at first jobs. Women do more work in family law than men across all cohorts, 38.5% of women versus 11.0% of men in the second through 59th cohorts ($p < 0.01$), and 29.8% of women versus 13.9% of men in the 60th–69th cohorts ($p < 0.01$). In sum, a smaller proportion of women in the 60th–69th cohorts chose family law, and the gap between men and women is still noticeable in this area, albeit narrowing. In other areas, Women were more likely than men to choose personal bankruptcy in the second through 59th cohorts, at 18.5% versus 4.1% respectively ($p < 0.01$), compared with 12.3% and 5.8% respectively in the 60th–69th cohorts ($p = 0.091$). The second through 59th cohorts also showed a difference in multiple sectors, at 5.9% for men and 12.3 for women ($p = 0.07$).

Summary

The income gap that appears to have widened during affiliation at first jobs was found to have only further expanded during affiliation at second jobs, particularly in the second through 59th cohorts, even taking into account men in these cohorts having been at these jobs longer on average than women. On the other hand, there is a difference even among the 60th–69th cohorts between men and women in these jobs from first- to last-year incomes, showing how lawyers in these jobs face such income gaps throughout their affiliation. The only noticeable tendency in practice fields was that women are more likely to work in family law, suggesting that women lawyers working in fields considered less lucrative may be one factor in this seemingly ever-present and growing income gap, though by no means the only one.

4.3.2.2 From Law Firm to In-House

Reasons for Changing Jobs

Fourty respondents, 27 male and 22 female, said that their second jobs involved moving from law firms to corporate in-house positions. Note that only nine, or 18.4%, of whom are in the second through 59th cohorts, indicating that the very phenomenon of in-house lawyer jobs has been expanding steadily since 2000. There are no noticeable gender differences in reasons cited for changing jobs among respondents who moved in-house from a second law firm job, except that more men than women in the 60th–69th cohorts cited job satisfaction, at 63.6% and 27.8% respectively ($p < 0.05$). By contrast, nearly 68.3% of male and 72.2% of female respondents in these cohorts cited work-life balance. As shown above, more women than men in these cohorts moved in-house from law firms, and these results suggest that one factor may be that women put more store in work-life balance.

Firm Size and Position

In Japan, some lawyers surrender their legal licenses when they start working in-house. All respondents in this category maintained theirs, however. Another 10, or 20.4%, worked in departments other than legal, again with no particular gender differences shown, one each male and female in the second through 59th cohorts, four each in the 60th–69th cohorts. When they started work, the averages were 3.75 men and 5.25 women in the second through 59th cohorts, versus 3.53 for men and 3.11 for women in the 60th–69th cohorts. At the end of employment, by contrast, these values were 5.00 for men and 5.5 for women in the second through 59th cohorts and 7.94 for men and 4.72 for women in the 60th–69th cohorts. While no gender differences are evident, it is clear that men in some of the later cohorts work for firms that are hiring more in-house lawyers. Nor were gender differences found by sector in the 60th–69th cohorts, with some 30% in manufacturing, seven each male and female, approximately another 30% in finance or insurance, seven men and five women, and 10% in telecommunications, four men and one woman, suggesting that these sectors are more actively hiring lawyers than others.

First-Year Income

Estimated average annual salaries are derived for in-house as for law firm jobs and resulting differences in income due to moving from law firms to corporations examined. Unlike the group that moved from one law firm to another, no gender differences were found among respondents who took in-house counsel positions. While estimated difference in income due to changing jobs was JPY2.5 million for men and -JPY3.5 million for women in the second through 59th cohorts, there were only five men and four women in this category. Also, the standard deviation for men was substantial, at 11.5 million vs. 4.4 million for women. Nor was there a statistically significant difference in men's and women's estimated first-year average incomes, at JPY17.2 million and JPY9.5 million respectively. Again, the standard deviations were large, though clearly more prominent for men at 12.9 million, versus 2.0 million for women, nor were any statistically significant differences found. All respondents earned more than JPY7 million in their first year at these jobs, with one male and three female lawyers earning JPY7–ten million, three males and one female JPY10–15 million, and one male more than JPY15 million. Hence, no clear income disparity is found here unlike law firms, despite the small sample size.

In the 60th–69th cohorts, by contrast, change in income due moving in-house from law firms was JPY0.05 million for men and -JPY0.91 million for women, with 22 male and 18 female respondents, a standard deviation of 4.1 million for men and 4.2 million for women, and no statistically significant differences found. No statistically significant gender differences were found by income bracket. One each male and female reported earning less than JPY5 million, four men, or 18.2%, and eight women, or 44.4%, JPY5–seven million, eight men, or 36.4%, and six women, or 33.3%, JPY7–ten million, seven men, or 31.8%, and two women, or 11.1%, JPY10–15 million, and two men, or 9.1%, and one woman, or 5.6%, more than JPY15 million. Although women appear to be more skewed toward the JPY5–seven million range than men, there is no overall trend toward income polarization versus respondents who moved among law firms, which may contribute to resulting lower gender disparity.

Duration of Employment and Last-Year Income

Average employment was 4.4 years for men and 4.8 years for women in the second through 59th cohorts, showing no statistically significant difference. Nor was any statistically significant difference found in estimated last-year income in these cohorts, which was JPY25.2 million for men and JPY13.6 million for women, owing to respective standard deviations of 28 million and 7.8 million. Average first- and last-year income difference was JPY8 million for men and JPY4.1 million for women, again statistically insignificant despite indications that income for some male lawyers rose significantly. By bracket, again, no one earned less than JPY7 million, with one male and two females reporting JPY7–ten million, and two males and one female each reporting JPY10–15 million and more than JPY15 million, with no significant gender differences found.

In the 60th–69th cohorts, average duration of employment was 3.3 years for men and 3.6 years for women, showing no statistically significant difference. Nor was any statistically significant difference found in estimated last-year income in these cohorts, which was JPY11 million for men and JPY9.3 million for women, despite men being paid more than women. By bracket, one woman, or 5.6%, reported less than JPY5 million, two men, or 9.5%, and four women, or 22.2% JPY5–seven million, 10 men, or 47.6%, and seven women, or 38.9%, JPY7–ten million, six men, or 28.6%, and five women, or 27.8%, JPY10–15 million, and three men, or 14.3%, and one woman, or 5.6%, more than JPY15 million, with no statistically significant differences.

Summary

In the final analysis, no single gender difference was identified in either the second through 59th cohorts or the 60th–69th cohorts, whether in first–year income, duration of employment, last-year income, or change in income during employment. This shows that in-house lawyers do not evince the kind of gender disparity found among lawyers in law firms.

4.3.3 Third Job Overview

There were 256 respondents whose first job was in a law firm and responded as having had at least three jobs. Of these, 157 were from the second through 59th cohorts, and the other 99 the 60th–69th cohorts. Of men in the former cohorts, 114, or 95%, moved to law firms, five, 4.2%, went in-house, and one, or 0.8%, elsewhere, whereas of women in these cohorts, 33, or 89.2%, moved to law firms, one, or 2.7%, went in-house, two, or 1.3%, into government, and one, or 2.7%, elsewhere. Conversely, of men in the latter cohorts, 65, or 82.3%, moved to law firms, 10, or 12.7%, went in-house, three, or 3.8%, into government, and one, or 1.3%, elsewhere, whereas of women in these cohorts, 14, or 70.0%, moved to law firms, five, or 25%, went in-house, and one, or 5.0%, into government.

Of the 147 respondents in the second through 59th cohorts whose third job is at a law firm, 108 men and 30 women moved from another law firm, two women from in-house jobs, five men and one woman from government, and one from elsewhere. Of the 79 respondents in the 60th–69th cohorts whose third job is at a law firm, 55 men and 11 women moved from another law firm, two men from in-house jobs, six men and two women from government, and two men and one woman from elsewhere. This data shows that law firms are still the primary third job destination, providing a framework for gender-based examination of respondents who moved twice between law firms.

4.3.3.1 Third Law Firm Job Reasons for Moving, Sizes, and Positions

This section examines the 204 respondents consistently working in law firms, of whom 108 men and 30 women are in the second through 59th cohorts and 55 men and 11 women in the 60th–69th cohorts. Significant gender differences among reasons for changing jobs again were found only for work-life balance" in the second through 59th cohorts, which six women, or 20%, cited, versus four men, or 38% (Fisher's Exact Test, $p < 0.05$). In Term 2-59, The most cited reason overall in these cohorts was open own firm, with 45 men and nine Women 9, followed by workplace relations, with 32 men and four women, job satisfaction, with 17 men and three women, and higher income, with 13 men and no women. Reasons given in the 60th–69th cohorts were similar, with 18 men and two women citing open own firm, followed by workplace relations, with 11 men 11 and two women 2, job satisfaction, with 12 men 12 and no women, work-life balance, with nine men and three women, and higher income, with six men and no women. Seventeen men and six women respondents gave other as a reason without further specification.

No statistically significant gender-based gender differences were found in sizes of law firms that respondents moved to. Average numbers of partners and associates in such firms were 4.65 and 33.19 for men and 5.96 and 11.75 for women respectively in the second through 59th cohorts, and 2.18 and 2.21 for men and 1.78 and 0.83 for women respectively in the 60th–69th cohorts. Nor were gender differences found in positions within firms in the the 2-59 cohort group, with partners comprising 84.6% of male lawyers and 74.1% of female lawyers in the second through 59th cohorts and 72.5% of male lawyers and 55.6% of female lawyers in the 60th–69th cohorts. In short, the majority of respondents in both categories are partners in third law firm jobs with no statistically significant differences, despite women's lower percentages.

4.3.3.2 Third Law Firm Job Income and Field of Practice

As noted above, no statistically significantly gender differences were found concerning sizes of law firms respondents moved to or their positions once hired. Significant differences did emerge concerning income, however. Comparisons of last-year income at second law firm jobs with first-year income third firm jobs are as follows. Estimated changes in income due to changing firms were 0.98 million for men and 0.41 million for women in the second through 59th cohorts, with no statistically significant difference. This suggests noticeably lesser gender disparities in these job than changing from a first law to a second law firm job, again, as described above. Notwithstanding, average estimated first-year income in these jobs shows significant gender differences, at JPY17.9 million for men and JPY10.5 million for women. There are also differences in fields of practice, with women continuing to tend to focus on family law more than men, at 36.7% and 11.5% respectively ($p < 0.01$). More men than women also concentrate on accidents, though not to a statistically significant degree, at 11.5% and zero percent respectively (Fisher's Exact Test, $p = 0.07$). Men in these cohorts were also employed at these jobs longer than women, at 12.0 and 7.3 years respectively.

Gender differences are also evident in last-year income at these jobs, possibly owing to these differences in practice and seniority, at JPY22.8 million for men and JPY12.8 million for women, achieving statistical significance (Independent Sample Test, $p < 0.05$). By bracket, 10.6% of ment and 15.4% of women report less than

JPY5 million, 6.4% of men and 11.5% of women JPY5–seven million, 9.6% of men and 26.9% of women JPY7-ten million, 19.1% of men and 19.2% of women JPY10-15 million, and 54.3% of men and 26.9% of women more than JPY15 million. Remarkably, more than 50% of men earn more than JPY15 million, whereas more than 50% of women earn less than JPY10 million. On average, men's incomes rose JPY4.6 million, versus JPY2.8 million for women, which is again statistically insignificant.

Conversely, in the 60th–69th cohorts, statistically, no gender gap was found in terms of income or duration of law firm affiliation. Estimated changes in income due to moving between law firms was JPY0.25 million for men and -JPY1.1 million for women, again, statistically insignificant, with standard deviations of 4.1 million for men and 2.6 million for women. Average estimated first-year income was JPY8.3 million for men and JPY5.0 million for women, achieving statistical significance. By bracket, 21.8% of men and 54.5% of women reported less than JPY5 million, and 30.9% of men and 36.4% of women JPY5-seven million. In short, women make up 90.9% of the under JPY7 million brackets. While these distributions are only modestly statistically significant (Fisher's Exact Test, $p = 0.085$), they do show that most female lawyers who changed jobs three times are in disproportionately lower income brackets than their male counterparts.

Regarding field of practice, unlike the second through 59th cohorts, both men and women in these cohorts worked more in family law, at 21% and 27.3% respectively, showing no gender difference. By contrast, more women than men focused on accidents, 36.4% versus 7.3% respectively (Fisher's Exact Test, $p < 0.05$). Average duration of these jobs was 2.2 years for men and 2.6 years for women, with no significant difference. Nor are there significant differences between men and women in last-year income, at estimated averages of JPY8.3 million for men and JPY6.1 million for women, although it is unclear whether this is because there were no differences in practice or duration of affiliation or because affiliation was relatively short for both men and women. By bracket, 19.6% of men and 36.4% of women report less than JPY5 million, 31.4% of men and 45.5% of women JPY5–seven million, 21.6% of men and 9.1% of women JPY7–ten million, 13.7% of men and zero percent of women JPY10–15 million, and 13.7% of men and 9.1% of women more than JPY15 million. No statistically significant differences were found in these analyses either, although women are thus again skewed slightly more toward the lower end of the income spectrum. On average, men's incomes rose JPY0.66 million, and women's JPY1.0 million, over the course of their affiliation, again showing no statistically significant differences.

4.3.3.3 Summary

Consistent with first and second law firm jobs, gender differences in income were found over the course of affiliation in the second through 59th cohorts, despite no statistically significant differences in firm size. Conversely, only first-year income showed differences in the 60th–69th cohorts. In addition, the trend that more women concentrate on family law than men, which had been consistent thus far, was not confirmed in these cohorts. It is unclear from the data whether this reflects law firm and legal market trends or whether trends have yet to stabilized owing to these respondents still being relatively early in their careers.

4.3.3.4 Third Jobs for Respondents Whose Second Jobs Were Not Law Firms

Following is an overview of the third jobs of those few respondents whose second jobs were not law firms. It is assumed that only those who moved from second jobs responded with third jobs, meaning that those who have not moved are still at their second jobs when the survey was conducted. It is reasonable to assume that there some respondents who have no positive reason to change jobs, although verification is impossible owing to there being no questions about reasons for remaining at a given job.

Of the few members of the second through 59th cohorts who had changed jobs once, five men and four women moved in-house, seven men and one woman went into government, and one man elsewhere. Only three of the nine in-house lawyers had a third job, one man moving to another in-house position and two women to law firms, leaving six still in-house. Seven of the eight government lawyers also changed jobs a second time, five men and one woman moving to law firms and the remaining male elsewhere. The one man whose second job was elsewhere also moved to a law firm.

In the 60th–69th cohorts, 61 chose second jobs other than law firms, 22 men and 18 women moving in-house, 11 men and five women into government, and four men and one woman elsewhere. Of those whose second placement was in-house, eight changed jobs again, two men to law firms, and five men and one woman to other in-house positions. Of those 16 whose second placement was in government, 13 changed jobs again, six men and two women to law firms, two men and one woman in-house, and two men elsewhere in government. Two of the men and the one woman whose second jobs were elsewhere moved to law firms. Again, it is striking that 32 of the 40 who second jobs were in-house did not change jobs again, with significantly more women moving from first law firm jobs to in-house positions, while only one changed jobs a second time, and even then to another corporate in-house position.

4.4 Women Lawyers' Career Paths

4.4.1 How Women Change Jobs

Figure 4.1 shows career paths of women lawyers in the second through 59th cohorts, and Fig. 4.2 career paths of those in the 60th–69th cohorts. Lawyers in the former cohorts would follow the traditional career paths of working at law firms and, in principle, moving to other law firms when changing jobs. Indeed, among 98 women

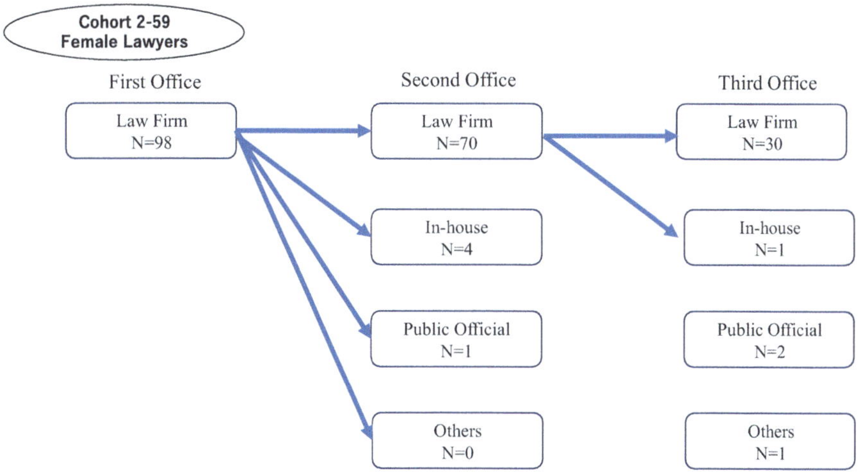

Fig. 4.1 Women Lawyers' Career Paths, Second Through 59th Cohorts

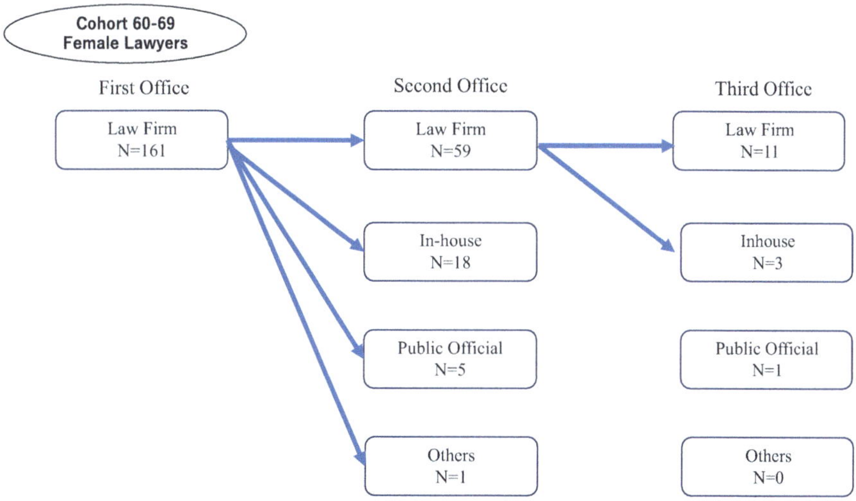

Fig. 4.2 Women Lawyers' Career Paths, 60th–69th Cohorts

lawyers in this category, 75, or 76.5%, changed jobs once, of which 70 moved to second law firms, 39 of which became partners. Of these 75, 34, or 48.6%, moved from second to third law firms, and 20 of these are partners. The aforementioned fact that many of them work primarily in family law and the significant disparity in their income compared with that of male lawyers following similar career paths remain, however.

Figure 4.2 shows more diverse career paths for women lawyers, although the main path is still from one law firm to another. Seventy-eight of the 161 respondents in this category are still at their first law firm jobs, indicative of the relative youth as of this writing of the 60th–69th cohorts. Of those who moved to the second workplace, Significantly fewer of those who have changed jobs have moved to other law firms than their predecessors, with the rest moving to in-house corporate counsel positions. While the gender gap in law firm jobs appears to be narrowing compared to the second through 59th cohorts, men still consistently earn more than women in first through third law firm jobs, including last-year incomes even for similar durations of affiliation.

4.4.2 How Job Changes Affect Income

Figure 4.3 traces estimated incomes of lawyers in the first and last years of their first through third law firm jobs by gender, with "x" marking inflection points of statistically significant gender differences. As described above, male lawyers in the second through 59th cohorts are more economically successful than female lawyers, to a statistically significant degree. By contrast, for the 60th -69th cohorts, the income gap found in the 60th–69th cohorts to span from last years at first law firm jobs to first years at third law firm jobs disappears in last years at third law firm jobs. It is unclear whether this is due to these cohorts comprising relatively young lawyers, as mentioned above, although it should be noted that 11 female and 51 male lawyers in these cohorts had changed law firm jobs twice when the survey was conducted.

Figure 4.3 shows that on the whole, the 60th–69th cohorts are not earning as much as their predecessors. Nor is the gender gap as large, which may or may not contribute to these overall lower earnings. Notwithstanding, there is a gender gap in

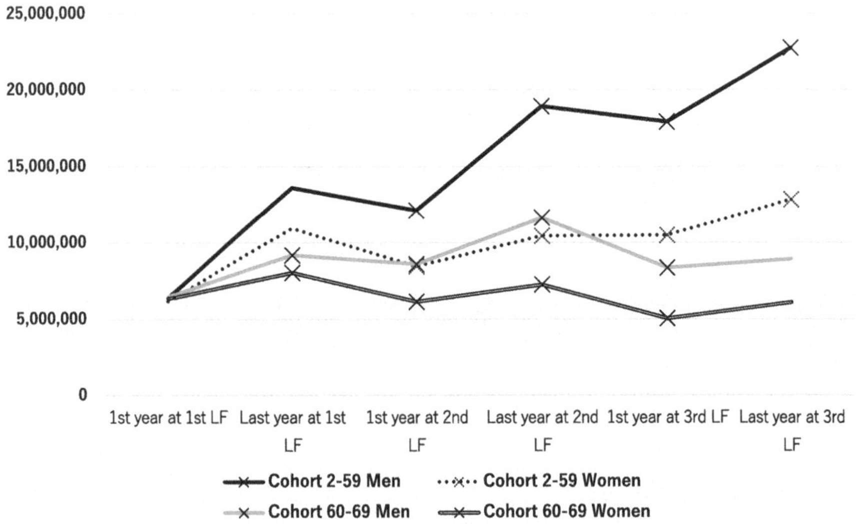

Fig. 4.3 Gender Disparities in Estimated Income Trends

estimated last-year income among these cohorts at first law firm jobs in the categories with the most respondents, which widens further after moving to second law firms. It is possible that the overall slope is simply more gradual than in the second through 59th cohorts.

On the other hand, no such gender disparity was found among in-house lawyers, despite there being relatively few respondents in this category. Men and women alike who moved to such jobs frequently cited work-life balance as their reason for doing so, and the results suggest that they are treated equally at these jobs. The study also found that lawyers who moved to in-house counsel tended not to return to law firms.

4.4.3 Prospects for Women Lawyers in Japan

The questionnaire concludes by asking respondents whether they currently wish to change jobs, and if so, where they would like to work and why. The results shed light on female lawyers' future careers. In the second through 59th cohorts, 10 men and three women, or 2.3%, and 89 respondents, or 11.4%, in the 60th–69th cohorts, answered yes. Also in the latter cohorts, 497, or 63.9%, answered no, and 192, or 24.7%, that they were unsure. Women in these cohorts stood out, with 33, or 18.9%, answering yes, versus 102, or 58.3%, answering no, and 40, or 22.9%, that they were unsure. Women are thus statistically more likely than men to want to change jobs ($p < 0.01$). Furthermore, 21, or 63.6%, of the women who answered yes in these cohorts answered that they hoped to move in-house, again achieving statistical significance (Fisher's Exact Test, $p < 0.01$).

The most common reason given by respondents in these cohorts answering yes was higher income, by 28 men and 14 women, or 46.2%, followed by job satisfaction, by 21 men and 18 women, or 42.9%, work-life balance, by 13 men and 16 women, or 31.9%, workplace relations, by 18 men and 8 women, or 28.6%, and open own firm, by 20 men and one woman, or 23.1%. Women chose work-life balance significantly more often ($p < 0.01$).

The survey reveals that more women than men in the 60th–69th cohorts want to change jobs to become in-house lawyers, with many of them citing work-life balance as a reason. As shown above, there is no gender disparity in income for in-house lawyers. Additionally, they are protected by Japan's Equal Employment Opportunity Law once they are employed by corporations, as well as receiving corporate employment benefits. These factors help in-house jobs foster better work-life balance than typical law firm jobs. It thus seems likely that many more women lawyers will move in-house, subject to demand.

As the above comparison of cohorts shows, the gender gap in law firms will narrow, albeit slowly, over time, as the 60th–69th cohorts attain leadership in bar associations. Greater participation by women lawyers is still the primary factor in encouraging gender equality in the legal community, however. Such a sea change would drive talent to in-house jobs for some time to come, forcing law firms to offer more women-friendly situations to remain competitive. In conclusion, the gender disparity in Japan's legal community will not be eliminated for some time yet, as structural changes are required.

References

American Bar Association (2021), Profile of the Legal Profession 2021. https://www.abalegalprofile.com/. Retrieved October 20, 2023.

Epstein C (1981), Women in Law, Basic Books, New York.

JFBA (Japan Federation of Bar Associations), (Nihon Bengoshi Rengokai) (2022) Bengoshi Hakusho 2022 (White Paper on Attorneys 2022), Nihon Bengoshi Rengokai, Tokyo.

Kyoko Ishida (2011), Josei bengoshi no tokucho (Characteristics of women lawyers), in JFBA, Bengoshi Gyomu no Keizai Kiban ni Kansuru Hokokusho (Survey Report on the Economic Basis of Legal Practice), Jiyu to seigi, 62 (6): 27–28.

Kyoko Ishida (2015), Raifu ibento to senmonshoku seikatsu jenda no shiten kara (Life events and professional life through the lens of gender), in Sato I, Hamano R, eds., Hendoki no nihon no bengoshi (Japanese Lawyers in a Time of Transition), 178–196.

Kyoko Ishida (2016), Why Female Lawyers Get Less: Multiple Glass Ceilings for Japanese Female Lawyers, Hastings International and Comparative Law Review, 39: 411–439.

Mayumi Nakamura (2015), Bengoshi no waku raifu balansu (Lawyers' Work-life Balance), Akashi publishing, Tokyo.

Naikakuhu, Danjo Kyodo Sankaku Kyoku (Cabinet Office, Gender Equality Bureau), (2023) Danjo Kyodo Sankaku Hakusho 2023 (Gender Equality White Paper 2023). https://www.gender.go.jp/about_danjo/whitepaper/r05/zentai/html/zuhyo/zuhyo01-14.html. Retrieved October 20 2023.

Mibuchi Y, Nagaishi Y, Sato K, Kaji C, Yamamoto K, Uno K, Wakana M, Dohi S, Ishikawa E, Owaki M, Matsuo K, Kasahara I, and Ito M (1983) Josei Horitsuka: Kakudai suru Shin Jidai no Katsudo Bun-ya (Women Lawyers: a New Era of Expanding Fields of Endeavor), Yuhikaku, Tokyo.

Miyazawa S (2001) The Politics of Judicial Reform in Japan: The Rule of Law at Last? Asian-Pacific Law & Policy Journal, 2: 88.

Kyoko Ishida is Professor at Waseda Law School, Tokyo, where she has been teaching since 2009. She received her LL.M in 2003 and Ph.D. in 2006 from the School of Law, University of Washington. Her research interests include lawyers' professional obligations, gender in law, and access to justice. Her publications include *Unpopular or Unfamiliar Dispute Resolution? How Japanese People View ADR* (Asian Pacific Mediation Journal Vol. 1, 2019), *Why Does Surname Matter? Past, Present, and Future Prospect of Family Law from a Gender Perspective in Japan*, (Journal of Korean Law Vol. 18, 2018), *Deterioration or refinement? Impacts of an increasing number of lawyers on the lawyer discipline system in Japan* (International Journal of the Legal Profession Vol. 24, 2017), and *Ethics and Regulations of Legal Services Providers in Japan* (VDM Publishing, 2011).

Chapter 5
The Relationship Between Educational Institutions and Legal Careers

Daisuke Mori

Abstract This chapter examines the relationship between educational institutions and legal careers in Japan. We divided the survey data into two groups: respondents in the first through 59th and 60th–69th legal apprenticeship cohorts, which roughly correspond, respectively, to before and after the establishment of Japan's modern law school system. Categories analyzed by university and law school include locations, initial annual income, the number of lawyers, and fields of specialization, at first law firm jobs. The results showed various changes from the first through 59th cohorts to the 60th–69th cohorts. For example, regarding the number of lawyers at law firms where graduates had their first jobs, academic inequalities, among schools and within given schools alike, grew more among the 60th–69th cohorts than the first through 59th cohorts, with the widening inequalities among schools in this regard in recent years clarified by further subdividing the 60th–69th cohorts into the 60th–65th and the 66th–69th cohorts.

5.1 Introduction

Graduating from a highly ranked university is believed to be associated with future success in the job market. Empirical analyses in various countries, including Japan (Ono 2004; Kawaguchi and Ma 2008), have shown a strong correlation between graduating from highly ranked universities and subsequent success in the labor market.

Lawyers are no exception. Heinz et al. (2005) surveyed Chicago lawyers and found that high-ranking law school graduates were more likely to work for and become partners in large US law firms (Heinz et al. 2005, pp. 57–60). According to Watson's (2016) interview with a Japanese lawyer, there is a lawyer recruitment

D. Mori (✉)
Kumamoto University Faculty of Law, Kumamoto, Japan
e-mail: mdai@kumamoto-u.ac.jp

M. Murayama (ed.), *The Japanese Legal Profession in Transition*, Economics, Law, and Institutions in Asia Pacific,
https://doi.org/10.1007/978-981-97-2692-9_5

hierarchy in Japan in which alumni of elite schools, such as the University of Tokyo and Kyoto University, receive priority over alumni of lower-ranking colleges and universities (Watson 2016, p. 34).

There are several empirical studies on the relationship between Japanese lawyers and their universities or law schools, but each has its limitations, as follows.

Nakazato et al. (2010) used 2004 tax data in Japan to analyze what factors affect lawyers' income, such as talent or geographic location. The results showed that those who graduated from the University of Tokyo earned higher income than others. However, this analysis is limited in that the data are only from before the establishment of Japan's modern law school system, and the number of universities whose impact is being considered is limited.

Nakamura (2014), using census data collected by the Japan Federation of Bar Associations (JFBA) in 2010, examined whether differences in gender and the law school from which one graduated made a difference in the size of the graduate's first law firm. The results showed that, for some schools, there was a disparity in the size of the law firms where graduates were employed. Furthermore, this disparity tended to increase with the passage of time and the introduction of the New Bar Exam. However, this study had a limitation in that the only dependent variable was the size of the graduate's first law firm. Additionally, schools were anonymized for survey integrity purposes.

Fujimoto et al. (2017) surveyed Japanese lawyers in the 67th legal apprenticeship cohort and analyzed the effects of the universities and law schools they attended on their income and where law firms they worked at were located. The analysis showed that there were significant differences in mean income across universities and law schools, and in particular, the mean income of the University of Tokyo Law School alumni was significantly higher than those of alumni of Chuo University Law School and other law schools. Alumni of the law schools of the University of Tokyo Law School, Keio Law School, and Waseda Law School are more likely to be affiliated with law firms located in the 23 wards that comprise central Tokyo. However, this study has the limitation of focusing only on lawyers in one specific legal apprenticeship cohort.

This chapter will analyze the relationship between educational institutions (the university or law school from which one graduated) and legal careers, using more variables, universities and law schools, and cohorts than these previous studies. The remainder of this chapter is organized as follows. First, we examine our data to determine which universities and law schools the majority of respondents graduated from, as well as gender ratios thereof. Second, for those respondents who graduated from university or law school (hereinafter "graduates" or "alumni"), we analyze locations, initial annual income, the number of lawyers, and fields of specialization, at first law firm jobs, by their alma mater. Third, we examine changes in recent years and other issues including studying abroad and the adoption of the Preliminary Bar Exam. The chapter concludes with a summary and a discussion of possible future research.

5.2 Universities and Law Schools in the Data

5.2.1 Number of Lawyers by University and Law School

Respondents are divided, for the purposes of analysis, into the first through 59th and 60th–69th legal apprenticeship cohorts. The term "legal apprenticeship" refers to mandatory one- to two-year courses for legal accreditation at the Legal Training and Research Institute (LTRI) after passing the bar exam.

The legal apprenticeship cohort is often used as a measure of how long a lawyer has been practicing law in Japan. The first cohort of lawyers began their training at LTRI in 1947, meaning that adding 1946 to cohort numbers yields starting years for such legal apprenticeships.

The survey data is separated as described above because the 60th cohort refers to legal apprenticeships in 2006, the year when the first graduates of the modern law schools began legal apprenticeships. Before these graduate schools for legal education were established in 2004, the bar exam was open to all applicants. By contrast, the New Bar Exam system that commenced in 2006 made graduating from these new law schools a prerequisite for taking the bar exam.[1] Comparing the first through 59th cohorts with the 60th–69th cohorts thus shows the situations before and after these reforms. Accordingly, the analysis focuses primarily on universities for lawyers in the first through 59th cohorts and the new law schools for those in the 60th–69th cohorts,[2] as the last schools lawyers graduated from were considered to be the most significant.[3]

According to the survey data, there were 614 lawyers in the first through 59th cohorts. The seven universities with the most lawyer alumni from these cohorts are the University of Tokyo and Chuo University, with 104, or 16.9%, apiece; Waseda University, with 80, or 13.0%; Kyoto University, with 57, or 9.3%; Keio University, with 43, or 7.0%; Hitotsubashi University, at 21, or 3.4%; and Osaka University, at 20, or 3.2%.[4] This chapter focuses on these universities, beginning with thumbnail sketches as follows.

[1] For details on the establishment of modern law schools and the New Bar Exam in Japan, see Matsui (2013, pp. 11–18), Watson (2016, pp. 16–24) and Murayama (2020, p. 757).

[2] Even after the establishment of the modern law schools, the Old Bar Exam, which had no restrictions on eligibility, coexisted with the New Bar Exam. Essentially, only law school graduates of the new law schools were eligible for the New Bar Exam, and this coexistence continued until 2010. The Preliminary Bar Exam, which also had no restrictions on eligibility, was instituted in 2011 (see also Sect. 5.5.1 of this chapter). Hence, while some lawyers in the 60th–69th cohorts became lawyers without having graduated from law school, they are excluded hereinafter except in Sect. 5.5.1.

[3] Fujimoto et al. (2017, p. 97) utilized multiple regression analysis to examine the impact of various factors on income. They found that being an alumnus of the University of Tokyo or Waseda law schools was significant in the 67th cohort, while graduating from either university's undergraduate law faculties was not.

[4] Omura et al. (2005, p. 40) refer to the top five of these universities as the "big five."

The University of Tokyo is a public national university located in Tokyo. It is the highest-ranked national university in Japan and holds a top position in the hierarchy of Japanese universities.[5] It also holds the record for the most students passing the bar exam annually between 1970 and 2019, with an average ranking of 1.32 (Ikeda and Yoshida 2020, p. 24).

Chuo University is a private university located in Tokyo. It is part of the second tier of such universities in the Tokyo metropolitan area, behind Waseda and Keio.[6] Many of its alumni have passed the bar exam, and it and the University of Tokyo are regarded as "a clique of two universities dividing the judicial world into two." Between 1970 and 2019, it has been second only to the University of Tokyo in the number of times it has topped the annual list of students passing the bar exam, with an average ranking of 2.86 (Ikeda and Yoshida 2020, p. 24).

Waseda University, another private university located in Tokyo, is one of the top-tier private universities in Japan. As for bar exams, the number of successful applicants has increased since 1970, topping the list for the first time in 1983 and ranking first consecutively in 2004 and 2005, just before the commencement of the New Bar Exam. As a result, it had the third-highest number of successful applicants for the bar exam annually since 1970, with an average ranking of 2.88 (Ikeda and Yoshida 2020, p. 24).

Keio University, another private university in Tokyo, ranks with Waseda in the top tier of such schools in Japan. In bar exams, Keio University has been ranked behind Waseda University. Since the 1980s, it and Kyoto University, the university described immediately below, have been competing for fourth and fifth places, entering the top three for the first time in 1998 and becoming regular in the top three since the beginning of the twenty-first century (Ikeda and Yoshida 2020, p. 25).

Kyoto University is a public national university located in Kyoto. It is considered the second-highest-ranked national university in Japan after the University of Tokyo. The average ranking of students passing the bar exam in 1970–2019 is 3.96 (Ikeda and Yoshida 2020, p. 24).

Hitotsubashi University is a public national university located in Tokyo. It is the third highest-ranked national university in Japan, after the University of Tokyo and Kyoto University (Ramseyer and Rasmusen 2015, p. 123).

Osaka University is a public national university located in Osaka. It is the second-highest ranked national university in the Kansai region after Kyoto University.

For lawyers in the first through 59th cohorts, graduates of universities other than these seven were divided into three groups: prestigious national universities, with 58 students, or 9.5%; other public universities, with 34 students, or 5.5%; and other private universities, with 93 students, or 15.1%, resulting in 10 school groups.[7]

[5] See Kawaguchi and Ma (2008, p. 186). For more information on the rankings of various Japanese universities and law schools, see Ramseyer and Rasmusen (2015, pp. 121–137).

[6] Ramseyer and Rasmusen (2015, p. 122) described the US equivalents to the University of Tokyo and Chuo University as Princeton and Vanderbilt, respectively.

[7] Nakamura (2014) employs a similar classification. In this study, the universities from which the respondents graduated were divided into a total of 11 categories: seven schools with the largest

Prestigious national universities include five historic and challenging public national universities: Kyushu University, Tohoku University, Nagoya University, Hokkaido University, and Kobe University. These universities rank highly among national universities after the University of Tokyo, Kyoto University, Hitotsubashi University, and Osaka University. In the survey data, Kyushu ranked eighth, with 16 students, or 2.6%; Tohoku University, ranked ninth, with 11 students, or 1.8%; and Nagoya, Hokkaido, and Kobe University, ranked 11th, with 10 students, or 1.6%, apiece. Other public universities include all universities established or operated by national and local governments.

The survey data shows 688 lawyers in the 60th–69th cohorts. The seven new law schools with the most graduates in these cohorts were Keio, with 64 students, or 9.3%; Chuo, with 56 students, or 8.1%; Kyoto University, with 50 students, or 7.2%; the University of Tokyo, with 49 students, or 7.1%; Waseda, with 33 students, or 4.8%; Meiji University, with 31 students, or 4.5%; and Osaka University, with 29 students, or 4.2%. These overlap with the universities with the most graduates in the first through 59th cohorts, with the exception of Meiji.

Because Hitotsubashi instead of Meiji is included in the seven universities in the first through 59th cohorts, we will include Hitotsubashi, with 26 students, or 3.8%, rather than Meiji University in the seven law schools, to facilitate comparison with the first through 59th cohorts, and Meiji University will be included in the "other private universities" group.[8] As with universities, we divided respondents who are not alumni of these seven law schools into three groups: prestigious national universities, with 96 respondents, or 13.9%; other public universities, with 70 respondents, or 10.2%; and other private universities, with 215 respondents, or 31.3%, resulting in 10 school groups.[9]

As can be gleaned from the above, there is considerable overlap between the top universities in the first through 59th cohorts and the 60th–69th cohorts. Most major universities instituted law schools as affiliated graduate schools in 2004 when the new law school program was established, without discontinuing their existing undergraduate law degree programs (Matsui 2013, pp. 10–11; Murayama 2020, p. 758). The question arises: What, then, is the relationship between the undergraduate degree programs and the new law schools for lawyers in the 60th–69th cohorts?

Table 5.1 shows the relationship between undergraduate and law schools. Each cell gives the percentage of graduates from a given law school, on the y-axis, who

---

number of graduates among the respondents (three national and four private schools, with each university renamed to obscure its specific identity), and categories including "other former imperial universities" (similar to prestigious national universities), "other public universities," "other private universities," and "foreign universities." The study assesses their impact on the size of the first law firms examined.

[8] Note that Hitotsubashi University has the highest cumulative bar exam pass rate among law schools in Japan for the period 2005–2018 (MOJ 2020).

[9] The numbers of graduates from law schools of prestigious national universities are as follows: Kobe ranks eighth with 27 respondents, or 3.9%; Hokkaido is in tenth place with 22 respondents, or 3.2%; Kyushu in 11th place with 19 respondents, or 2.8%; and Nagoya is in 12th place with 17 respondents, or 2.5%.

Table 5.1 Law school graduates by undergraduate campus

Law school \ University	Tokyo	Chuo	Waseda	Kyoto	Keio	Hitotsubashi	Osaka	Prestigious	Public	Private	Total	*n*
Tokyo	65.3	4.1	8.2	4.1	6.1	0.0	0.0	4.1	0.0	8.2	100	49
Chuo	7.4	25.9	3.7	0.0	14.8	7.4	1.9	9.3	5.6	24.1	100	54
Waseda	24.2	3.0	33.3	6.1	3.0	6.1	3.0	3.0	6.1	12.1	100	33
Kyoto	4.0	0.0	2.0	66.0	4.0	0.0	6.0	8.0	2.0	8.0	100	50
Keio	11.3	12.9	9.7	3.2	40.3	4.8	0.0	3.2	3.2	11.3	100	62
Hitotsubashi	7.7	0.0	7.7	3.8	15.4	46.2	0.0	3.8	3.8	11.5	100	26
Osaka	3.4	3.4	0.0	10.3	13.8	10.3	17.2	6.9	10.3	24.1	100	29
Prestigious	7.4	2.1	8.4	6.3	0.0	1.1	2.1	42.1	12.6	17.9	100	95
Public	10.0	7.1	8.6	4.3	2.9	2.9	2.9	10.0	25.7	25.7	100	70
Private	4.7	8.1	12.8	4.3	4.3	1.9	0.9	6.2	12.8	44.1	100.1	211

Numbers in the table except the last column are row percentages. Row totals may not add up to 100% owing to rounding. $\chi^2 = 830.16, p = 0.000$

were previously alumni of the undergraduate programs, on the x-axis. For example, 65.3% of the 49 graduates of the University of Tokyo Law School were University of Tokyo undergraduate alumni.

Law school graduates are likely to be alumni of the university to which the law school they graduated from is affiliated. The diagonal gray cells in Table 5.1 represent undergraduates of given universities who went on to law school at the same universities. For most universities, this gray cell represents the highest percentage.

However, every law school also includes some percentage of alumni from other universities. The percentages of alumni who are from the same university and from different universities vary from one law school to another. For example, the top public national law schools, such as the University of Tokyo and Kyoto University, have a notably high percentage of undergraduates from the same university, followed by Hitotsubashi University, which is also a top public national law school. By contrast, private universities such as Keio, Waseda, and Chuo University generally have a lower percentage of students from their own universities than public national universities. These law schools include many students from other public and private universities. Among public national universities, Osaka University, which is located in Osaka rather than Tokyo, has a lower percentage of students from its own university and a relatively large percentage of students from Tokyo campuses such as Keio and Hitotsubashi, as well as from nearby schools such as Kyoto University.

5.2.2 Universities, Law Schools, and Gender

This section analyzes the genders of graduates from the first through 59th cohorts and the 60th–69th cohorts.[10] In the first through 59th cohorts, 513, or 84.9%, were male, and 91, or 15.1%, were female, whereas 527, or 78.1%, were male, and 148,

[10]Those who chose "do not wish to answer" among the gender options were excluded from the analysis.

or 21.9%, were female in the 60th–69th cohorts, indicating that the percentage of females had statistically significantly increased ($\chi^2 = 9.87$, $p = 0.002$).[11]

In the first through 59th cohorts, there are statistically significant gender differences in graduation by university ($\chi^2 = 20.73$, $p = 0.012$). The universities with the smallest percentages of female respondents were the University of Tokyo alumni, at 6.7%, followed by Kyoto and Waseda, at 8.9% apiece, prestigious national universities, at 12.3%, and Osaka, at 15.0%. By contrast, Keio University and Chuo University have relatively high percentages of female alumni, at 24.4% and 21.0%, respectively, while other public universities have 26.5% and other private universities have 19.6%.

Conversely, in the 60th–69th cohorts, gender differences by law school were small and not statistically significant ($\chi^2 = 3.20$, $p = 0.954$). In all schools, females now account for 15–30% of the total: 26.5% at the University of Tokyo, 21.4% at Chuo University, 24.2% at Waseda, 25.0% at Kyoto, 22.2% at Keio, 16.0% at Hitotsubashi, 19.2% at Osaka, 20.8% at prestigious national universities, 16.2% at other public universities, and 23.2% at other private universities.

5.3 Universities, Law Schools, and Legal Career

5.3.1 Types of First Jobs

This section examines types of first jobs for college and law school graduates: working as an in-house lawyer or in a law firm.[12] Statistically significant differences were found in first job percentages between the first through 59th cohorts and the 60th–69th cohorts overall ($\chi^2 = 28.44$, $p = 0.000$). In the first through 59th cohorts, 538, or 98.9%, of the first jobs were in law firms, with only six, or 1.1%, in corporations, whereas in the 60th–69th cohorts, 632, or 92.4%, were in law firms, and 52, or 7.6%, were in corporations.[13] This finding suggests that the prevalence of in-house lawyers is increasing.[14]

---

[11] R 4.2.1 was used for statistical analysis in this chapter. Chi-square test *p*-values were computed by Monte Carlo simulation because there may be cells with small expected frequencies in chi-square tests.

[12] In addition to the options "law firm" and "corporation," the questionnaire included options "public office" and "other." "Public offices" include national ministry, prefecture, municipality, court and prosecutor's office. "Other" includes assemblyman, university teacher, NPO, labor union, and policy secretary. However, these are excluded from the results due to small response sizes.

[13] Sixty-five graduates in the first through 59th cohorts chose government as their first jobs, versus 3 in the 60th–69th cohorts, most likely due to 32 respondents having chosen the courts and 30 prosecutor's offices in the first through 59th cohorts. In other words, the reason for the higher number of respondents in the first through 59th cohorts compared to the 60th–69th cohorts is probably that judges and prosecutors often leave their positions to work for law firms only after a certain amount of time has passed since they became judges or prosecutors.

[14] According to JILA (2023a, b), as of 2001, only 66 lawyers worked in-house, in a total of 39 companies. That represented less than 0.4% of all lawyers at the time. The reason for the small

There was no statistically significant difference in first job percentages by university in the first through 59th cohorts ($\chi^2 = 13.88$, $p = 0.104$). In-house jobs represented 4.4%, 2.2%, and 2.0% of these jobs for alumni of the University of Tokyo, Kyoto, and prestigious national universities, respectively, and 0% for the rest.

In the 60th–69th cohorts, there was also no statistically significant difference in first job percentages by law school ($\chi^2 = 7.24$, $p = 0.616$). However, unlike in the first through 59th cohorts, in the 60th–69th cohorts, a certain percentage of respondents in all law schools work for corporations. Numbers and percentages of law school graduates working for corporations are four, or 8.3%, for the University of Tokyo, three, or 5.4%, for Chuo, five, or 15.2%, for Waseda, five, or 10.0% for Kyoto, five, or 7.8%, for Keio, one, or 3.8%, for Hitotsubashi, three, or 10.7%, for Osaka, three, or 3.2%, for prestigious public national universities, five, or 7.1%, for other public national universities, and 18, or 8.4% for other private universities.

In the following sections, we analyze only those who had first jobs at law firms and exclude in-house lawyers from the analysis.

5.3.2 *Locations of First Law Firm Jobs*

Table 5.2 shows the locations of graduates' first law firm jobs.[15] The "Overall" row shows that the percentage of graduates going to law firms in Tokyo and Osaka decreased from the first through 59th to the 60th–69th cohorts, while that going to "high court locations" and "other locations" increased.[16] There are several possible explanations for this finding. First, there were more graduates from prestigious national universities and other public and private law schools in the 60th–69th cohorts than in the first through 59th cohorts. Many of these law schools are located in "high court locations" or "other locations," and many graduates go directly to work for law firms located in those locations. Second is the impact of the efforts by the JFBA and others to reduce lawyers' underrepresentation and maldistribution. The JFBA calls the district court jurisdictions where one or no lawyers are registered as "zero-one lawyer areas." To eliminate this problem, the JFBA established the "Sunflower Fund" by collecting funds from its member lawyers, and in 2000,

---

number of in-house lawyers until this time was that lawyers were required by law to obtain prior permission from their local bar association to take such in-house jobs. The number has risen considerably after this requirement was replaced with an after-the-fact reporting requirement in 2003 (Foote 2019, p. 163). As of June 2023, 1429 companies employed a total of 3184 lawyers, who represented 7.1% of all lawyers.

[15] "High" in Table 5.2 refers to the high court locations other than Tokyo and Osaka, including Sapporo, Sendai, Nagoya, Hiroshima, Takamatsu, and Fukuoka, which are also regional urban population centers. "Other" includes everywhere else. Responses choosing Aichi, which was also offered in the survey, are included in "High," owing to low percentages for most universities and law schools.

[16] Bushimata (2018, p. 133) notes that the extreme concentration of lawyers in Tokyo and Osaka has eased, albeit slightly, in the decade 2006–2016.

opened "Sunflower Fund Law Offices" throughout Japan.[17] A certain number of graduates in the 60th–69th cohorts were employed by these law offices.

In many cases, graduates are employed by law firms located near their alma mater. For example, the University of Tokyo, Chuo University, Waseda University, Keio University, and Hitotsubashi University are located in Tokyo, and many of their graduates are employed by law firms in Tokyo. Similarly, many graduates from Osaka University are employed by law firms in Osaka. The prestigious national universities are located in the "high court locations" or "other locations," and many of their graduates are employed by law firms located in those locations.[18]

However, among schools located in Tokyo, some schools have a relatively high percentage of students employed in Tokyo, while others have a low percentage. The top national and private schools such as the University of Tokyo and Keio University have a particularly high percentage of graduates working in Tokyo, while Chuo University, Waseda University, and Hitotsubashi University have a lower percentage working in Tokyo, with many going to "other locations."[19] Additionally, for Kyoto University, although its location, Kyoto, is included in the "other locations" in Table 5.2, many graduates go to Osaka, a larger city nearby. In the 60th–69th cohorts, however, more graduates from Kyoto University went to Tokyo instead.

5.3.3 *Initial Annual Income at First Law Firm Jobs*

Table 5.3 shows summary statistics of initial annual pre-tax income at first law firm jobs.[20] In the first through 59th cohorts, the University of Tokyo had the largest mean, while Chuo University had the smallest.[21] The top private universities such as Keio and Waseda tended to have relatively large means, while other public universities and other private universities tended to have small means. However, only the

---

[17] For more information on these efforts, see Foote (2019, pp. 158–160).

[18] The prestigious national universities are in Sapporo, Sendai, Nagoya, Fukuoka, and Kobe, many of which are also high court locations. See also footnote 15.

[19] Bushimata (2018, p. 136) also divides the group of graduates of law schools located in Tokyo into those who were employed in Tokyo, high court locations other than Tokyo, and other locations, but Table 6.2 further shows that the size of these percentages varies by law school.

[20] Respondents were offered brackets of less than JPY three million, JPY 3–five million, JPY 5–seven million, JPY 7–ten million, JPY 10–15 million, JPY 15–20 million, JPY 20–30 million, JPY 30–50 million, JPY 50–100 million, and more than JPY 100 million. JPY 30–50 million and JPY 50–100 million were excluded as outliers since only one respondent apiece chose either in the survey. Summary statistics were computed for the remainder by taking middle numbers for each range, i.e., JPY 1.5 million, JPY four million, JPY six million, JPY 7.5 million, JPY 12.5 million, JPY 17.5 million, and JPY 25 million, respectively.

[21] The University of Tokyo also had the largest median, and Chuo had the smallest.

Table 5.2 Locations of first law firm jobs

1st–59th cohorts							60th–69th cohorts						
	Location							Location					
University	Tokyo	Osaka	High	Other	Total	*N*	Law school	Tokyo	Osaka	High	Other	Total	*N*
Tokyo	81.6**	2.3**	9.2	6.9**	100	87	Tokyo	84.1**	0.0*	6.8*	9.1**	100	44
Chuo	64.8**	3.4**	13.6	18.2	100	88	Chuo	58.5*	0.0**	11.3	30.2	100	53
Waseda	56.8	6.8	13.5	23.0	100	74	Waseda	71.4**	0.0†	7.1	21.4	100	28
Kyoto	17.8**	40.0**	1.3	28.9	100	45	Kyoto	31.1	28.9**	15.6	24.4	100	45
Keio	82.1**	2.6**	5.1†	10.3†	100	39	Keio	72.9**	1.7*	5.1**	20.3	100	59
Hitotsubashi	63.2	5.3	5.3	26.3	100	19	Hitotsubashi	44.0	4.0	8.0	44.0	100	25
Osaka	5.3**	63.2**	5.3	26.3	100	19	Osaka	20.0*	52.0**	16.0	12.0†	100	25
Prestigious	16.7**	8.3	45.8**	29.2	100	48	Prestigious	9.9**	14.3	47.3**	28.6	100	91
Public	32.3*	22.6†	12.9	32.3	100	31	Public	26.2**	10.8	16.9	46.2**	100	65
Private	42.4†	17.6	14.1	25.9	100	85	Private	39.6	9.6	16.8	34.0†	100	197
Overall	51.8	12.7	14.6	20.9	100	535	Overall	41.9	10.6	18.1	29.4	100	632

Numbers in the table except the last column are row percentages. Row totals may not add up to 100%, owing to rounding. $\chi^2 = 203.20$, $p = 0.000$ in the first through 59th cohorts, and $\chi^2 = 204.27$, $p = 0.000$ in the 60th–69th cohorts. The asterisks and daggers in the table are based on the adjusted standardized residuals († $p < 0.1$, * $p < 0.05$, ** $p < 0.01$)

University of Tokyo was statistically significantly larger than the overall mean, and Chuo University was statistically significantly smaller.[22]

By contrast, more schools in the 60th–69th cohorts had means varying statistically significantly from the overall mean than in the first through 59th cohorts.[23] Looking at individual schools, similar to the first through 59th cohorts, the University of Tokyo Law School had the largest mean value. Moreover, Keio University Law School was also statistically significantly larger than the overall mean, and other public and private schools were statistically significantly smaller.

Additionally, Mean Log Deviation (MLD), a measure of inequality, was employed to directly capture disparities among universities and law schools.[24] The MLD value is zero for a perfectly equal distribution, and larger the greater the inequality. It can be decomposed into inequalities between and within groups.[25] The groups here are the ten groups of universities and law schools also used in Tables 5.1 through 5.7: Tokyo, Chuo, Waseda, Kyoto, Keio, Hitotsubashi, Osaka, Prestigious, Public, and Private. Hereinafter, these groups will be referred to as the "school groups."

Figure 5.1 shows the MLD of income and its decomposition in the first through 59th and 60th–69th cohorts. The MLD of income for the first through 59th cohorts is 0.175. The decomposition shows that the within-school-group inequality is 0.163 and the between-school-group inequality is 0.011. The MLD of income for the 60th–69th cohorts is 0.102. The decomposition shows that the within-school-group inequality is 0.089 and the between-school-group inequality is 0.012. Hence, although within-school-group inequality has decreased, between-school-group inequality increases, albeit slightly.

---

[22] Multiple comparisons of means by school groups with the overall mean are made by Analysis of Means (ANOM) with heterogeneous variances. The null hypothesis for ANOM is that the group mean equals the overall mean. The alternative hypothesis for ANOM is that the group mean is different from the overall mean. For more information on ANOM, see Nelson et al. (2005) and Pallmann and Hothorn (2016).

[23] Owing to timespans involved and resulting disparities in monetary value, no comparison was made as to whether annual income was higher in the first through 59th or the 60th–69th cohorts. It also obviates any necessity for determining whether respondents' answers are in modern or older monetary values.

[24] For the details on MLD, see, for example, Haughton and Khandker (2009, pp. 106–107).

[25] MLD is characterized by making such decompositions easier than other measures of inequality, such as the Gini coefficient.

Table 5.3 Initial annual income at first law firm jobs

1st–59th cohorts							60th–69th cohorts						
University	Mean	*SD*	0%	50%	100%	*N*	Law school	Mean	*SD*	0%	50%	100%	*N*
Tokyo**	779	408	150	850	1750	87	Tokyo**	872	305	400	850	1250	44
Chuo**	491	291	150	400	1250	88	Chuo	553	241	150	600	1250	52
Waseda	681	345	150	600	1750	72	Waseda	691	289	400	600	1250	28
Kyoto	621	221	150	600	850	45	Kyoto†	720	249	400	600	1250	45
Keio	736	337	150	600	1750	39	Keio**	781	382	150	600	2500	59
Hitotsubashi	550	396	150	600	1750	19	Hitotsubashi	620	264	150	600	1250	25
Osaka	634	374	150	600	1750	19	Osaka	596	169	400	600	1250	25
Prestigious	588	368	150	600	2500	47	Prestigious	597	197	150	600	1250	91
Public	556	316	150	600	1250	31	Public**	525	227	150	600	1250	65
Private	592	305	150	600	1750	84	Private**	552	257	150	600	1750	197
Overall	629	346	150	600	2500	531	Overall	622	279	150	600	2500	631

Numbers in the table are in JPY ten thousand. The asterisks and daggers on the tableside were based on Analysis of Means (ANOM) († $p < 0.1$, * $p < 0.05$, ** $p < 0.01$). "0%" is the minimum, "50%" is the median, and "100%" is the maximum

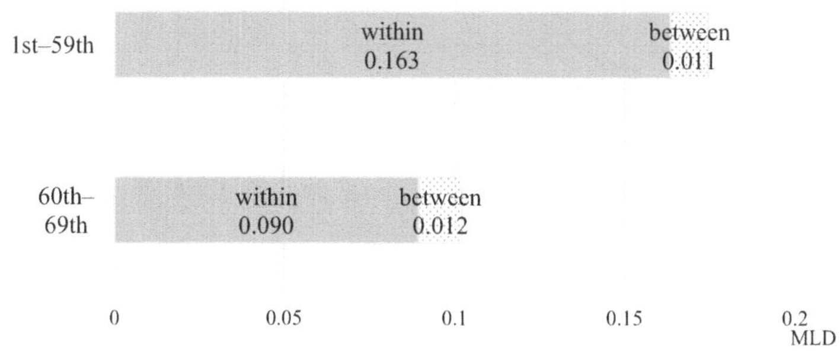

Fig. 5.1 Mean Log Deviation (MLD) of income and its decomposition

5.3.4 *Number of Lawyers at First Law Firm Jobs*

Table 5.4 shows summary statistics on the number of lawyers at law firms where graduates had their first jobs.[26] The number of lawyers is treated as indicative of firm size; the more lawyers, the larger the firm.

In terms of the overall change from the first through 59th cohorts to the 60th–69th cohorts, the mean number of lawyers in law firms nearly tripled, from 9.8 to 26.3,[27] while medians did not change much. Thus, while many graduates in the 60th–69th cohorts joined law firms that were not different in size from the small law firms in the first through 59th cohorts, some graduates joined larger law firms than those in the first through 59th cohorts. Many Japanese lawyers have traditionally worked in small law firms (Murayama 2020, p. 755). While it is likely that many still exhibit this tendency today, there has been some change from this trend.

In the first through 59th cohorts, the University of Tokyo stands out in Table 5.4 for its mean number of lawyers, and the difference from the overall mean is statistically significant. However, the large standard deviation and relatively small median signify that a few graduates are admitted to large firms and many more work in smaller firms. Chuo University, Osaka University, prestigious national universities, and other public and private universities had smaller means for lawyers, and the differences from the overall mean were statistically significant.

In the 60th–69th cohorts, the University of Tokyo again stood out in terms of the mean number of lawyers, and the difference from the overall mean was statistically significant. Similar to the first through 59th cohorts, Osaka University, the prestigious national universities, and other public and private universities had smaller

[26] The number of lawyers in the law firm is calculated by adding the number of managing lawyers and the number of non-managing lawyers. The number of lawyers includes the respondents themselves. The response format is to write the numbers directly into the survey form for the number of managing lawyers and the number of non-managing lawyers.

[27] Welch's test showed a significant difference between the mean number of lawyers in the first through 59th cohorts and that in the 60th–69th cohorts ($p = 0.000$).

Table 5.4 Number of lawyers at first law firm jobs

1st–59th cohorts							60th–69th cohorts						
University	Mean	*SD*	0%	50%	100%	*N*	Law school	Mean	*SD*	0%	50%	100%	*N*
Tokyo**	29.2	52.2	1	7	240	76	Tokyo*	119.2	168.2	2	20.5	540	32
Chuo**	4.4	3.4	2	3	24	77	Chuo	12.4	42.3	1	4	300	49
Waseda	7.8	8.7	2	5	50	66	Waseda	15.0	24.9	1	7	120	24
Kyoto	7.1	6.6	2	4	28	44	Kyoto	69.0	150.5	1	6	500	40
Keio	13.9	21.4	2	6	110	35	Keio	59.6	127.2	1	8	500	54
Hitotsubashi	7.6	6.7	2	5	25	16	Hitotsubashi	35.5	76.1	1	5.5	350	24
Osaka**	3.1	1.1	2	3	5	17	Osaka*	10.1	21.1	1	4	105	23
Prestigious**	3.4	2.0	1	3	13	47	Prestigious**	9.6	19.8	2	4	130	89
Public**	4.2	3.7	2	3	20	28	Public**	6.8	8.9	1	4	52	61
Private**	5.2	4.9	1	4	25	77	Private**	10.8	38.2	1	4	480	175
Overall	9.8	23.6	1	4	240	483	Overall	26.3	80.3	1	5	540	571

Numbers in the table represent the number of respondents. The asterisks and daggers on the tableside are based on ANOM († $p < 0.1$, * $p < 0.05$, ** $p < 0.01$). "0%" is the minimum, "50%" is the median, and "100%" is the maximum means for lawyers, and the differences from the overall mean were statistically significant. However, the difference between schools with the largest mean number of lawyers and those with the smallest number of lawyers was larger in the 60th–69th cohorts than in the first through 59th cohorts. For example, the difference in the first through 59th cohorts between the University of Tokyo, with the largest mean number of lawyers, at 29.2, and Osaka, with the smallest mean number of lawyers, at 1.5, was 16.3, while that in the 60th–69th cohorts between the University of Tokyo, with the largest mean number of lawyers, at 119.2, and other public universities, with the smallest mean number of lawyers, at 6.8, was 112.4.

Inequality between schools in terms of the number of lawyers in graduates' first law firm jobs is also measured with MLD.[28] Figure 5.2 shows the MLD of the number of lawyers at first law firm jobs and its decomposition. The MLD in Fig. 5.2 is much larger than the one in Fig. 5.1. This indicates that inequality is more apparent in the number of lawyers in law firms where graduates take their first jobs than in the initial annual income at such jobs.

For the number of lawyers in law firms where graduates take their first jobs, unlike the initial annual income at such jobs, overall inequality and both within-school-group and between-school-group inequalities increased considerably in the 60th–69th cohorts compared to the first through 59th cohorts. According to Fig. 5.2, from the first through 59th cohorts to the 60th–69th cohorts, the overall inequality increased from 0.704 to 1.365, the within-school-group inequality increased from 0.412 to 0.907, and the between-school-group inequality increased from 0.292 to 0.458.

5.3.5 *Specializations at First Law Firm Jobs*

Table 5.5 shows whether each lawyer has fields of specialization at their first law firm jobs.[29] Survey respondents were asked to select up to three fields that accounted for at least one-third of their income, if any.[30] For example, in the first through 59th

[28] MLD can measure inequality in the distribution of various data other than income. For example, Borooah (2016) measured inequality in the distribution of inter-constituency vote shares and decomposed inter-constituency inequality by the states to which the constituencies belong.

[29] JFBA (2014) states that it is preferable that lawyers refrain from labeling fields of specialization, owing to difficulty in defining objective, impartial standards that would avoid misunderstanding on the part of clients. Therefore, many Japanese lawyers use other labels such as "fields of emphasis" instead. For the sake of consistency and clarity, however, this chapter will use the term "fields of specialization." For more information on surveying Japanese lawyers' fields of specialization, see Foote (2019, p. 161).

[30] Because this is a multiple-answer question, Table 5.5 analyzed the question in the following manner. Each choice of fields of specialization was converted into a binary variable of "selected or not selected," and a cross table was created with it and the university or law school. A chi-square test was then conducted. The asterisks and daggers at the top of the table are based on this chi-square test. If the chi-square test was significant at the 10% level, an adjusted standardized residual

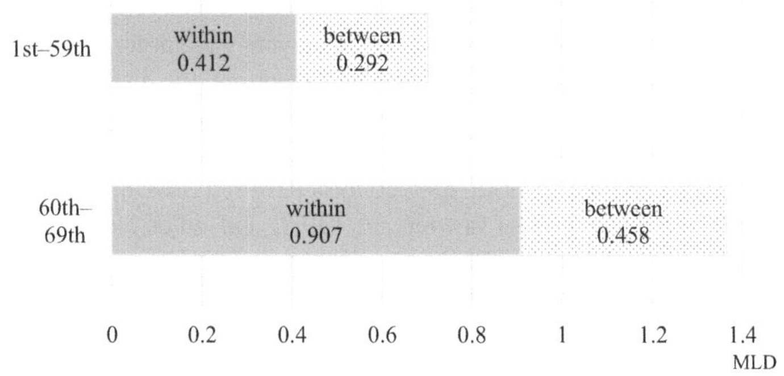

Fig. 5.2 MLD of the number of lawyers at first law firm jobs and its decomposition

cohorts in Table 5.5, the figure for "Labor" at the University of Tokyo is 4.7, meaning that 4.7% of the University of Tokyo graduate respondents in those cohorts chose labor law as their field of specialization.[31]

In Table 5.5, the "Overall" row percentage of "None" is slightly lower in the 60th–69th cohorts than in the first through 59th cohorts, but still just under half of the lawyers do not have fields of specialization. Only in a few fields, such as traffic accidents, did the "Overall" row percentage increase statistically significantly.[32] All of this reinforces the tendency for Japanese lawyers to be characterized as "generalists" (Murayama 2020, p. 755).[33]

In the first through 59th cohorts, the University of Tokyo has a significantly lower percentage of respondents with "None" in their field of specialization and a significantly higher percentage in "M&A" and "Intl" than the other universities. It has been pointed out that it is difficult for lawyers whose practice focuses on general

---

was calculated for the cross table concerned. The asterisks and daggers in the cells are based on these residuals.

[31] Numbers in the table are percentages of university and law school graduates who selected fields at the top of the table, with multiple choices of fields allowed. The asterisks and daggers at the top of the table are based on the chi-square test, and those in the cells are based on adjusted standardized residuals († $p < 0.1$, * $p < 0.05$, ** $p < 0.01$). In Table 5.5, "None" corresponds to no field of specialization, "Labor" to labor law, "Medical" to medical malpractice, "Traffic" to traffic accidents, "Family" to family law, "Real" to real property, "Loans" to consumer loans, "Personal" to personal bankruptcy, "Criminal" to criminal cases, "IP" to intellectual property rights, "Finance" to financial law, "M&A" to mergers and acquisitions, "Biz" to business bankruptcy, "Intl" to international transactions, and "Tax" to tax affairs. "Other fields of specialization," which is also an option in the survey, is omitted from the table.

[32] This is based on the results of a chi-square test, in which each choice of fields of specialization was converted into a binary variable of "selected or not selected" and cross-tabulated with the "first through 59th cohorts or 60th–69th cohorts" option. Those significant at the 5% level were "Labor" ($p = 0.011$), "Medical" ($p = 0.022$), "Traffic" ($p = 0.001$), and "Real" ($p = 0.006$).

[33] Bushimata (2018, p. 148) notes that the overall degree of specialization in law practice in Japan remains low even in recent times.

Table 5.5 Specializations at first law firm jobs

1st–59th cohorts																
University	Field															
	None*	Labor	Medical	Traffic†	Family†	Real	Loans	Personal	Criminal	IP	Finance	M&A**	Biz	Intl*	Tax	*N*
Tokyo	38.8**	4.7	3.5	5.9	7.1†	9.4	3.5	3.5	1.2	5.9	10.6	14.1**	5.9	14.1**	1.2	85
Chuo	52.3	2.3	0.0	10.5	14.0	12.8	8.1	11.6	4.7	3.5	7.0	0.0*	3.5	3.5	1.2	86
Waseda	59.5	1.4	1.4	17.6**	9.5	6.8	4.1	5.4	4.1	0.0	4.1	1.4	6.8	4.1	0.0	74
Kyoto	65.9†	4.5	2.3	9.1	6.8	4.5	4.5	2.3	0.0	0.0	2.3	0.0	0.0	0.0	2.3	44
Keio	55.3	5.3	2.6	2.6	5.3	5.3	0.0	0.0	2.6	0.0	0.0	7.9	7.9	7.9	2.6	38
Hitotsubashi	44.4	5.6	0.0	27.8**	16.7	11.1	0.0	5.6	0.0	5.6	5.6	11.1	11.1	5.6	0.0	18
Osaka	68.4	0.0	5.3	5.3	21.1	5.3	15.8	10.5	5.3	0.0	0.0	0.0	0.0	0.0	0.0	19
Prestigious	62.5	2.1	2.1	8.3	18.8	6.2	6.2	4.2	0.0	4.2	4.2	0.0	2.1	4.2	0.0	48
Public	53.3	0.0	6.7	6.7	16.7	13.3	6.7	6.5	9.7	0.0	0.0	0.0	6.7	0.0	0.0	30
Private	43.5†	4.7	2.4	8.2	22.4**	14.1	4.7	5.9	3.5	7.1	8.2	3.5	7.1	3.5	0.0	85
Overall	52.4	3.2	2.3	9.7	13.3	9.5	5.1	5.7	3.0	3.2	5.5	4.0	5.1	5.1	0.8	527
60th–69th cohorts																
Law school	Field															
	None	Labor	Medical	Traffic†	Family*	Real	Loans	Personal	Criminal	IP	Finance**	M&A**	Biz	Intl**	Tax	*N*
Tokyo	36.4	11.4	0.0	4.5*	2.3*	6.8	0.0	0.0	0.0	4.5	20.5**	20.5**	2.3	22.7**	2.3	44
Chuo	55.8	5.8	1.9	19.2	9.6	3.8	3.8	3.8	1.9	3.8	3.8	3.8	7.7	0.0†	0.0	52
Waseda	46.4	0.0	0.0	10.7	7.1	7.1	10.7	7.1	7.1	7.1	14.3*	3.6	0.0	7.1	0.0	28
Kyoto	32.6	14.0	0.0	16.3	11.6	9.3	2.3	4.7	7.0	2.3	9.3	7.0	4.7	7.0	2.3	43
Keio	37.3	6.8	0.0	8.5†	15.3	11.9	0.0	1.7	1.7	5.1	13.6**	15.3**	6.8	13.6**	0.0	59
Hitotsubashi	44.0	8.0	0.0	16.0	12.0	4.0	4.0	4.0	0.0	0.0	0.0	0.0	0.0	16.0*	0.0	25
Osaka	50.0	8.3	0.0	25.0	8.3	4.2	8.3	4.2	0.0	4.2	0.0	0.0	0.0	4.2	0.0	24
Prestigious	52.7	7.7	0.0	26.4*	18.7†	1.1	7.7	8.8	7.7	1.1	2.2	0.0*	1.1	1.1†	0.0	91
Public	57.1	3.2	1.6	17.5	1.6**	4.8	7.9	4.8	7.9	4.8	1.6	1.6	1.6	1.6	0.0	63
Private	48.5	5.2	1.0	19.1	18.0**	4.1	5.7	8.2	6.7	2.1	2.1*	1.0**	5.7	1.0†	0.5	194
Overall	47.4	6.6	0.6	17.5	12.8	5.1	5.1	5.8	5.1	3.0	5.5	4.3	3.9	5.1	0.5	623

Numbers in the table are percentages of university and law school graduates who selected fields at the top of the table, with multiple choices of fields allowed. The asterisks and daggers at the top of the table are based on the chi-square test, and those in the cells are based on adjusted standardized residuals († $p < 0.1$, * $p < 0.05$, ** $p < 0.01$)

civil affairs to enter the fields of international and corporate legal affairs because international and corporate legal affairs require a certain level of experience in acquiring deep and broad specialized knowledge and understanding of the overall business (Hori 2000, p. 34).[34] By contrast, some universities have graduates who specialize in traffic accidents and family laws. Graduates specializing in traffic accidents tended to be from Waseda and Hitotsubashi, whereas graduates specializing in family law tended to be from other private universities.

In the 60th–69th cohorts, Keio, one of the top private law schools, also sent out graduates specializing in M&A and international transactions, as did the University of Tokyo. In addition to these law schools, Waseda Law School has more graduates specializing in financial law than any other school. These fields can be summarized as those related to international and corporate legal affairs.[35] These fields are also associated with an increase in the size of law firms. In these fields, law firms tend to be large because of the large volume of work and the advantages of collaboration thereon (Hori 2000, p. 34). By contrast, prestigious public national universities have a higher percentage of graduates specializing in traffic accidents and other private universities in family law. Conversely, some law schools in the 60th–69th cohorts had fewer graduates specializing in traffic accidents and family law. For traffic accidents, the University of Tokyo and Keio University had statistically significantly fewer graduates specializing in traffic accidents, at the five and 10% levels, respectively, while for family law, the University of Tokyo had statistically significantly fewer graduates specializing in family law at the 5% level. These results may indicate growing differentiation in specialty by school.

5.4 Recent Changes in the 60th–65th Vs. 66th–69th Cohorts

We examined recent changes in the environment surrounding new lawyers by dividing the data for the 60th–69th cohorts into two halves: the 60th–65th and the 66th–69th cohorts. Owing to space limitations, only the annual income and office size were compared.

The dividing line is that the 66th cohort, beginning in 2012, is the first after the Old Bar Exam was discontinued. Cohorts from this point on comprise only LTRI trainees who passed the New Bar Exam, intended as mentioned above for graduates

[34] As for international transactions, there have long been law offices specializing in this field, called *shōgai jimusho* (Foote 2019, p. 155; Nagashima and Zaloom 2007, pp. 138–139).

[35] According to Murayama (2020, p. 766), large business law firms in Japan have three main divisions: corporate law, financial law, and litigation and business bankruptcy. Lawyers in these offices tend to work in one of these divisions and often specialize in more than one. They may move to another one of these divisions but seldom work in fields other than these three.

of the modern law schools. The switch to the modern law school program was thus completed by this time.[36]

Table 5.6 shows the summary statistics for the initial annual income at first law firm jobs for the 60th–65th and 66th–69th cohorts. The overall mean annual income was slightly lower in the 65th–69th cohorts than in the 66th–69th cohorts, and Welch's test was statistically significant ($p = 0.001$).[37]

The difference between law schools is larger in the 66th–69th cohorts than in the 60th–65th cohorts, with graduates from the top national law schools, the University of Tokyo, Kyoto University, and Hitotsubashi University, seeing their annual income rise in the 66th–69th cohorts compared to the 60th–65th cohorts, while those from the others saw their income fall across the board. By way of illustration, in the 60th–65th cohorts, the difference between Keio graduates, who had the highest average annual income, at JPY 8.37 million, and Chuo graduates, who had the lowest, at JPY 5.73 million, was JPY 2.64 million. By contrast, in the 66th–69th cohorts, this difference had increased such that graduates of the University of Tokyo had the highest average annual income, at JPY 9.42 million, which was fully twice that of the lowest, other public universities' graduates, at JPY 4.71 million. Additionally, whereas in the 60th–65th cohorts only other private universities were statistically significantly lower than the overall mean at the 10% level, in the 66th–69th cohorts other public and private universities alike were statistically significantly lower at the 1% level, and prestigious national universities were statistically significantly lower at the 10% level.

We analyzed the inequality between schools using MLD. The MLD for the 60th–65th cohorts was 0.105, with a within-school-group inequality of 0.097 and a between-school-group inequality of 0.008. The MLD for the 66th–69th cohorts was 0.094, with a within-school-group inequality of 0.068 and a between-school-group inequality of 0.026. Thus, while overall income inequality is slightly smaller in the 66th–69th cohorts than in the 60th–65th cohorts, the decrease is mainly in within-school-group inequality, with a slight increase in between-school-group inequality.

Table 5.7 shows the summary statistics for the number of lawyers at first law firm jobs for the 60th–65th and 66th–69th cohorts. Comparing the overall mean of the number of lawyers between the 60th–65th and 66th–69th cohorts, there was little change, and Welch's test was not statistically significant ($p = 0.530$).

However, the difference between law schools is larger in the 66th–69th cohorts than in the 60th–65th cohorts: the mean number of lawyers who are graduates of the

[36] Other events that occurred during this period include the simultaneous reduction of enrollment caps at many law schools in 2010, and the fact that some law schools stopped accepting applications after this time. In 2009, the Ministry of Education, Culture, Sports, Science, and Technology (MEXT) encouraged each law school to reduce their admissions by between 20 and 30% (Watson 2016, pp. 31–32). Moreover, based on two criteria, the bar exam pass rate and the ratio of total applicants to successful applicants for the entrance exam, MEXT has begun to reduce financial subsidies to poorly performing law schools (Watson 2016, p. 32). This led to eight law schools stopping admitting new students in 2013.

[37] Unlike Table 5.3 and footnote 23, Table 5.6 compares income because the period in question is short enough for monetary values not to have changed significantly.

Table 5.6 Initial annual income at first law firm jobs, 60th–65th and 66th–69th cohorts

60th–65th cohorts							66th–69th cohorts						
Law school	Mean	*SD*	0%	50%	100%	*N*	Law school	Mean	*SD*	0%	50%	100%	*N*
Tokyo†	818	307	400	850	1250	25	Tokyo**	942	295	400	850	1250	19
Chuo	573	257	150	600	1250	32	Chuo	520	214	150	600	850	20
Waseda	750	303	400	725	1250	16	Waseda	612	260	400	600	1250	12
Kyoto	669	192	400	600	1250	27	Kyto*	797	306	400	850	1250	18
Keio†	837	443	150	600	2500	35	Keio	700	255	400	600	1250	24
Hitotsubashi	592	287	150	600	1250	12	Hitotsubashi	646	249	400	600	1250	13
Osaka	672	217	600	600	1250	9	Osaka	553	123	400	600	850	16
Prestigious	644	207	400	600	1250	59	Prestigious†	511	145	150	600	850	32
Public	584	278	150	600	1250	31	Public**	471	152	150	500	600	34
Private†	597	290	150	600	1750	124	Private**	475	163	150	400	850	73
Overall	652	297	150	600	2500	370	Overall	578	246	150	600	1250	261

Numbers in the table are in JPY ten thousand. The asterisks and daggers on the table side are based on ANOM († $p < .1$, * $p < .05$, ** $p < .01$). "0%" is the minimum, "50%" is the median, and "100%" is the maximum

Table 5.7 Number of lawyers at first law firm jobs, 60th–65th and 66th–69th cohorts

60th–65th cohorts							66th–69th cohorts						
Law school	Mean	*SD*	0%	50%	100%	*N*	Law school	Mean	*SD*	0%	50%	100%	*N*
Tokyo	76.2	123.3	2	19	400	20	Tokyo†	190.9	211.0	2	72	540	12
Chuo	16.7	53.9	1	4	300	30	Chuo**	5.7	3.2	1	5	11	19
Waseda†	10.3	12.6	2	7	40	13	Waseda	20.6	34.3	1	8	120	11
Kyoto	43.8	116.0	1	6	450	26	Kyoto	115.9	196.0	2	9	500	14
Keio	65.5	132.1	1	8	500	33	Keio	50.4	121.7	2	8	470	21
Hitotsubashi	50.2	101.4	1	5	350	12	Hitotsubashi	20.8	36.8	3	6	130	12
Osaka**	6.6	4.7	1	6	13	9	Osaka	12.4	27.0	1	4	105	14
Prestigious**	10.7	23.8	2	4	130	57	Prestigious**	7.6	9.4	2	4	47	32
Public**	6.8	9.7	1	3.5	52	30	Public**	6.8	8.2	1	4	44	31
Private	12.6	47.2	1	4	480	110	Private**	7.8	12.2	2	4	83	65
Overall	24.5	73.5	1	5	500	340	Overall	29.0	89.5	1	5	540	231

Numbers in the table represent the number of respondents. The asterisks and daggers on the table side are based on ANOM († $p < 0.1$, * $p < 0.05$, ** $p < 0.01$). "0%" is the minimum, "50%" is the median, and "100%" is the maximum

top national law schools, the University of Tokyo and Kyoto University, has increased in the 66th–69th cohorts compared to the 60th–65th cohorts, while other public and private law schools have not changed much, and some schools, such as Chuo University, saw a mean decrease. As a result, the difference in the 60th–65th cohorts between the highest mean, 76.2, for the University of Tokyo, and the lowest, 6.6, for Osaka University, was 69.6, while that same difference in the 66th–69th cohorts between the highest mean, 190.9, again for the University of Tokyo, and the lowest, 5.7, for Chuo, increased to 185.2. Additionally, while some schools in the 60th–65th cohorts were statistically significantly lower than the overall mean, none were significantly higher. In the 66th–69th cohorts, by contrast, the University of Tokyo had a statistically significantly higher mean at the 10% level.

We again analyzed the inequality between schools using MLD. The MLD for the 60th–65th cohorts was 1.322, with a within-school-group inequality of 0.986 and a between-school-group inequality of 0.336. The MLD for the 66th–69th cohorts was 1.420, with a within-school-group inequality of 0.683 and a between-school-group inequality of 0.736. Thus, although within-school-group inequality decreases, between-school-group inequality increases noticeably from the 60th–65th cohorts to the 66th–69th cohorts.

5.5 Other Concerns

5.5.1 Preliminary Bar Exam

As mentioned in Sect. 5.2.1, the New Bar Exam system that commenced in 2006 made graduating from the new law schools a prerequisite for taking the bar exam. Since 2011, however, the Preliminary Bar Exam has been available for those who cannot attend law school for financial or other reasons (Matsui 2013, p. 30; Watson 2016, p. 33). It is open to all, and there are no particular prerequisites. Passing qualifies applicants to sit for the bar exam without having to graduate from law school first.

In the survey data, 28 respondents passed the Preliminary Bar Exam in the 65th–69th cohorts,[38] 22 of whom were law school graduates. Of these 22 respondents, four, or 18.2%, graduated from the University of Tokyo, three, or 13.6%, from Kyoto University, two, or 9.1%, from Keio University, three, or 13.6%, from prestigious national universities, two, or 9.1%, from other public universities, and five, or 22.7%, from private universities. Of the other six respondents who passed the Preliminary Bar Exam without graduating from law school, three, or 50.0%, were from Keio University, and one each, or 16.7%, from the University of Tokyo, a prestigious national university, and another public university. It is thus likely that most of those who passed the Preliminary Bar Exam came from the highest-ranked

[38] A few respondents indicated that they passed the Preliminary Bar Exam after obtaining their legal license. We excluded them from the data.

national and private universities, such as the University of Tokyo, Kyoto, and Keio, although verification is difficult owing to small response sizes.

Those who pass the Preliminary Bar Exam have been considered popular among the large law firms. This is because the Preliminary Bar Exam is extremely difficult, and passing it becomes strong proof of being one of the best and brightest young candidates.[39] Those who pass are usually considered young, easily taught, and cognitively competent (Watson 2016, p. 34). According to the interviews cited in the Introduction, successful young Preliminary Bar Exam applicants are accordingly at the top of the recruitment hierarchy (Watson 2016, p. 34). Survey data were therefore examined for possible corroboration as follows.

We compared the initial annual income of those who passed the Preliminary Bar Exam at their first law firm jobs with that of the other respondents. The mean annual income of those who passed the Preliminary Bar Exam was JPY 7.66 million (SD = JPY 3.55 million, $N = 25$), whereas the mean annual income of the others was JPY 5.68 million (SD = JPY 2.49 million, $N = 286$). Welch's test revealed a statistically significant difference between them ($p = 0.011$).

We also compared the number of lawyers in law firms of the first jobs of those who passed the Preliminary Bar Exam with that of other respondents. The mean number of lawyers in law firms of the first jobs of those who passed the Preliminary Bar Exam is 148.2 ($SD = 197.3$, $N = 19$), whereas the mean number of lawyers in law firms of the first jobs of other respondents is 25.9 ($SD = 83.1$, $N = 255$). Welch's test revealed a statistically significant difference between them ($p = 0.000$).

Thus, when comparing those who passed the Preliminary Bar Exam with others, there were significant differences in the initial annual income and in the number of lawyers at first law firm jobs. The survey data thus duly corroborate the idea that applicants who pass the Preliminary Bar Exam are indeed popular with large law firms.

5.5.2 Study Abroad and Its Effect on Legal Careers

Some Japanese lawyers study abroad, chiefly in the US and UK. In the first through 59th cohorts, 62, or 11.1%, of the 560 respondents, whose first jobs were in law firms, went abroad to study.[40] 47, or 77.0%, went to the US, 10, or 16.4% to the UK, and four, or 6.5% to other countries.[41] By contrast, in the 60th–69th cohorts, 21, or 2.9%, of the 723 respondents whose first jobs were in law firms went abroad, 20, or 80%, to the US, and five, or 20%, to other countries.

[39] The pass rate for the Preliminary Bar Exam in 2022 is only 3.6%. See MOJ (2022).

[40] In order to analyze study abroad after becoming lawyers, those who went abroad to study before becoming lawyers are excluded from the data.

[41] Non-responses are excluded from the data.

One reason there are so few respondents in the 60th–69th cohorts studying abroad is that lawyers typically study abroad only after they have practiced law for a certain number of years, and respondents in the 60th–69th cohorts have not been lawyers for very long at the time of the survey. The survey data confirms that it takes a certain number of years after becoming a lawyer to go to study abroad; the mean number of years until they went abroad in the first through 59th cohorts was 8.0 years, which is quite a long period of time.

According to Hori (2000), lawyers from law firms that handle international and corporate legal affairs often gain experience studying abroad during their careers.[42] Additionally, law firms that handle international and corporate legal affairs tend to become larger (Hori 2000, p. 34). These findings are corroborated by the survey data as follows.

We examined the relationship between fields of specialization and studying abroad. In the first through 59th cohorts, among those whose first jobs were in law firms, 22 out of 30, or 73.3%, of those specializing in international transactions studied abroad, whereas only 38 out of 518, or 7.3%, of those not specializing in international transactions, indicating a statistically significant difference ($\chi^2 = 126.68$, $p = 0.000$). In fields of specialization other than international transactions, while relatively more lawyers studied abroad in M&A at 68.2%, few in other fields did so, for example, zero percent of those who specialize in traffic accidents. This trend held for the 60th–69th cohorts as well.[43]

Next, we compared the initial annual income at first law firm jobs between those who studied abroad and those who did not. In the first through 59th cohorts, those who studied abroad had a mean annual income of JPY 8.952 million (SD = JPY 3.773 million, $N = 62$), while those who did not had a mean annual income of JPY 5.926 million (SD = JPY 3.368 million, $N = 490$). Welch's test revealed a statistically significant difference in mean annual income between those who studied abroad and those who did not ($p = 0.000$). The same held for the 60th–69th cohorts.[44]

Furthermore, we compared the number of lawyers at first law firm jobs between those who studied abroad and those who did not. In the first through 59th cohorts,

[42] There is usually no clear distinction between offices that handle international transactions and offices that handle corporate legal affairs. Most international transactions are corporate legal affairs using English, and many lawyers handle both of them (Hori 2000, pp. 30–31).

[43] However, because those in the 60th–69th cohorts have only been practicing law for a short time at the time of the survey, overall percentages of lawyers in the 60th–69th cohorts studying abroad are necessarily lower than for those in the first through 59th cohorts. In the 60th–69th cohorts, 10 out of 37, or 27.0%, of those specializing in international transactions studied abroad, whereas only 11 out of 676, or 1.6%, of those not specializing in international transactions, indicating a statistically significant difference ($\chi^2 = 79.17$, $p = 0.000$). Again, while relatively more lawyers studied abroad in M&A, at 16.1%, few in other fields did so; for example, zero percent of those who specialize in accidents.

[44] In the 60th–69th cohorts, those who studied abroad had a mean annual income of JPY 10.643 million (SD = JPY 4.114 million, $N = 21$), while those who did not had a mean annual income of JPY 6.184 million (SD = JPY 2.673 million, $N = 701$), indicating a significant difference in these means ($p = 0.000$).

the mean number of lawyers in law firms joined by those who studied abroad was 28.3 ($SD = 47.1$, $N = 52$), while the mean number of lawyers in law firms joined by those who did not study abroad was 6.9 ($SD = 15.4$, $N = 445$). Welch's test revealed a statistically significant difference ($p = 0.000$). The same held yet again for the 60th–69th cohorts.[45]

In short, as described above, many lawyers specializing in international and corporate legal affairs have studied abroad. Those who have studied abroad earn a higher annual income than those who have not and work in larger law firms with more lawyers on average than those who have not.

5.6 Conclusion

This chapter has examined the relationship between educational institutions and legal careers in Japan. The findings can be summarized as follows:

Gender of Graduates In the first through 59th cohorts, females accounted for only a small percentage of graduates, and there were large differences between universities. In the 60th–69th cohorts, females accounted for a larger percentage, and there were only small differences between law schools.

Types of First Jobs There was no clear difference in the trend by university and law school, with more students working in-house in the 60th–69th cohorts than in the first through 59th cohorts.

Locations of First Law Firm Jobs The percentage of graduates going to law firms in Tokyo and Osaka decreased from the first through 59th to the 60th–69th cohorts, while that going to law firms in regional cities and other areas increased. Although many graduates are employed by law firms located near their alma mater, the percentage of graduates who are employed there varies by university and law school.

Initial Annual Income at First Law Firm Jobs In the 60th–69th cohorts, there were more schools where the mean annual income was significantly higher or lower than the overall mean income compared to the first through 59th cohorts. In terms of inequality in annual income measured by MLD, between-school-group inequality slightly increased from the first through 59th cohorts to the 60th–69th cohorts, though within-school-group inequality decreased.

[45] In the 60th–69th cohorts, the mean number of lawyers in law firms joined by those who studied abroad is 143.3 ($SD = 165.1$, $N = 17$), while the mean number of lawyers in the law firms joined by those who did not is 25.0 ($SD = 78.9$, $N = 638$), indicating a significant difference in these means ($p = 0.000$).

Number of Lawyers at First Law Firm Jobs While many graduates in the 60th–69th cohorts joined law firms that were not different in size from the small law firms in the first through 59th cohorts, some graduates joined larger law firms than those in the first through 59th cohorts. In terms of inequality in the number of lawyers measured by MLD, both within-school-group and between-school-group inequalities increased from the first through 59th cohorts to the 60th–69th cohorts.

Fields of Specialization at First Law Firm Jobs In the first through 59th cohorts, the University of Tokyo had more graduates specializing in international and corporate legal affairs, whereas many graduates specialized in traffic accidents and family law at other universities. In the 60th–69th cohorts, many graduates specialized in international and corporate legal affairs at top private law schools in addition to the University of Tokyo. These schools have significantly fewer graduates specializing in traffic accidents and family law, suggesting a growing differentiation in specialties among schools.

When comparing the 60th–65th and 66th–69th cohorts, which is a comparison of more recent years, between-school-group inequality slightly increased from the 60th–65th cohorts to the 66th–69th cohorts with respect to initial annual income at first law firm jobs, whereas between-school-group inequality escalated considerably with respect to the number of lawyers in their first law firms.

When comparing those who passed the Preliminary Bar Exam and others, there were significant differences in the initial annual income and in the number of lawyers at first law firm jobs. When comparing lawyers who have studied abroad and those who have not, there were also significant differences in the initial annual income and in the number of lawyers at first law firm jobs. Additionally, lawyers specializing in international and corporate legal affairs were more likely to study abroad than others.

Finally, we discuss future research directions. Although the analysis in this chapter shows that there are differences in the subsequent careers of lawyers depending on their educational institutions, this only represents a correlation, and it is unclear from the analysis alone whether there is a causal relationship. For example, although a higher percentage of graduates from highly ranked law schools joined large law firms, it is not clear whether this means that "the people who joined large law firms chose to go to highly ranked law schools" or "they joined large offices as a result of their education at highly ranked law schools." To clarify this, it is necessary to measure and control individual abilities in some way or by using methods such as quasi-experiments.[46] Using such methods to analyze the impact of educational institutions on legal careers will be a future task.

[46] For studies on general occupations in Japan employing these methods, see Ono (2004) and Kawaguchi and Ma (2008).

References

Borooah VK (2016) Votes, Parties, and Seats: A Quantitative Analysis of Indian Parliamentary Elections, 1962–2014. Palgrave Macmillan, Switzerland.

Bushimata A (2018) Shinjin Bengoshi to Bengoshi Kai no Kōzōteki Henka wo Megutte: Gyōmu Bunseki no Chiken kara [Concerning Structural Changes for New Lawyers and the World of Lawyers: Based on Information regarding Fields of Practice]. In: Foote DH, Hamano R, Ota S (eds) Hō no Keikenteki Shakaikagaku no Kakuritsu ni Mukete [Toward Empirical Social Science of Law]. Shinzansha, Tokyo, pp. 133–152.

Foote DH (2019) 'Lawyers in Every Corner of Society': A Progress Report. In: Foote DH, Hamano R, Ota S (eds) Hō no Keikenteki Shakaikagaku no Kakuritsu ni Mukete [Toward Empirical Social Science of Law]. Shinzansha, Tokyo, pp. 153–174.

Fujimoto R, Ishida K, Bushimata A, Ageishi K (2017) Dai 67 Ki Bengoshi no Kyaria Tenkai: 2016 Nen Dai 1 Kai Yūsō Chōsa Dēta no Tahenryō Kaiseki [Career Trajectory of the 67th Cohort of Japanese Attorney: Multivariate Analysis of the First Mailing Survey]. Nagoya Daigaku Hōseironsyū 275: 45–110.

Haughton J, Khandker SR (2009) Handbook on Poverty and Inequality. World Bank, Washington, D.C.

Heinz JP, Nelson RL, Sandefur RL, Laumann EO (2005) Urban Lawyers: The New Social Structure of the Bar. University of Chicago Press, Chicago.

Hori, Y (2000) Bengoshi no Gyōmu no Tayōka to Kyaria Keisei no Bunka: Nihon ni okeru Senmonshoku no Rōdō Shijō ni kansuru Ichikōsatsu [Diversification of Lawyers' Work and Differentiation in Career Formation: A Reflection on the Professional Labor Market in Japan]. Nihon Rōdō Kenkyū Zasshi 42(8): 26–35.

Ikeda H, Yoshida E (2020) SPECIAL FEATURE: Shihō Shiken Gōkakusha ga Ooi Daigaku: 50 Nenkan no Hensen to Hōsō 3 Toppu no Sotsugyō Daigaku [SPECIAL FEATURE: Universities with the Most Bar Admissions: 50 Years of Change and the 3 Top Graduating Universities of the Legal Profession]. Bengoshi Dotto Komu 52: 23–29.

Japan Federation of Bar Associations (JFBA) (2014) Gyōmu Kōkoku nikansuru Shishin [Guidelines for Adverting of Lawyers' Services]. https://www.nichibenren.or.jp/library/ja/jfba_info/rules/pdf/kaiki/kaiki_no_45-2_160620.pdf (Retrieved February 24, 2024).

JILA (Japan In-House Lawyers Association) (2023a) Kigyōnai Bengoshisū no Suii (2001nen-2023nen) [Shifts in the Number of In-House Lawyers (2001-2023)]. https://jila.jp/wp/wp-content/themes/jila/pdf/transition.pdf (Retrieved February 24, 2024).

-------- (2023b)Kigyōnai Bengoshi wo Ooku Kakaeru Kigyō Jōi 20sha (2001nen-2023nen) [Top 20 Companies Employing the Largest Number of In-House Lawyers (2001-2023)]. https://jila.jp/wp/wp-content/themes/jila/pdf/company.pdf (Retrieved February 24, 2024).

Kawaguchi D, Ma W (2008) The Causal Effect of Graduating from a Top University on Promotion: Evidence from the University of Tokyo's 1969 Admission Freeze. Economics of Education Review 27: 184–196.

Matsui S (2013) Turbulence Ahead: The Future of Law Schools in Japan. Journal of Legal Education 62(1): 3–31.

MOJ (Ministry of Justice) (2022) Reiwa 4 Nen Shihō Shiken Yobi Shiken [2022 Preliminary Bar Exam]. https://www.moj.go.jp/content/001384104.pdf (Retrieved February 24, 2024).

---------- (2020) Hōka Daigakuin Betsu Shihō Shiken Ruikei Gōkakushasūtou (Ruikei Gōkakuritsujun) [Cumulative Number of Students who have Passed the Bar Exams by Law School, in Order of Cumulative Passing Rate]. https://www.moj.go.jp/content/001332215.pdf (Retrieved February 24, 2024).

Murayama M (2020) Japan: Towards Stratification, Diversification and Specialisation. In: Abel RL, Hammerslev O, Sommerlad H, Schultz U (eds) Lawyers in 21st-Century Societies: Vol. 1: National Reports. Hart Publishing, Oxford, pp.753–774.

Nagashima Y, Zaloom EA (2007) The Rise of the Large Japanese Business Law Firm and Its Prospects for the Future. In: Foote DH (ed) Law in Japan: A Turning Point. University of Washington Press, Seattle, pp.136–152.
Nakamura M (2014) Legal Reform, Law Firms, and Lawyer Stratification in Japan. Asian Journal of Law and Society 1(1): 99–124.
Nakazato M, Ramseyer JM, Rasmusen EB (2010) The Industrial Organization of the Japanese Bar: Levels and Determinants of Attorney Income. Journal of Empirical Legal Studies 7(3): 460–489.
Nelson PR, Wludyka PS, Copeland KAF (2005) The Analysis of Means: A Graphical Method for Comparing Means, Rates and Proportions. Society for Industrial and Applied Mathematics, Philadelphia.
Omura M, Osanai S, Smith M (2005) Japan's New Legal Education System: Towards International Legal Education? Journal of Japanese Law 10(20): 39–54.
Ono H (2004) College Quality and Earnings in the Japanese Labor Market. Industrial Relations 43(3): 595–617.
Pallmann P, Hothorn LA (2016) Analysis of Means (ANOM): A Generalized Approach Using R. Journal of Applied Statistics 43(8): 1541–1560.
Ramseyer JM, Rasmusen EB (2015) Lowering the Bar to Raise the Bar: Licensing Difficulty and Attorney Quality in Japan. Journal of Japanese Studies 41: 113–142.
Watson A (2016) Changes in Japanese Legal Education. Journal of Japanese Law 21(41): 1–54.

Daisuke Mori is an Associate Professor in the Faculty of Law, Kumamoto University, Japan. He obtained his LL.M. in Sociology of Law from the University of Tokyo, and his LL.M. in Law and Economics from George Mason University. His areas of interest include Law and Economics, Law and Statistics, and Empirical Legal Studies. His recent publication is *Policing, Labor Market, and Crime in Japan: Evidence from Prefectural Panel Data* (Asian Journal of Criminology Vol.18, 2023, coauthored with Tomokazu Nomura and Yoshiki Takeda).

Chapter 6
From Professionalism to Consumerism

Masayuki Murayama

6.1 Backlash

As we saw in Introduction and Chap. 1, when the number of bar examination passers began to exceed 2000 per annum in 2007, lawyers began to voice their opposition to the policy of increasing the population of lawyers. In 2008, the Japan Federation of Bar Associations (JFBA) proposed to slow down the implementation of the population policy. In 2012, the JFBA issued proposals to reduce the number of bar examination passers to 1500 and to consider a further reduction, investigating the maturity of the new training system and the real demand for lawyers. The increase in the number of lawyers admitted to practice raised concerns about maintaining "the quality of legal professionals", increasing incompetent lawyers due to the lack of on-the-job training, and decreasing the number of people who aspired to be legal professionals. The proposal cited 6 local bar associations and regional federations demanding the reduction of the number of bar exam passers to 1500 and 10 local bar associations demanding the reduction to 1000 (JFBA 2012).[1]

In the first year of the new bar examination, the pass rate was 48%, much lower than 80% that the Justice System Reform Council (JSRC) had envisioned, and the pass rate further decreased to 24% in 2011, as the number of graduates from law schools increased. In 2012, The Ministry of Internal Affairs and Communications

[1] Local bar associations out of urban centers were more strongly opposed to the increase of people passing the bar exam. On the 'rent' that lawyers in rural areas obtained in the old bar exam system, see Nakazato et al. (2006). Rent in this context is interest or profit obtained by monopolization, more than the market price.

M. Murayama (✉)
Organization for the Strategic Coordination of Research and Intellectual Properties, Institute of Law and Social Sciences, Meiji University, Tokyo, Japan

M. Murayama (ed.), *The Japanese Legal Profession in Transition*, Economics, Law, and Institutions in Asia Pacific,
https://doi.org/10.1007/978-981-97-2692-9_6

issued a policy review of the new lawyer population policy and bitterly criticized the quality of the professional education at new law schools, arguing that the 2000 newly qualified lawyers created an over-supply of private attorneys (Somusho 2012).[2] In 2013, the government decided to withdraw the target of 3000 as the number of lawyers who could be permitted to pass the bar exam. In 2015, Ministry of Education, Culture, Sports, Science and Technology (MEXT) cut subsidies to law schools whose pass rates were below the average. As the pass rate of the new bar exam was lower than initially expected, some law schools had already begun to have difficulties in obtaining students. This reduction in enrollments had adverse financial implications: many law schools chose to close down or stopped admission (Murayama 2020, p. 761). In 2020, there were only 35 law schools, fewer than a half of 74 law schools in 2005. The number of applicants of law schools sharply decreased from 72,800 in 2004 to the lowest number of 8058 in 2018. In 2022, 10,633 students were enrolled in law schools (JFBA 2022, p. 40).

Since the new law school system began to work from 2004, some elements of the recruitment system of legal professionals returned to the old ones. As we saw in Chap. 1, the introduction of the preliminary bar examination made it possible, from 2011, to pass the bar exam without a law degree, just like the old bar exam.[3] The old bar exam could be taken as many times as applicants wanted, but the new bar exam limited law school graduates to three times within five years after graduation. The JFBA opposed this trial limit. Now the 5 year limit is maintained but applicants can attempt the bar exam every year. Under the old bar exam, trainees at the Legal Training and Research Institute (LTRI) were provided with a monthly salary and fringe benefits. In 2011, the salary for the trainees was replaced by loan without interest for 10 years. But in 2017, a reduced amount of salary was revived, including benefits for relocation and housing.[4]

These restorations were intended to regain the popularity of the legal profession as a professional career for young people. Since the first students graduated from the law schools and more than 2000 passed the bar exam in 2007, negative information was spread on the mass media and on the Internet: low pass rates of the bar exam indicated the poor quality of education at law school. The negative media reported that as there were too many LTRI graduates, they would be unable to find jobs and they could not get on-the-job training so that they would become incompetent lawyers. It was asserted that lawyers were more likely to engage in

[2] The JFBA issued a comment on the Ministry's report and mostly agreed with it (JFBA 2012b).

[3] Unless applicants have acquired considerable legal knowledge, they would not be able to pass the preliminary bar examination. But applicants do not have to have a LL.B. to take the preliminary bar exam. The old bar exam could be also taken by those without a LL.B. Therefore, in theory, applicants are not expected to have legal knowledge. In reality, prep schools are thriving for the preliminary bar examination, very much like for the old bar exam.

[4] There were three reasons presented for reinstating the payment of the monthly salary: (1) LTRI trainees were required to concentrate on the training and were prohibited from doing any other work; (2) Trainees had a financial burden from the loan, three million Yen, which was considered onerous for lawyers; (3) The number of undergraduate law students and, in particular, applicants to law schools, had both decreased.

wrongdoings because they faced too much competition,[5] and that legal practice was no longer a job in which a high income could be earned.

It is not clear whether and to what extent these negative campaigns (Nikkei 2011; Asahi 2015) affected the image of the legal profession as a career for young people. But the number of applicants to the law schools continued to decrease in the 2010s. What was more worrisome was the decrease of undergraduate law students (Murayama 2020, p. 762, footnote 10). For example, it used to be more difficult to be admitted to the Faculty of Law at the University of Tokyo than the Faculty of Economics and that of Letters, but the score of the admission test for Law became lower than that for Letters in 2017 (Nikkei Riskilling 2021). This change was taken to indicate the unpopularity of the legal profession and the national public administration (Asahi 2016).[6] It was reported that elite high school graduates did not choose law as their major at universities, as stability and high-income of legal practice were not guaranteed any more (Asahi 2016). The editorial of a major national newspaper expressed its concern with young people's avoidance of the legal profession, in criticizing the performance of law schools (Yomiuri 2019).

Although the number of bar exam passers decreased from 2049 in 2013 to 1525 in 2018, 13 bar associations asked the government for a further reduction of bar exam passers in 2019, arguing that the harmful effects of the over-supply of lawyers were not yet eliminated and that the bar exam was conducted in considering the quantity of passers more important than the quality of passers (Saitama Bengoshikai 2019). The number of bar exam passers continued to fall to 1403 in 2022 (JFBA 2022, b, p. 41).

6.2 Competition and Stratification

According to our findings shown in this book, what prompted the backlash was the increasing competition and stratification among law firms. The increase of bar exam passers benefitted large law firms, typically the Big Five, to grow further, thus making the stratification of law firms even more conspicuous. The growth of large business law firms reflected increasing competition among law firms practicing mainly for business clients. The stratification resulted from competition which started among business law firms.

Ota (Chap. 2) found that, when the annual number of newly registered lawyers exceeded 500 in 1996, movement for career change among lawyers was activated. This was the time when business law firms began to grow by dealing with increasing number of international transactions and M&A cases. Although the number of bar

[5] In fact, the percentage of disciplined lawyers decreased (Ishida 2017, pp. 243–57).

[6] The number of Tokyo University graduates who passed the examination for national public officials for major career track has declined significantly in recent years, from 459 persons in 2015 to 193 persons in 2023, though Tokyo University had the largest number of passers, followed by Kyoto University (Jinjiin 2015, 2023).

exam passers increased gradually before the establishment of law schools, many new lawyers were employed by law firms mainly in Tokyo. Mori (Chap. 5) found that, before the establishment of law schools, the average annual income was not significantly different among graduates of national and private universities, except those of one national university which was significantly higher and those of one private university which was significantly lower. This indicates that, though the stratification began among business law firms, trying to employ best graduates of the national university, the gradual increase of bar exam passers did not have significant disrupting impact on legal practice in general before the JSR.

Law Schools were established in 2004 and the number of bar exam passers exceeded 2000 in 2006. Mori (Chap. 5) found that, after the establishment of law schools, competition became stronger as graduates of more schools had significantly higher or lower annual income than before the establishment of law schools. Five years after the establishment of law schools was a transitional period in which both the old and new bar exam were conducted. If we divide the period after the establishment of law schools in the former 5 years and the latter 5 years, the average annual income was lower in the latter half than in the former half. Income differences among universities became larger in the latter half than in the former.

As the number of bar exam passers increased, corporations began to actively employ lawyers for in-house positions.[7] Some lawyers began to venture into business. The social fields where lawyers work clearly expanded. However, the above findings indicate that competition not only became stronger but also widespread among law firms. There were temporarily too many LTRI graduates for law firms in Tokyo. The surplus LTRI graduates moved to other areas, much to the objection of members of the local bar associations. These 'newcomers' disrupted the established practice of experienced lawyers in those areas.[8] The backlash against the increase of

---

[7] The percentage of women lawyers is high among in-house lawyers (Ishida, Chap. 4), contributing to gender diversification in the legal profession, but the percentage of LTRI women graduates has stagnated between 20% and 30% for 20 years since 2000 (JFBA 2022a, p. 44). This is partly a reflection of Japanese society where the fixed gender roles have been accepted for decades, though they finally began to change just recently. The fact that women lawyers' income did not increase or even decrease by moving to another position, reported by Sugino in Chap. 3, shows that law firms do not have a system for women lawyers to pursue their lifetime careers, as do men lawyers.

[8] A lawyer in Tokyo explained well about changes of legal practice in a local prefecture in 2012. The following interview was made, concerning the relationship between lawyers in Tokyo and those in local prefectures after the East Japan Earthquakes, but the situation described by him could be also applied to prefectures other than those in Northeast Japan where bar associations demanded to decrease the annual number of bar exam passers. 2012 was the year when the JFBA president, who proposed to reduce the number of bar exam passers, was elected after two elections.

> Lawyers in Northeast Japan, such as Fukushima, do not want Tokyo lawyers to come. After the disaster, a law firm that acted in a large number of consumer loan cases in Tokyo chartered a bus to visit shelters and distributed their name cards. Viewing this kind of incident, the local bar association was worried that Tokyo lawyers would take cases away. Lawyers in Northeast Japan, including Iwate and Aomori, used to have a certain number of clients, even though the number was small, and they secured income and maintained their social status as local elites. There was a balance of that kind in their life. But since about ten years

bar exam passers was particularly strong in bar associations out of Tokyo,[9] as lawyers of these bar associations had kept stable legal practice for long time.

6.3 Lawyers' Public Image

Despite the backlash against the increase of the lawyer population, there is some evidence that the quality of lawyers is in fact becoming better. Ota asked experienced lawyers to evaluate the performance of lawyers who represented 191 civil litigation cases in 2010. He found that the evaluated quality of representation in civil litigation was higher for less experienced lawyers than for experienced lawyers. The group of lawyers which included new law school graduates showed more highly evaluated quality than the groups of more experienced lawyers (Ota 2014, pp. 132–156). Foote also compared litigants' evaluations of their lawyers in 2007 and 2018 and found that the overall evaluation was better in 2018 than 2007 and that the lawyers in their 60s and 70s were evaluated lower than those in their 20s and 30s and those in their 40s and 50s (Foote 2023). Ramseyer and Rasmusen argued that, as the opportunity cost of becoming a lawyer decreased by increasing the number of bar exam passers, the quality of lawyers who passed the new bar exam must have been higher (Ramseyer and Rasmusen 2015).

Survey results indicate that the public image of lawyers has not deteriorated but may have become better.

An internet survey on images of lawyers was conducted in January 2009. According to the survey results, people considered that lawyers were not allies nor enemies of common people, the weak, or justice, and that it could not be said that lawyers were respectable, or could be admired or were kind. Lawyers were considered to be foreign to and unrelated with everyday life of common people. And the

---

> ago, the number of lawyers began to increase and it was getting difficult for them to maintain that kind of life. But such influence would be severe for lawyers of advanced age and young age. Middle aged lawyers have their own basis for practice and are not affected by such influence so much. They did not actively seek clients and they could simply wait for relatively big cases to come in. That's their way of practice. Once you get used to such style of practice, you cannot change it easily. For cases related with the disaster, we have to renounce the initial fee and get only several percentage of damages as our fee, when we obtain damages from the other side. Then, the fee would be small. As they are not used to making much effort for such small cases, they do not want to do that. At the same time, local lawyers are concerned that Tokyo lawyers will take big cases, while leaving such small cases to them.

Some words are changed in translation from the original paper. The Interview was conducted on January 25, 2012 (Murayama 2014).

[9] Lawyers of bar associations neighboring Tokyo and other urban centers were afraid of the "invasion" of Tokyo and other urban lawyers. Lawyers in rural centers did not welcome "alien" lawyers. Lawyers can get clients anywhere in Japan and many lawyers do, but jurisdictions of local bar associations are considered as virtual boarders of legal practice among local lawyers.

image of lawyer's work was litigation ('Hoso no Shitsu' Kenkyukai 2011, pp. 11, 18). The Justice System Reform Council (JSRC) wanted to make lawyers equivalent to home doctors for everyday life of people, but even as recent as 2009, people seemed to keep the traditional image of lawyers.

We conducted a questionnaire survey in February to March 2021, concerning the public image of lawyers and the trust in lawyers in comparison with trust in persons in general.[10]

As our questions were not the same as the 2009 survey, precise comparisons are impossible, but our survey results show that the public has basic trust in lawyers but also are realistic to see that the work of a lawyer is no more than business. We asked respondents to evaluate five statements in a six stage Likert scale, from "not agree at all" to "agree very much". The median is 3.5. "It is the mission for lawyers to serve clients" has the highest average score, 4.64, while "The work of a lawyer is no more than business" and "it is better to ask a lawyer to deal with a legal problem even if it costs money" both have high average scores, 4.30. Yet "Retaining a lawyer does not bring a result worth the cost" has an average score of 3.95 and "Lawyers do not always work hard for clients" has that of 3.75. People seem to support the positive image of lawyers more than the negative ones, but also realistically saw lawyers as making money by using special knowledge to deal with legal issues.

We also asked two versions of 17 questions, one on lawyers and the other on persons in general. The two versions were randomly assigned to respondents. Seventeen scales were integrated to three scores on integrity, deceptiveness, and selfishness. There was no significant difference on integrity, but scores on lawyers were significantly higher on deceptiveness and selfishness. Apparently, people considered that lawyers were less deceptive and selfish than people in general.

We consider that images of lawyers have been changing since TV advertisements of law firms appeared in the 2000s. Some TV commercials present lawyers as allies of the weak. There have been TV dramas where lawyers appear tireless champions for justice and the weak. Lawyers also increasingly appear on variety TV programs.[11] Their appearance on TV made lawyers and legal practice more accessible to the general public who now more or less understand how lawyers work.

Our survey results also show that people understand the peculiar relationship between a client and a lawyer as principal and agent relationship and the need to find a reliable lawyer to retain. In the 2020 survey, we presented 13 items of information on lawyers and asked respondents to evaluate the importance of each item in

---

[10] We conducted a preliminary survey on the Internet in January 2021 and a main survey on 2500 randomly chosen Japanese men and women from 20 to 69 years old. We sent out questionnaires by mail but respondents could answer either by mail or on the website. Nine hundred and seventy two persons sent back effective responses and the response rate was 38.9% (Murayama et al. 2024).

[11] A TV program, Gyoretu no Dekiru Houritu Sodanjo, in English, Legal Consultation Center Where People Make a Line, started in 2002 and it became a very popular program with high viewer ratings. Four private attorneys appeared in the program and one of them, a most popular lawyer, later became the governor of Osaka prefecture. In the program, he sometimes criticized bar associations and ways of other lawyer's legal practice. He was both popular and unpopular. Good or bad, the program made lawyers and their work much accessible to the general public.

a six stage Likert scale, that would influence them in deciding which lawyer to consult. The highest item was "clear criteria of lawyer's fee" (5.0), and the second was "specializing in the field of the respondent's problem" (4.9) while the third was "never been disciplined by the bar association" (4.8). These results show that people would like to find a competent and honest lawyer, yet they also want to understand for what they pay. When we added another item, introduction from a family or a friend to a lawyer, it was considered less important than the other three items. This result indicates that people search an appropriate lawyer with their own initiative.

6.4 Legal Service in the Digital Age

Although lawyers still rely on personal networks to obtain new clients, people out of these networks increasingly want to get legal advice from lawyers and retain them. Therefore, people want to get information about lawyers. In our 2020 survey, we asked respondents to evaluate advertisements on commuting trains/buses, on TV/radio, and on the Internet in six stage Likert scales. Respondents were most positive about advertisements on the Internet (77.5%), then on trains/buses (66.4%), and lastly on TV/radio (63.7%). It is clear that a majority of people do not have a negative view of advertisements by lawyers.

We also asked the same question on introducing lawyers and law firms on Internet home pages. The answer was most positive with 51.1% rather agreed, 28.2% agreed and 9.4% agreed very much, in total 88.7% showing positive attitudes to Internet home pages. People seem to consider that advertising on the Internet is good, but, that just giving information on lawyers and law firms is even better. These findings clearly show that people want to have information on lawyers and, when necessary, they want to choose an appropriate lawyer by themselves.

As we saw in the Introduction, Bengoshi Dot Com was a small company in 2005. But it expanded rapidly to have a half of the registered lawyers of Japan as their members. When it started, Bengoshi Dot Com looked a risky venture, but it is now a part of the Japanese legal practice landscape.[12] Another portal site for introducing lawyers, Coconala Horitsu Sodan (Legal Consultation Here), is expanding its service. This is a comprehensive consultation portal site for various different kinds of professional services with three million members. The legal division of this portal site gives member lawyers their service to help create their home pages for free of charge. They say they have more than 4000 lawyers as members and receive more than 20,000 queries each month.

As law firms specialized in criminal defense advertise their practice on the Internet, lawyers who accumulated experience of criminal defense set up an Internet

[12] The president of Bengoshi Dot Com ran as a candidate of the Liberal Democratic Party for the Upper House of the Diet and became a member of the House of Councilors from 2016. In 2022, he did not run for his re-election but came back to the company with political ties with the governing party and national bureaucracy.

site to warn people about how to choose a good criminal defense lawyer. In this way, the Internet has become a major forum for people to get information about lawyers and law firms not only in criminal defense but also in other many legal fields related to everyday life of the people.[13]

Lawyers are not professionals aloof from people any more, but are trading in providing legal services to people who need them. We can see on the Internet how people try to behave as wise consumers. People ask many questions of various kinds on Q&A websites and lawyers give not only basic information but also more detailed information on their home pages. We can see from information exchanged on the websites of legal firms, that the general public are trying to find out as much as they can about legal services, including their costs, so as to make an informed decision concerning retaining a lawyer.

6.5 Against the Backlash

The changes that the increase of lawyers has brought are indeed real ones. The Big Five firms are growing and corporations will continue to employ lawyers, even if the pace may be slowing down. Not only the image of lawyers but also the ways of their practice have changed and these changes are not reversible.

MEXT began to restructure the training process of legal professionals in cooperation with the Ministry of Justice (MOJ) and the Supreme Court (SC). In addition to the restoration of the elements of the old recruitment system, MEXT approved an express course for future legal professionals. Universities set up an early graduation program of three-year undergraduate education in law, which is connected to a two-year program at law schools. In this way, students could choose a three-year program in law, instead of a 4-year ordinary program, and, including 2 years at a law school, could take the bar exam after 5 years from entering a university for undergraduate education. This 5 year program, called the legal professional course, started in 2020.

Moreover, MEXT announced in 2020 that it would allow law school students to take the bar exam before graduation from 2023. This means that graduates of the express program can enter the LTRI training program immediately after graduation from law schools. This new opportunity aimed to increase the number of applicants to law schools and seemed to have some effect in doing so.[14] While 8341 persons

[13] A lawyer practicing in a prefecture with a High Court told us that young people did not watch TV anymore and that they use social networking services (SNS) to look for information. Another lawyer in Tokyo told us that he obtained new clients through SNS. He has acquired an increasing number of clients with legal problems through the Internet. Roundtable discussion organized by our research project, 6 January 2023.

[14] MEXT emphasized that students in the legal professional course could become legal professionals only in 6 years if they could pass the bar exam before graduation from law schools (MEXT 2023a).

applied for the entrance examinations for 32 law schools in 2021, the number increased to 12,174 in 2023 (MEXT 2023b). The results of the latest bar exam were just announced by MOJ. The number of bar exam passers increased from 1403 in 2022 to 1781 in 2023. The number of currently enrolled law school students who passed the bar exam in 2023 was 637, 36% of all the passers (MOJ 2023). The MEXT new express program seems to be successful in increasing the number of bar exam passers.

As the number of law schools decreased and the student admission capacity was reduced, the pass rate of the bar exam began to improve. The pass rate of the bar exam was less than 30% until 2018, but it began to increase from 33.6% in 2019 to 45.5% in 2022 (JFBA 2022, p. 42) and 45.3% in 2023 (MOJ 2023).

In 2021, the Japan In-House Lawyers Association (JILA) issued the president's announcement, proposing to increase the number of passers of the bar exam and raise the pass rate. It argued that the real reason for the unpopularity of law schools was that the low pass rate would not match the time and financial cost to take the bar exam.[15] It requested the reinstatement of the number of bar exam passers to 2000 and a 70% pass rate by "working on" the law school admission capacity, the number of preliminary bar exam passers, etc. JILA argued that the need for legal services was increasing, showing that the number of in-house lawyers had been increasing, on average, by more than 200 lawyers every year in the 2010s, and concluded that the number of lawyers was not enough to satisfy the current demand (JILA 2021).

The latest Corporate Law Department survey report verified the claim that more lawyers are needed. According to the report, 36% of corporations with law departments wanted to employ lawyers by any possible means and 23% of them wanted to employ lawyers if possible, while 18% of them wanted to employ LTRI graduates by any possible means and 14% if possible. Only 4% of them do not intend to employ lawyers anymore and 14% of them do not intend to employ LTRI graduates (Yoneda 2022, p. 224). There is a strong demand to employ more lawyers among corporations with law departments.

From what occurred following the period when the number of bar exam passers became more than 2000, it would be safe to assume that the internal politics of the JFBA could influence the future number of bar exam passers. Although the JSRC report emphasized that the number of legal professionals who actually work in various fields of society is to be decided by the market principle (JSRC 2001, Chap. III, Part 1, 1), the number of bar exam passers has been talked about as if the concerned could fix the number, as the three branches of the legal profession (the SC for judges, the MOJ for public prosecutors, and the JFBA for lawyers), had done before the Justice System Reform.

In fact, the attitudes of the JFBA president could have affected the reduction of the number of bar exam passers.[16] The JFBA president is elected by JFBA members

[15] Ramseyer and Rasmusen argued that the high opportunity cost of becoming a lawyer would result in aspirants abandoning seeking the career (Ramseyer and Rasmusen 2015, pp. 1–36).

[16] The JFBA's policy to expand the lawyer population in the 1990's was also initiated by a JFBA president who led the JFBA to issue the declaration for the justice system reform (JFBA 1990). He

for a 2 year term. According to the JFBA Rules, in order to be elected as president, a candidate must obtain (1) the largest number of votes among candidates and (2) the majority votes from more than one third of local bar associations, which means 18 local bar associations, at least (JFBA 1949, Art. 61).

Though the JFBA declared the necessity of increasing lawyers in 1990 (JFBA 1990) and supported the JSRC policy in 2000 (JFBA 2000), there were members of local bar associations who were strongly opposed to the increase of lawyers. When the annual number of bar exam passers exceeded 2000, LTRI graduates who could not find jobs in Tokyo left Tokyo and disrupted the established practice of experienced lawyers in local cities, as we saw above. Local lawyers skeptical of the JFBA policy began to voice their opposition more strongly. In the election to choose the JFBA president in 2010, two lawyers of the Tokyo Bar Association ran for president. One lawyer was from the mainstream of the JFBA, while the other was opposed to the JSRC policy of increasing lawyers. The two running candidates could not satisfy the requirement for victory at the first and second voting. The first candidate who won the majority votes did not get the majority from one third of the bar associations. This was the first time that the JFBA could not choose its president by the first election. There was a re-election in which the second candidate won the election. Year after next, in 2012, the president issued the JFBA proposal to decrease the number of bar exam passers to 1500. The number of bar exam passers was the largest in 2012, and since then, it has been decreasing until 2022.

This JFBA president lost the next presidential election in 2012 to a mainstream candidate, but this time again, the latter won in the re-election after the second voting. Since then, three presidents of the mainstream group were elected at the first voting. But in 2020, a mainstream Tokyo lawyer lost the presidential election to a lawyer whose bar association's president issued a joint announcement to further reduce the number of bar exam passers from 1500 (Saitama Bengoshikai et al. 2019). In 2022, three candidates ran for the president and a candidate from the Tokyo Bar Association won the election. But the third candidate pushed a policy to reduce the number of bar exam passers to 1000. He lost, but the events of the JFBA presidential elections indicate that the internal political balance of the JFBA is not stable enough to support the JSRC population policy of legal professionals.

The JFBA issued its response to the population policy of legal professionals in 2022 at the end of the last presidential term. It pointed out (1) the difficulty which LTRI graduates faced in finding employment in 2012 had been greatly improved and there was not a clear relationship between the increase of lawyers and the decrease of lawyers' income, (2) the civil justice reform was still in progress and the insurance for lawyer's fee and JLSC service had been expanding to various sectors of people's life.[17] In addition, the JFBA was responsible for further expanding fields of lawyers' activities, sending lawyers to jurisdictions with few lawyers, and

later became a member of JSRC.

[17] A lawyer's fee is now included in most insurance policies for traffic accidents and more general accidents.

increasing diversities of lawyers, including increasing the number of women lawyers. Moreover, (3) the JFBA did not find a decrease in the quality of LTRI graduates and noted that it is important to administer the legal professional training system with stability, in order to increase the number of aspirants to become legal professionals. The JFBA concluded that there was no real basis to propose a further reduction of bar exam passers from 1500 (JFBA 2022b).

Politics inside the JFBA is complicated with different political ideologies, professional interests, and visions for the future. In general, business and conservatives support de-regulation, while labor and the left are against de-regulation. But this is not always the case when considering de-regulation of lawyers: the Democratic Party of Japan (DPJ) was in power from 2009 to 2012, when the lawyer population policy began to be reconsidered.[18] But also members of the conservative Liberal Democratic Party (LDP), voiced their opposition to the increase of lawyers.[19] The JFBA has a political organization, legally independent of JFBA, Nihon Bengosi Seiji Renmei (Japan Political Federation of Private Attorneys), whose purpose is to conduct political activities and research on political institutions, in order to achieve the purposes of the JFBA and local bar associations.[20] This political federation holds meetings with all political parties from the Liberal Democratic Party to the Japan Communist Party and endorses politicians of different parties for national elections.[21] They also make political donations, though the method and amounts are not known. These kinds of routine political activities might have some significant effect upon attitudes of Diet members and public officials of the MEXT and MOJ.

But the future of the lawyer population policy is likely to be influenced by attitudes of lawyers who are graduates of new law schools and now make up half of the lawyer population. As experienced lawyers who were most impacted by new LTRI graduates are going to retire, the new generations will decide which way the JFBA goes, narrowing or widening entry to the profession.

The bar exam results in 2023 might be a sign for the increase of passers in future, even if a pace of increase is slow. Yet, even if the number of bar exam passers continues to be around 1500, the job market of lawyers will continue to be active.[22] The Big Five firms will continue to recruit the best 150 or so LTRI graduates every

[18]According to a lawyer who knew lawyer members of the DPJ's cabinet said that the Chief Cabinet Secretary was "skeptical" of the population policy. Interview with a senior lawyer of Japan Political Federation of Private Attorneys in July 2017.

[19]There were inside criticisms of those who opposed the population policy because the Justice System Reform had been proposed and legislated by the LDP.

[20]The president has been appointed from among former presidents of the JFBA.

[21]When the JFBA officially demanded the reduction of bar exam graduates to 1500 in 2012, there were 36 lawyers in the Diet, 21 lawyers (4.5%) of the Representatives in the lower house and 12 lawyers (4.8%) of the Councilors in the upper house (Kokusei Joho Center 2012, pp. 23–24). In 2022, the number of lawyers was similar, 35 in total, 20 in the lower house and 15 in the upper house (JFBA 2022a, p. 140).

[22]Chapter 2 shows that when the number of bar exam graduates increased from 500 to 750, the job market of lawyers began to move.

year.[23] Mass process law firms will also grow and keep their business. But it is possible that there will not be enough number of legal professionals who would go to positions other than private practice at law firms. Corporations may find it difficult to employ enough number of lawyers. The SC and MOJ may also have difficulties in recruiting future judges and prosecutors.[24] In retrospect, the deregulation policy leading to the Justice System Reform had been pushed by Keizaidoyukai (Japan Association of Corporate Executives), one of the two national business managers associations. Two attempts of the justice system reform, one failed in the 1960s, and one half-successful from the 2000s, were initially triggered by the insufficient number of LTRI graduates who would become judges and public prosecutors (Foote 2019, pp. 154–155; Murayama 2020, pp. 755, 756). Therefore, how the business sector, SC and MOJ would react could be a key to changes in future. The JSRC vision of the shape of the country has been far from realized, but whether the current level of bar exam passers will exert pressure for lawyers to expand their legal practice to new fields has yet to be seen.

References

Asahi (Asahi Shinbun) (Asahi News) (2015) Bengoshi Chokai Saita 101ken Azukarikin Ryuyo Medatsu Sakunen (101 Lawyers disciplined last year, record high, notable misappropriation of clients' funds), February 21, morning edn, 37.

------ (2016) Globe 178, Nyushi to Erito, Todai Hogakubu no Choraku (Globe 178, Entrance Examination and Elites, Downfall of Tokyo University Faculty of Law), 6 March, morning edn, 6.

Foote D (2019) 'Lawyers in Every Corner of Society': A Progress Report. In: Foote D, Hamano R, Ota S, eds., Toward Empirical Social Science of Law, Shinzansha, Tokyo, pp. 153–174.

Foote D (2023) Bengoshi ni taisuru Sosho Tojisha no Hyoka—10 Nen de Hyoka wa do Kawattaka—(Litigants' Evaluations of Their Lawyers: How Did Their Evaluations Change in 10 Years). In: Sato I, Abe M, Ota S, eds., Gendai Nihon no Hunso Katei to Shiho Seisaku: Minji Hunso Zenkoku Chosa 2016-2020 (Disputing Process and Judicial Policy of Modern Japan: National Survey of Civil Disputes in 2016-2020), Tokyo Daigaku Shuppankai (The University of Tokyo Press), Tokyo.

'Hoso no Shitsu' Kenkyukai (Research Group on the Quality of Legal Professionals), eds. (2011) Nihonjin no Bengoshi Imeji (The Image of Lawyers among the Japanese), Shoji Homu, Tokyo

Ishida K (2017) Deterioration or refinement? Impact of an increasing number of lawyers on the lawyer discipline system in Japan, Int J Legal Profession, 24 (3): 243–57.

---

[23] A Big Five firm partner was confident in his firm's ability to recruit the best LTRI graduates. When the number of bar exam graduates was decreasing, a partner of a Big Five firm said, "It doesn't matter. We will get the best 30 or so anyway". Interview with a partner at a Big Five firm, August 9, 2017.

[24] Foote expected that, while the Big Five firms would keep attracting recruits and national Ministries would find little difficulty in attracting lawyers, the SC would not be able to recruit enough LTRI graduates, and corporations also may have difficulty in recruiting enough in-house lawyers. He also questioned whether needs for lawyers in public bodies other than national Ministries, international organizations, NPOs and labor unions as well as in rural areas with few lawyers, would be satisfied (Foote 2019, pp. 169–170).

JFBA (1949) Nihon Bengoshi Rengokai Kaisoku (JFBA Rules). https://www.nichibenren.or.jp/library/pdf/jfba_info/rules/kaisoku/kaisoku_no_1r.pdf. Retrieved September 25, 2023.
------ (1990) Dai 41 Kai Nichibenren Teiki Sokai Hokoku (Report of the 41th JFBA General Meeting), Jiyu to Seigi, 41 (8): 114–117.
------ (2000) Danwa—Shihoseido Kaikaku Shingikai "Chukan Hokoku" no Happyo ni Atatte—(Statement on the Occasion of JSRC Interim Report Announcement), https://www.nichibenren.or.jp/document/statement/year/2000/2000_13.html. Retrieved 25 September 25, 2023.
------ (2012a) Hohsoh Jinkoh Seisaku ni kansuru Teigen (Proposal Concerning Policy on Numbers of Legal Professionals), March 15. https://www.nichibenren.or.jp/library/ja/opinion/report/data/2012/opinion_120315.pdf. Retrieved August 29, 2023.
------ (2012b) Somusho 'Hoso Jinko no Kakudai oyobi Hoso Yosei Seido no Kaikaku ni kansuru Seisaku Hyoukasho' ni kansuru Nichibenren Komento (JFBA Comments on Policy Evaluation Report on the Expansion of Population of Legal Professionals and the Institutional Reform of Training for Legal Professionals), April 20. https://www.nichibenren.or.jp/document/statement/year/2012/120420_3.html. Retrieved August 29, 2023.
------ (2022a) Bengoshi Hakusho (White Paper on Attorneys), Nihon Bengoshi Rengokai, Tokyo.
------ (2022b) Current Direction on Policy Regarding the Number of Legal Professionals: Results of the Review for Further Reduction in the Number of Successful Bar Examinees, 17 March. https://www.nichibenren.or.jp/en/document/opinionpapers/220317.html. Retrieved September 16, 2023.
JILA (2021) "Shiho Shiken Gokakusha no Zoka to Gokakuritsu no Josho wo Motomeru Rijicho Seimei (President's Call for More Successful Bar Exam Applicants and Higher Pass Rates). https://jila.jp/wp/wp-content/uploads/2021/08/seimei20210826.pdf. Retrieved August 31, 2023.
Jinjiin (National Personnel Authority), (2015) Kokka Komuin Saiyo Sogoshoku Shiken 2015, Gokakusha Saita ha "Todai" 459 Nin (Examination for National Public Officials for Major Career Track 2015, the Largest Group of Passers is "Tokyo University" 459 Persons). https://resemom.jp/article/2015/07/31/26076.html. Retrieved October 11, 2023.
------ (2023) 2023 Nendo Kokka Komuin Saiyo Sogoshoku Shiken (Haru) no Gokaku Happyo (Announcement of Examination Results for National Public Officials for Major Career Track in Spring 2023). https://www.jinji.go.jp/kisya/2306/C12-2023saigo_shiryo.pdf. Retrieved August 30, 2023.
JSRC Justice System Reform Council (JSRC) (Shiho Seido Kaikaku Shingikai) (2001) Recommendations of the Justice System Reform Council: For a Justice System to Support Japan in the 21st Century. https://japan.kantei.go.jp/policy/sihou/singikai/990612_e.html. Retrieved August 12, 2023.
Kokusei Joho Center (National Politics Information Center) (2012) Kokkai Giin Yoran (Directory of Diet Members), Kokusei Joho Center, Tokyo.
MEXT (Ministry of Education, Culture, Sports, Science and Technology) (Monbukagakusho) (2023a) Hoso Kosu no Shokai (Introduction to the Legal Professional Course). https://www.mext.go.jp/content/20230327-mxt_senmon02-100001054_2.pdf. Retrieved June 5, 2024.
------ (2023b) Hoka Daigakuin Shigansha Su (The Number of Applicants for Law Schools). https://www.mext.go.jp/content/20231106-mxt_senmon02-000030546_7-4.pdf. Retrieved June 5, 2024.
MOJ (Ministry of Justice) (Homusho) (2023) Reiwa 5 Nen Shiho Shiken no Saiten Kekka (Scoring Results of the Bar Examination in 2023). https://www.moj.go.jp/content/001405789.pdf. Retrieved November 16, 2023.
Murayama M (2014) There Are Few Cases around Here: Lawyers' Response to Nuclear Compensation Issues and Structural Problems of the Japanese Legal System, Paper submitted at International Sociological Association World Congress in Yokohama in July 2014.
------ (2020) Japan: Toward Stratification, Diversification and Specialization. In: Abel R, Hammerslev O, Sommerlad H, Schultz U, Lawyers in 21st-Century Societies, Volume 1: National Reports, Hart Publishing, Oxford, New York, pp. 753–774.

Murayama M, Ota S, Foote D, Sugino I, Ii T, Ishida K, Mori D, Kabashima H (2024) Kyodo Kenkyu: Bengoshi eno Shinrai to Sentaku (Research Collaboration: Trust in Lawyers and Selection of Lawyers), Ho to Shakai Kenkyu (Study of Law and Society), 9: 113-155.
Nakazato M, Ramseyer J, Rasmusen E (2006) The Industrial Organization of the Japanese Bar: Levels and Determinants of Attorney Incomes, Discussion Paper No.559, Harvard Law School.
Nikkei (Nihon Keizai Shinbun) (Japan Economic Newspaper) (2011) Bengoshi Chokai Shobun Sakunen Saita no 80 Ken (80 Lawyers Disciplined Last Year, Record High), 3 March, evening edn, 14.
Nikkei Reskilling (2021) Todai ni Ihen, Bun3 ga Bun1 wo Gyakuten: Kanban Gakubu ni Magarikado (Unusual for the University of Tokyo, Faculty of Letters Took Over Faculty of Law: Turning Point for the Leading Faculty). https://reskill.nikkei.com/article/DGXZQOLM1675B0W1A111C2000000/. Retrieved August 30, 2023.
Ota S (2014) Bengoshi no Minji Sosho ni okeru Performance Hyoka: Hoso no Shitsu no Jisshoteki Kenkyu (Performance Evaluation of Lawyers in Civil Litigation: Empirical Study of the Quality of Legal Professionals), Tokyo Daigaku Hoka Daigakuin Law Review (University of Tokyo Law School Law Review), 9: 132–156.
Ramseyer J, Rasmusen E (2015) Lowering the Bar to Raise the Bar: Licensing Difficulty and Attorney Quality in Japan, J Japanese Studies, 41 (1): 1–36.
Saitama Bengoshikai, Chibaken Bengoshikai, Tochigiken Bengoshikai, Yamanashiken Bengoshikai, Naganoken Bengoshikai, Hyogoken Bengoshikai, Toyamaken Bengoshikai, Yamaguchiken Bengoshikai, Oitaken Bengoshikai, Sendai Bengoshikai, Yamagataken Bengoshikai, Akita Bengoshikai, Sapporo Bengoshikai (Saitama Bar Association, Chibaken Bar Association, Tochigiken Bar Association, Yamanashiken Bar Association, Naganoken Bar Association, Hyogoken Bar Association, Toyamaken Bar Association, Yamaguchiken Bar Association, Oitaken Bar Association, Sendai Bar Association, Yamagataken Bar Association, Akita Bar Association, Sapporo Bar Association) (2019) Shiho Shiken Gokakusha Su no saranaru Genin wo Motomeru 13 Bengoshikai Kaicho Kyodo Seimei (Joint Statement by Presidents of 13 Bar Associations Calling for Further Reductions in Successful Bar Exam Applicants). https://www.saiben.or.jp/proclamation/000884.html. Retrieved August 31, 2023.
Somusho (2012) Hoso Jinko no Kakudai oyobi Hoso Yosei Seido no Kaikaku ni kansuru Seisaku Hyoukasho (Policy Evaluation Report on the Expansion of Population of Legal Professionals and the Institutional Reform of Training for Legal Professionals). https://www.soumu.go.jp/main_content/000159698.pdf. Retrieved August 26, 2023.
Yomiuri (Yomiuri Shinbun) (Yomiuri News) (2019) Shasetsu: Susumu Hoso Banare: Shiho no Kiban ga Yuragi kanenai (Editorial: Increasing Separation from the Legal Profession: The of the Judiciary Could Be on a Shaky), September 29, morning edn.
Yoneda K (ed) (2022) Kaisha Homubu: Dai12ji Jittaichosa no Bunseki Hokoku (Corporate Legal Departments: Report of Analyses of 12th Survey Results), Shoji Homu, Tokyo.

Masayuki Murayama is Professor Emeritus of Meiji University and Chiba University. He obtained his Ph.D. in Sociology of Law from the University of Tokyo. He studied in LL.M. Program and the Jurisprudence and Social Policy Program at the University of California, Berkeley and visited The Centre for Socio-Legal Studies, Oxford, Centre de Sociologie des Organisations, Paris, Institut fuer Rechtssoziologie, Freie Universitaet, Berlin, and Columbia Law School. He is an empirical researcher and has conducted empirical research on the police, criminal justice process, family mediation, civil disputes and access to justice, and the legal profession.

Appendix A: Survey Outline and Data

This survey was approved by the Ethics Committee on Human Research of Meiji University on August 17, 2018 (No.25).

1.1 Outline

The purpose of this survey is to obtain retrospective data from individual attorneys concerning their career changes, and to facilitate analysis of historical changes of legal practice in Japan. What follows is an outline of the questionnaire. An English rendering of the complete original Japanese questionnaire is given in Appendix B. We thank Daniel Foote for reviewing it.

The questionnaire consists of three major parts. In the first part, we asked all respondents year of birth, gender, education, social experience, accreditation, first work as legal professional, present position, study abroad, how many times they have changed jobs to date, etc. This part aimed at obtaining basic information by which we could analyze their careers.

In the second part, we asked all respondents to choose one of the four sectors according to their first career: law firm, corporation, public office, or other, this last including academic positions. For each sector, we tried to obtain as much relevant data as possible, but we had to trade off the number of questions against the possibility of low response rates. We wanted to ask about respondents' entire careers, but we limited ourselves to up to seven career changes. In case a respondent had more than seven career changes, the respondent was asked to answer about the latest career in the seventh career page. This is the central part of the questionnaire and has 28 pages.

The third part is the last page of the questionnaire, divided into twosections. In the first, we asked all respondents who currently practiced at law firms, questions concerning recent changes of legal practice. In the second, we asked to all respondents about their desire to move from the current positions.

M. Murayama (ed.), *The Japanese Legal Profession in Transition*, Economics, Law, and Institutions in Asia Pacific, https://doi.org/10.1007/978-981-97-2692-9

The universe of our survey is private attorneys who were registered by the JFBA in 2017. We randomly chose 3500 lawyers as our sample. We sent, by mail, the questionnaire with our request of cooperation twice: 9 November 2018 and 6 December 2018. Each time, we sent a reminder postcard approximately a week after the questionnaire was sent out. Although we sent our questionnaire by mail, respondents could choose either to send back their answers by mail or to answer to the questionnaire on the website. We sent both the URL and QR code of the website so that respondents could answer either with a computer or a tablet. We asked respondents to answer the questionnaire by 31 December 2018, but the website was closed on 31 January 2019.

1.2 Data

The number of respondents was 1478, but the number of effective responses was 1477, thus the response rate was 42.2%.[1] 814 (55.1%) of the respondents answered by mail, while 663 (44.9%) of them answered on the website. As nationwide surveys of lawyers tended to have low response rates, often less than 20%, we tried to obtain a higher response rate, 40%, if possible. We fortunately succeeded to obtain even a higher response rate. The availability of answering via the website might have contributed to the high response rate.[2]

Following is an examination of to what extent the data is representative of the universe of registered private attorneys.

1.2.1 Age

Respondents in their 1930s are significantly overrepresented and those in their 50s underrepresented, as is shown in Table A.1.

[1] We conducted data cleaning thoroughly. We tried to keep the original responses as much as possible. Even when responses were wrong in light of experience but when we could not deny the possibility of the responses in theory, we kept the responses as such. When responses were logically inconsistent, we corrected the data only insofar as we found some basis to change the original responses to other responses. Even in this case, we corrected the data only when we could find logically clear responses, and we did not correct the data, based on inference by experience. When responses were logically inconsistent and also when we could not find logically clear responses, we made the responses invalid. The reason why numbers of responses vary in analyses in this book is that no-answers exist in answers and that such invalid answers also exist.

[2] The Japan In-House Lawyers Association (JILA) twice sent out an email to ask their members to cooperate in answering to our survey just before we sent out the questionnaire. The Japan Law Foundation (JLF) put an article about our survey in their newsletter before our survey was distributed. Their support must have contributed to improving the response rate. We thank the JILA and the JLF for their support. We also thank Yoshiyuki Matsumura, Tadahisa Sakamoto, Masaaki Haga, Kazuhiko Yamamoto, Ryo Fujimoto, Aya Yamada, Ryota Kosai, Hideaki Irie, and Ken-ichi Yoneda as well as the Japan Federation of Bar Associations for their support for the survey.

Table A.1 Age of the lawyers in the universe and of the respondents

	Age						Total
	20s	30s	40s	50s	60s	70 or Older	
Universe[a]	2933	13,033	9221	4297	4522	4974	38,980
	7.5%	33.4%	23.7%	11.0%	11.6%	12.8%	100.0%
Respondents	105	543	361	137	153	168	1467
	7.2%	37.0%	24.6%	9.3%	10.4%	11.5%	100.0%
Standardized residual	−0.51	2.37	0.75	−1.94	−1.32	−1.4	–

[a] As of March 31, 2017. *Source*: JFBA (2017), Bengoshi Hakusho (White Paper on Attorneys), p. 31

Table A.2 Gender of the lawyers in the universe and of the respondents

	Gender			Total
	Men	Women	Don't Want Answer	
Universe[a]	31,801	7179	–	38,980
	81.6%	18.4%	–	100.0%
Respondents	1174	277	16	1467
	80.0%	18.9%	1.1%	100.0%
Standardized residual	−0.66	0.41	–	–

[a] As of March 31, 2017. *Source*: JFBA (2017), Bengoshi Hakusho (White Paper on Attorneys), p. 33

1.2.2 Gender

Table A.2 shows the gender distribution in the universe and among the respondents. Women are slightly overrepresented, but it is not statistically significant.

1.2.3 Legal Training and Research Institute (LTRI) Cohort

Since the LTRI training program began in 1947, graduates of the program have been grouped by the term of the program, such as the first term, second term etc. In Table A.3, as the number of respondents before 20th Term is small, all respondents whose term is from second to 19th are in one category. Compared to the universe, the respondents are overrepresented in the 60 s and underrepresented in the 20s and 40s.

1.2.4 Local Bar Association Membership

In Table A.4, local bar associations are classified into those in Tokyo, Osaka, or Nagoya, and other prefectures with and without High Courts, respectively. We compared the distribution of lawyers in the universe and among the respondents. Although the lawyers in the Tokyo/Osaka/Nagoya bar associations are underrepresented, it is not statistically significant.

Table A.3 Term of LTRI program in the universe and among the respondents

	Term of LTRI Program						
	2–19	20–29	30–39	40–49	50–59	60–69	Total
Universe[a]	1667	3264	3382	4048	7759	18,323	38,443
	4.3%	8.5%	8.8%	10.5%	20.2%	47.7%	100.0%
Respondents	54	88	118	127	258	789	1434
	3.8%	6.1%	8.2%	8.9%	18.0%	55.0%	100.0%
Standardized residual	−1.04	−3.06	−0.73	−1.95	−1.85	4.04	–

[a] As of March 31, 2017. They were calculated from the numbers in JFBA (2017), Bengoshi Hakusho (White Paper on Attorneys), p. 32

Table A.4 Bar Association membership in the universe and among the respondents

	Bar Assocation			
	Tokyo/Osaka/ Nagoya	Others Prefectures with High Courts	Others Prefectures without High Courts	Total
Universe[a]	24,618	3200	11,162	38,980
	63.2%	8.2%	28.6%	100.0%
Respondents	893	135	449	1477
	60.4%	9.1%	30.4%	100.0%
Standardized residual	−1.30	1.25	1.27	–

[a] As of March 31, 2017. *Source*: JFBA (2017), Bengoshi Hakusho (White Paper on Attorneys), p. 33

Table A.5 Distribution among sectors in the universe and among the respondents

	Sector of Practice			
	Law Firm	Corporation	Public Office/Other	Total
Universe[a]	36,588	1931	461	38,980
	93.9%	5.0%	1.2%	[b]100.1%
Respondents	1342	111	22	1476
	90.9%	7.5%	1.5%	[b]99.9%
Standardized residual	−1.14	4.44	1.09	–

[a] The number of lawyers at law firms is on 31 March 2017, at corporations on 30 June 2017, at Public Offices on 1 June 2017, and at Law Schools on 1 May 2017. *Source*: JFBA (2017), Bengoshi Hakusho [White Paper on Attorneys] pp.33, 126, 132, 135

[b] Rounding error

1.2.5 Sector of Practice

In Table A.5, the number of lawyers practicing at law firms, at corporations and in public offices/other are compared between the universe and the respondents. As the number of respondents in others is small, public office and others are combined. Apparently, lawyers at corporations are significantly overrepresented among the respondents.

In summary, in our data, lawyers in their 30s, in their 60th–69th LTRI cohort, and employed by corporations are overrepresented in comparison with the universe. As the number of in-house lawyers increased rapidly in these last 10 years, these overrepresentations are related to each other. But otherwise, significant bias was not found.

Appendix B: Questionnaire

M. Murayama (ed.), *The Japanese Legal Profession in Transition*, Economics, Law, and Institutions in Asia Pacific, https://doi.org/10.1007/978-981-97-2692-9

ID in the right column is necessary to send a gratitude and a quick report of survey results. Please do not cut it off.

I D (Barcode) attached

National Survey on Diversification in Lawyers' Practice

Though the questionnaire is thick, at the shortest you can finish by answering questions on just three pages. Even at the longest, you can complete it in 10 to 15 minutes. You can answer with a personal computer, smart phone or tablet. Please look at the separate sheet "Request for Cooperation".

We will not identify your name and we will use your answers as quantitative data. **We will use your ID to send you a token of our gratitude and to send you a quick report of survey results, if you would like to receive it. Afterwards, the research company will delete the personal information.**

We plan to use the survey results as quantitative data for our research as well as secondary analyses by collaborative bodies for research, and to deposit the data at archives for further analyses by researchers.

◆Please circle the number indicating what you would like to receive as gratitude from us.

1. **QUO Card worth 3,000 Yen (We will send you by mail)**
2. **Contribution worth 3,000 Yen (Donation through Japan Red Cross "Relief for Heavy Rainfall Disaster in July 2018", "Relief for Earthquake Disaster in Hokkaido Iburi East Region in September 2018"**

◆If you would like to receive a quick report of survey results, we will send it to you. Please check below if you would like to have one.

□ I would like to receive a quick report. (ID will be deleted after a quick report is sent out)

Please answer from the following page.
<Requests in Responding>
- Please choose one response unless instructed otherwise.
- In the case (Multiple Answers Possible) is written, please choose all applicable responses.
- Please write appropriate numbers in the items that call for year (in or Showa・Heisei) and number of persons (persons).

**Funding : Japan Society for the promotion of Science, Basic Research (A) (17H00964)
Japan Law Foundation (Research No.135)
Minji Hunso Shori Kenkyu Kikin (Foundation for Research on Civil Dispute Resolution**

**Research Team : Shozo Ota (University of Tokyo), Daniel H. Foote (University of Tokyo)
Isamu Sugino (Ochanomizu University), Kyoko Ishida (Waseda University)
Takayuki Ii (Senshu University), Daisuke Mori (Kumamoto University)
Masayuki Murayama (PI, Meiji University)
Collaborative Researcher : Yoshiyuki Matsumura (Hokkaido University)
Tadahisa Sakamoto (Tohoku University), Masaaki Haga (Keio University)
Kazuhiko Yamamoto (Hitotsubashi University), Akira Fujimoto (Nagoya University)
Aya Yamada (Kyoto University), Ryota Kosai (Ehime University)
Hideaki Irie (Kyushu University), Kenichi Yoneda (Kagoshima University)
Collaborative Bodies : Japan Federation of Bar Associations, Japan In-House Lawyers Association
Research Agency: Nippon Research Center Co., Ltd.**

Please put the completed questionnaire into the enclosed envelope and mail it by **November 25 (Sun)**. You do not have to use a postage stamp.

Questions of this page are for everybody to answer. From next page, please select applicable pages.
Within parentheses, please write year, university, etc. Also please choose applicable numbers.

1. When were you born? (in 19 or Showa・Heisei)
2. Gender 1. Male 2. Female 3. Do not wish to answer

3. Have you graduated from a university? 1. Graduated 2. Not graduated
3-1. For those who graduated from a university
Please provide information regarding your university, faculty, and year of graduation (If you graduated from more than one university or faculty, please answer with respect to the last)
(University:) (Faculty:) (graduated in or in Showa・Heisei)

4. Before becoming qualified as a legal professional, did you work or raise a child?
1. Yes 2. No

5. Have you graduated from a law school?
1. No
2. Yes (If you have graduated from more than one law school, please answer with respect to the last)
(Law School :) (graduated in or in Showa・Heisei)

6. Have you passed the preliminary bar examination?
1. No 2. Yes (in or in Showa・Heisei)

7. How did you become qualified as a legal professional?
1. Passed the bar examination 2. Recognized as a legal professional under Article 5/6 of Attorneys Act

8. Year in which you passed the bar examination or became recognized by Article 5/6 (in or Showa・Heisei)

9. Did you take the Legal Training Program 1. I took (Term :) 2. I did not take

10. First career after becoming qualified as a legal professional : 1. Lawyer 2. Judge 3. Prosecutor 4. Other

11. When did you register as a lawyer for the first time? (In or in Showa・Heisei)

12. Which among the following is your present position? Please choose one.
1. Managing Lawyer at a Law Firm 2. Employed at a Law Firm 3. Other at a Law Firm 4. In-House at a Law Department 5. In-House at other position 6. Judge 7. Prosecutor 8. Other Public Official (except a law school teacher) 9. Other

13. Have you studied at a law school, a law faculty or a law-related graduate school in a foreign country?
If you have studied in a foreign country more than once, please answer with respect to the longest period of study.
1. No, I have not 2. Yes, I have (from to) or (from Showa・Heisei to)

Please answer by choosing your first position among law firm, corporation, public office and other, after you became qualified as a legal professional.

If you had more than one position, please choose the position with the highest income. If the incomes are the same, please choose the position that lasted for a longer period.

If you have moved, please choose the positions to which you, moved one by one.
It does not take much time to answer the questionnaire, as we ask you to choose applicable answers from the lists provided, except for items with respect to the year and the number of persons at the organization.

I. A

First Career【Law Firm】

1. Year you began to work：in Showa・Heisei
2. Location of Law Firm： 1.Tokyo Pref 2.Osaka Pref 3. Aichi Pref 4. Other region with a High Court 5. Other region without a High Court
3. Which was your first position among the following: 1. Employed Lawyer 2. Managing Lawyer (Member of a Legal Professional Corporation included) 3. Other
4. Roughly how many lawyers belonged to the law firm when you began to work? Managing Lawyer (persons) Non-Managing Lawyer (persons) 5. Roughly how many lawyers belonged to the law firm in your last year at the law firm? Managing Lawyer (persons) Non-Managing Lawyer (persons)
6. Which is the management style of the law firm among the following? (Multiple choice is possible) 1. Solo-practice 2. Cost sharing 3. Income sharing 4. Legal professional corporation 5. Other
7. Please choose one or more fields among the following if the income from the field accounted for one-third of your income or more (Except for item 1, you can choose up to three fields). 1. No such field 2. Labor Law 3. Medical Malpractice 4. Traffic Accidents 5. Family Law 6. Real Property 7. Consumer Loans 8. Personal Bankruptcy 9. Criminal 10. Intellectual Property 11. Finance 12. M&A 13. Business Bankruptcy 14. International Transactions 15. Tax Law 16. Other
8. When you began to work at this law firm, how much was your annual income before tax? A. Less than 3 million yen B. 3 million to less than 5 million C. 5million to less than 7 million D. 7 million to less than 10 million E. 10 million to less than 15 million F. 15 million to less than 20 million G. 20 million to less than 30 million H. 30 million to less than 50 million I. 50 million to less than 100 million J. 100 million or more
9. In the last year at this law firm, how much was your annual income before tax? A. Less than 3 million yen B. 3 million to less than 5 million C. 5million to less than 7 million D. 7 million to less than 10 million E. 10 million to less than 15 million F. 15 million to less than 20 million G. 20 million to less than 30 million H. 30 million to less than 50 million I. 50 million to less than 100 million J. 100 million or more
10.In which year did you end your work here？(In or Showa・Heisei) Still working→Go to Page 31

If you moved from this law firm, please answer by choosing the second career among 【law firm】、【corporation】、【public office】、【other】.

If you still work at this law firm, please go to the last page A 【law firm】.

Ⅰ. B

First Career【Corporation】

1. Year you began to work：in or Showa・Heisei
2. Location of corporation：1. Tokyo Pref 2. Osaka Pref 3. Aichi Pref 4. Other region with a High Court 5. Other region without a High Court
3. When you worked at the corporation, did you suspend your registration at the bar association? 1. Yes, I suspended 2. No, I did not suspend 3. I was not registered yet
4. In which of the following did you begin to work? 1. Law department 2. Other than law department
5. At the beginning of your work, how many legal professionals worked at the corporation? (persons) 6. At the end of your work, how many legal professionals worked at the corporation? (persons)
7. At the beginning of your work, how many employees worked at the corporation? 1. 1 to less than 50 persons 2. 50 to less than 100 persons 3. 100 to less than 300persons 4. 300 to less than 500persons 5. 500 to less than 1000 persons 6. 1000 or more persons
8. Which among the following is the industrial field of the corporation? Please choose one main field of the corporation. 1. Manufacture 2. Finance/Insurance 3. Construction 4 Information 5. Electricity/Gass/Water 6. Transportation/Mail Service 7. Wholesale/Retail sale 8. Real Property/Rental 9. Medical/Welfare 10. Other
9. When you began to work at this corporation, how much was your annual income before tax? A. Less than 3 million yen B. 3 million to less than 5 million C. 5million to less than 7 million D. 7 million to less than 10 million E. 10 million to less than 15 million F. 15 million to less than 20 million G. 20 million to less than 30 million H. 30 million to less than 50 million I. 50 million to less than 100 million J. 100 million or more
10. In the last year at this corporation, how much was your annual income before tax? A. Less than 3 million yen B. 3 million to less than 5 million C. 5million to less than 7 million D. 7 million to less than 10 million E. 10 million to less than 15 million F. 15 million to less than 20 million G. 20 million to less than 30 million H. 30 million to less than 50 million I. 50 million to less than 100 million J. 100 million or more
11. In which year did you end your work here ? (In or Showa・Heisei) Still working→Go to Page 31

If you moved from this corporation, please answer by choosing the second career among 【law firm】、【corporation】、【public office】、【other】.
If you still work at this corporation, please go to 【the last page】 B for Everybody.

Ⅰ. C

First Career【Public Office（Judge/Prosecutor included）】

（Teacher at a national and public university is classified as 'Other'）[Note: Teacher at a private university is classified as 'Other'. We added this warning, as an academic position at a national or public university could be considered as a position in 'public office'.]

1. Year you began to work：in or Showa・Heisei
2. Where in the following were you employed? 1．Court 2．Prosecutor's Office 3．National Ministry 4．Prefecture 5．Municipality 6．Other
3. Were you employed for a definite term? 1．Yes, for a definite term 2．No, not for a definite term
4. When you worked at this organization, did you suspend your registration at the bar association? 1．Yes, I suspended 2．No, I did not suspend 3．I was not registered yet
5. At the beginning of your work, how many legal professionals worked at this organization? (persons) 6. At the end of your work, how many legal professionals worked at this organization? (persons)
7. When you began to work in your office, how much was your annual income before tax? A. Less than 3 million yen B. 3 million to less than 5 million C. 5million to less than 7 million D. 7 million to less than 10 million E. 10 million to less than 15 million F. 15 million to less than 20 million G. 20 million to less than 30 million H. 30 million to less than 50 million I. 50 million to less than 100 million J. 100 million or more
8. In the last year in your office, how much was your annual income before tax? A. Less than 3 million yen B. 3 million to less than 5 million C. 5million to less than 7 million D. 7 million to less than 10 million E. 10 million to less than 15 million F. 15 million to less than 20 million G. 20 million to less than 30 million H. 30 million to less than 50 million I. 50 million to less than 100 million J. 100 million or more
9. In which year did you end your work here？（In or Showa・Heisei ） Still working→Go to Page 31

If you moved from this organization, please answer by choosing the second career among【law firm】、【corporation】、【public office】、【other】.
If you still work in this organization, please go to【the last page】B for Everybody.

Ⅰ. D

First Career【Other】

1. Year you began to work：in or Showa・Heisei
2. What was your job among the following? 1．Assemblyman（Politician） 2．University Teacher 3．NPO 4．Labor Union 5．Policy Secretary 6．Other
3. Were you employed for a definite term? 1．Yes, for a definite term 2．No, not for a definite term
4. When you worked here, did you suspend your registration at the bar association? 1．Yes, I suspend 2．No, I did not suspend 3．I was not registered yet
5. At the beginning of your work, how many legal professionals worked at this organization? (persons) 6. At the end of your work, how many legal professionals worked at this organization? (persons)
7. When you began to work at this organization, how much was your annual income before tax? A. Less than 3 million yen B. 3 million to less than 5 million C. 5million to less than 7 million D. 7 million to less than 10 million E. 10 million to less than 15 million F. 15 million to less than 20 million G. 20 million to less than 30 million H. 30 million to less than 50 million I. 50 million to less than 100 million J. 100 million or more
8. In the last year at this organization, how much was your annual income before tax? A. Less than 3 million yen B. 3 million to less than 5 million C. 5 million to less than 7 million D. 7 million to less than 10 million E. 10 million to less than 15 million F. 15 million to less than 20 million G. 20 million to less than 30 million H. 30 million to less than 50 million I. 50 million to less than 100 million J. 100 million or more
9. In which year did you end your work at this organization？（In or Showa・Heisei ） Still working→Go to Page 31

If you moved from this job, please answer by choosing the second career among【law firm】、【corporation】、【public office】、【other】.
If you still work in this office, please go to【the last page】B for Everybody.

II. A

Second Career【Law Firm】

1. Year you began to work ：in Showa・Heisei
2. Location of Law Firm： 1 .Tokyo Pref 2 .Osaka Pref 3 . Aichi Pref 4 . Other region with a High Court 5． Other region without a High Court
3. What is the main reason you moved here among the following? (Multiple choice is possible) 1. Better Income 2. Worthwhile Work 3. Human Relations 4. Work-Life Balance 5. To Have My Own Law Firm 6. Other
4. Which was your first position among the following: 1． Employed Lawyer 2． Managing Lawyer（Member of a Legal Professional Corporation included） 3． Other
5. Roughly how many lawyers belonged to the law firm when you began to work ? Managing Lawyer（ persons） Non-Managing Lawyer（ persons） 6. Roughly how many lawyers belonged to the law firm in your last year at the law firm ? Managing Lawyer（ persons） Non-Managing Lawyer（ persons）
7. Which is the management style of the law firm among the following? (Multiple choice is possible) 1． Solo-practice 2． Cost sharing 3． Income sharing 4． Legal professional corporation 5． Other
8. Please choose one or more fields among the following if the income from the field accounted for one-third of your income or more (Except for item 1, you can choose up to three fields). 1． No such field 2． Labor Law 3． Medical Malpractice 4． Traffic Accidents 5． Family Law 6． Real Property 7． Consumer Loans 8． Personal Bankruptcy 9． Criminal 10. Intellectual Property 11. Finance 12. M&A 13. Business Bankruptcy 14. International Transactions 15. Tax Law 16. Other
9. When you began to work at this law firm, how much was your annual income before tax? A. Less than 3 million yen B. 3 million to less than 5 million C. 5million to less than 7 million D. 7 million to less than 10 million E. 10 million to less than 15 million F. 15 million to less than 20 million G. 20 million to less than 30 million H. 30 million to less than 50 million I. 50 million to less than 100 million J. 100 million or more
10. In the last year at this law firm, how much was your annual income before tax? A. Less than 3 million yen B. 3 million to less than 5 million C. 5million to less than 7 million D. 7 million to less than 10 million E. 10 million to less than 15 million F. 15 million to less than 20 million G. 20 million to less than 30 million H. 30 million to less than 50 million I. 50 million to less than 100 million J. 100 million or more
11. In which year did you end your work here ?（In or Showa・Heisei ） Still working→Go to Page 31

If you moved from this law firm, please answer by choosing the third career among 【law firm】、【corporation】、【public office】、【other】.

If you still work at this law firm, please go to the last page A【law firm】.

II. B

Second Career【Corporation】

1. Year you began to work：in or Showa・Heisei
2. Location of corporation：1．Tokyo Pref 2．Osaka Pref 3．Aichi Pref 4．Other region with a High Court 5．Other region without a High Court
3. What is the main reason you moved here among the following? (Multiple choice is possible) 1. Better Income 2. Worthwhile Work 3. Human Relations 4. Work-Life Balance 5. Other
4. When you worked at the corporation, did you suspend your registration at the bar association? 1．Yes, I suspended 2．No, I did not suspend 3．I was not registered yet
5. In which of the following did you begin to work? 1．Law department 2．Other than law department
6. At the beginning of your work, how many legal professionals worked at the corporation? (persons) 7. At the end of your work, how many legal professionals worked at the corporation? (persons)
8. At the beginning of your work, how many employees worked at the corporation? 1．1 to less than 50 persons 2．50 to less than 100 persons 3．100 to less than 300persons 4．300 to less than 500persons 5．500 to less than 1000 persons 6．1000 or more persons
9. Which among the following is the industrial field of the corporation? Please choose one main field of the corporation. 1．Manufacture 2．Finance/Insurance 3．Construction 4 Information 5．Electricity/Gass/Water 6．Transportation/Mail Service 7．Wholesale/Retail sale 8．Real Property/Rental 9．Medical/Welfare 10. Other
10. When you began to work at this corporation, how much was your annual income before tax? A. Less than 3 million yen B. 3 million to less than 5 million C. 5million to less than 7 million D. 7 million to less than 10 million E. 10 million to less than 15 million F. 15 million to less than 20 million G. 20 million to less than 30 million H. 30 million to less than 50 million I. 50 million to less than 100 million J. 100 million or more
11. In the last year at this corporation, how much was your annual income before tax? A. Less than 3 million yen B. 3 million to less than 5 million C. 5million to less than 7 million D. 7 million to less than 10 million E. 10 million to less than 15 million F. 15 million to less than 20 million G. 20 million to less than 30 million H. 30 million to less than 50 million I. 50 million to less than 100 million J. 100 million or more
12. In which year did you end your work here？(In or Showa・Heisei) Still working→Go to Page 31

If you moved from this corporation, please answer by choosing the third career among【law firm】、【corporation】、【public office】、【other】.
If you still work at this corporation, please go to【the last page】B for Everybody.

II. C

Second Career【Public Office（Judge/Prosecutor included）】

（Teacher at a national and public university is classified as 'Other'）[Note: Teacher at a private university is classified as 'Other'. We added this warning, as an academic position at a national or public university could be considered as a position in 'public office'.]

1. Year you began to work：in or Showa・Heisei
2. Where in the following were you employed? １．Court ２．Prosecutor's Office ３．National Ministry ４．Prefecture ５．Municipality ６．Other
3. What is the main reason you moved here among the following? (Multiple choice is possible) 1. Better Income 2. Worthwhile Work 3. Human Relations 4. Work-Life Balance 5. Other
4. Were you employed for a definite term ? １．Yes, for a definite term ２．No, not for a definite term
5. When you worked at this organization, did you suspend your registration at the bar association? ２．Yes, I suspended ２．No, I did not suspend ３．I was not registered yet
6. At the beginning of your work, how many legal professionals worked at this organization? (persons) 7. At the end of your work, how many legal professionals worked at this organization ? (persons)
8. When you began to work in your office, how much was your annual income before tax? A. Less than 3 million yen B. 3 million to less than 5 million C. 5million to less than 7 million D. 7 million to less than 10 million E. 10 million to less than 15 million F. 15 million to less than 20 million G. 20 million to less than 30 million H. 30 million to less than 50 million I. 50 million to less than 100 million J. 100 million or more
9. In the last year in your office, how much was your annual income before tax? A. Less than 3 million yen B. 3 million to less than 5 million C. 5million to less than 7 million D. 7 million to less than 10 million E. 10 million to less than 15 million F. 15 million to less than 20 million G. 20 million to less than 30 million H. 30 million to less than 50 million I. 50 million to less than 100 million J. 100 million or more
10. In which year did you end your work here ?（In or Showa・Heisei ） Still working→Go to Page 31

If you moved from this organization, please answer by choosing the third career among【law firm】、【corporation】、【public office】、【other】.
If you still work in this organization, please go to【the last page】B for Everybody.

II. D

Second Career【Other】

1. Year you began to work：in or Showa・Heisei
2. What was your job among the following? 1. Assemblyman（Politician） 2. University Teacher 3. NPO 4. Labor Union 5. Policy Secretary 6. Other
3. What is the main reason you moved here among the following? (Multiple choice is possible) 1. Better Income 2. Worthwhile Work 3. Human Relations 4. Work-Life Balance 5. Other
4. Were you employed for a definite term? 1. Yes, for a definite term 2. No, not for a definite term
5. When you worked here, did you suspend your registration at the bar association? 1. Yes, I suspend 2. No, I did not suspend 3. I was not registered yet
6. At the beginning of your work, how many legal professionals worked at this organization? (persons) 7. At the end of your work, how many legal professionals worked at this organization? (persons)
8. When you began to work at this organization, how much was your annual income before tax? A. Less than 3 million yen B. 3 million to less than 5 million C. 5million to less than 7 million D. 7 million to less than 10 million E. 10 million to less than 15 million F. 15 million to less than 20 million G. 20 million to less than 30 million H. 30 million to less than 50 million I. 50 million to less than 100 million J. 100 million or more
9. In the last year at this organization, how much was your annual income before tax? A. Less than 3 million yen B. 3 million to less than 5 million C. 5 million to less than 7 million D. 7 million to less than 10 million E. 10 million to less than 15 million F. 15 million to less than 20 million G. 20 million to less than 30 million H. 30 million to less than 50 million I. 50 million to less than 100 million J. 100 million or more
10. In which year did you end your work at this organization ?（In or Showa・Heisei ） Still working→Go to Page 31

If you moved from this job, please answer by choosing the third career among【law firm】、【corporation】、【public office】、【other】.
If you still work in this office, please go to【the last page】B for Everybody.

[Note: From the third career to the fifth career, the questionnaire pages are exactly the same. Therefore, they are not shown here. The pages for the sixth and seventh careers have different directions to respondents. They are shown in the following pages.]

VI. A

6th Career【Law Firm】

1. Year you began to work：in Showa・Heisei
2. Location of Law Firm：１.Tokyo Pref ２.Osaka Pref ３.Aichi Pref ４.Other region with a High Court ５．Other region without a High Court
3. What is the main reason you moved here among the following? (Multiple choice is possible) 1. Better Income 2. Worthwhile Work 3. Human Relations 4. Work-Life Balance 5. To Have My Own Law Firm 6. Other
4. Which was your first position among the following : １．Employed Lawyer ２．Managing Lawyer（Member of a Legal Professional Corporation included） ３．Other
5. Roughly how many lawyers belonged to the law firm when you began to work? Managing Lawyer（ persons） No-Managing Lawyer（ persons） 6. Roughly how many lawyers belonged to the law firm in your last year at the law firm? Managing Lawyer（ persons） No-Managing Lawyer（ persons）
7. Which is the management style of the law firm among the following? (Multiple choice is possible) １．Solo-practice ２．Cost sharing ３．Income sharing ４．Legal professional corporation ５．Other
8. Please choose one or more fields among the following if the income from the field accounted for one-third of your income or more (Except for item 1, you can choose up to three fields). １．No such field ２．Labor Law ３．Medical Malpractice ４．Traffic Accidents ５．Family Law ６．Real Property ７．Consumer Loans ８．Personal Bankruptcy ９．Criminal 10．Intellectual Property 11．Finance 12．M&A 13．Business Bankruptcy 14．International Transactions 15．Tax Law 16．Other
9. When you began to work at this law firm, how much was your annual income before tax? A. Less than 3 million yen B. 3 million to less than 5 million C. 5million to less than 7 million D. 7 million to less than 10 million E. 10 million to less than 15 million F. 15 million to less than 20 million G. 20 million to less than 30 million H. 30 million to less than 50 million I. 50 million to less than 100 million J. 100 million or more
10. In the last year at this law firm, how much was your annual income before tax? A. Less than 3 million yen B. 3 million to less than 5 million C. 5million to less than 7 million D. 7 million to less than 10 million E. 10 million to less than 15 million F. 15 million to less than 20 million G. 20 million to less than 30 million H. 30 million to less than 50 million I. 50 million to less than 100 million J. 100 million or more
11. In which year did you end your work here？（In or Showa・Heisei ） Still working→Go to Page 31

If you moved from this law firm, please answer by choosing the 7th career among 【law firm】、【corporation】、【public office】、【other】. If you have moved more than 7 times, please answer by choosing the present career among 【law firm】、【corporation】、【public office】、【other】.

If you still work at this law firm, please go to the last page A【law firm】.

VI. B

6th Career【Corporation】

1. Year you began to work：in   or Showa・Heisei

2. Location of corporation：１．Tokyo Pref ２．Osaka Pref ３．Aichi Pref ４．Other with a High Co
５．Other without a High Court

3. What is the main reason you moved here among the following? (Multiple choice is possible)
1. Better Income   2. Worthwhile Work   3. Human Relations
4. Work-Life Balance   5. Other

4. When you worked at the corporation, did you suspend your registration at the bar association?
１．Yes, I suspended   ２．No, I did not suspend   ３．Not registered yet

5. In which of the following did you begin to work?
１．Law department   ２．Other than law department

6. At the beginning of your work, how many legal professionals worked at the corporation? (persons)
7. At the end of your work, how many legal professionals worked at the corporation?   (persons)

8. At the beginning of your work, how many employees worked at the corporation?
１．1 to less than 50 persons   ２．50 to less than 100 persons   ３．100 to less than 300persons
４．300 to less than 500persons   ５．500 to less than 1000 persons   ６．1000 or more persons

9. Which among the following is the industrial field of the corporation? Please choose one main field of the corporation.
１．Manufacture   ２．Finance/Insurance   ３．Construction
4 Information   ５．Electricity/Gass/Water   ６．Transportation/Mail Service
７．Wholesale/Retail sale   ８．Real Property/Rental   ９．Medical/Welfare
10. Other

10. When you began to work at this corporation, how much was your annual income before tax?
A. Less than 3 million   B. 3 million to less than 5 million   C. 5million to less than 7 million
D. 7 million to less than 10 million   E. 10 million to less than 15 million   F. 15 million to less than 20 million
G. 20 million to less than 30 million   H. 30 million to less than 50 million   I. 50 million to less than 100 million
J. 100 million or more

11. In the last year at this corporation, how much was your annual income before tax?
A. Less than 3 million   B. 3 million to less than 5 million   C. 5million to less than 7 million
D. 7 million to less than 10 million   E. 10 million to less than 15 million   F. 15 million to less than 20 million
G. 20 million to less than 30 million   H. 30 million to less than 50 million   I. 50 million to less than 100 million
J. 100 million or more

12. In which year did you end your work here？（In   or Showa・Heisei   ）
Still working→Go to Page 31

If you moved from this corporation, please answer by choosing the 7th career among 【law firm】、【corporation】、【public office】、【other】. If you have moved more than 7 times, please answer by choosing the present career among 【law firm】、【corporation】、【public office】、【other】.

If you still work at this corporation, please go to【the last page】B for Everybody.

VI. C

6th Career【Public Office（Judge/Prosecutor included）】

（Teacher at a national and public university is classified as 'Other'）

1. Year you began to work：in or Showa・Heisei
2. Where in the following were you employed? １．Court ２．Prosecutor's Office ３．National Ministry ４．Prefecture ５．Municipality ６．Other
3. What is the main reason you moved here among the following? (Multiple choice is possible) 1. Better Income 2. Worthwhile Work 3. Human Relations 4. Work-Life Balance 5. Other
4. Were you employed for a definite term? １．Yes, for a definite term ２．No, not for a definite term
5. When you worked at your office, did you suspend your registration at the bar association? ３．Yes, I suspended ２．No, I did not suspend ３．Not registered yet
6. At the beginning of your work, how many legal professionals worked here? (persons) 7. At the end of your work, how many legal professionals worked here? (persons)
8. When you began to work in your office, how much was your annual income before tax? A. Less than 3 million B. 3 million to less than 5 million C. 5million to less than 7 million D. 7 million to less than 10 million E. 10 million to less than 15 million F. 15 million to less than 20 million G. 20 million to less than 30 million H. 30 million to less than 50 million I. 50 million to less than 100 million J. 100 million or more
9. In the last year in your office, how much was your annual income before tax? A. Less than 3 million B. 3 million to less than 5 million C. 5million to less than 7 million D. 7 million to less than 10 million E. 10 million to less than 15 million F. 15 million to less than 20 million G. 20 million to less than 30 million H. 30 million to less than 50 million I. 50 million to less than 100 million J. 100 million or more
10. In which year did you end your work here？（In or Showa・Heisei ） Still working→Go to Page 31

If you moved from this office, please answer by choosing the 7th career among 【law firm】、【corporation】、【public office】、【other】. If you have moved more than 7 times, please answer by choosing the present career among 【law firm】、【corporation】、【public office】、【other】.
If you still work in this office, please go to 【the last page】 B for Everybody.

VI. D

6th Career【Other】

1. Year you began to work：in or Showa・Heisei
2. What was your job among the following ? 1. Assemblyman（Politician） 2. University Teacher 3. NPO 4. Labor Union 5. Policy Secretary 6. Other
3. What is the main reason you moved here among the following? (Multiple choice is possible) 1. Better Income 2. Worthwhile Work 3. Human Relations 4. Work-Life Balance 5. Other
4. Were you employed for a definite term? 1. Yes, for a definite term 2. No, not for a definite term
5. When you worked here, did you suspend your registration at the bar association? 1. Yes, I suspended 2. No, I did not suspend 3. Not registered yet
6. At the beginning of your work, how many legal professionals worked here? (persons)
7. At the end of your work, how many legal professionals worked here? (persons)
8. When you began to work here, how much was your annual income before tax? A. Less than 3 million B. 3 million to less than 5 million C. 5million to less than 7 million D. 7 million to less than 10 million E. 10 million to less than 15 million F. 15 million to less than 20 million G. 20 million to less than 30 million H. 30 million to less than 50 million I. 50 million to less than 100 million J. 100 million or more
9. In the last year at this corporation, how much was your annual income before tax? A. Less than 3 million B. 3 million to less than 5 million C. 5million to less than 7 million D. 7 million to less than 10 million E. 10 million to less than 15 million F. 15 million to less than 20 million G. 20 million to less than 30 million H. 30 million to less than 50 million I. 50 million to less than 100 million J. 100 million or more
10. In which year did you end your work here ?（In or Showa・Heisei ） Still working→Go to Page 31

If you moved from this job, please answer by choosing the 7th career among 【law firm】、【corporation】、【public office】、【other】. If you have moved more than 7 times, please answer by choosing the present career among 【law firm】、【corporation】、【public office】、【other】.
If you still continue to do this job, please go to 【the last page】 B for Everybody.

VII. A

7th Career【Law Firm】

If you have moved more than 7 times and the present position is in a law firm, please answer the questions below.

1. Year you began to work：in Showa・Heisei
2. Location of Law Firm：１.Tokyo Pref ２.Osaka Pref ３.Aichi Pref ４.Other with a High Court ５． Other without a High Court
3. What is the main reason you moved here among the following? (Multiple choice is possible) 1. Better Income 2. Worthwhile Work 3. Human Relations 4. Work-Life Balance 5. To Have My Own Law Firm 6. Other
4. Which is your first position among the following: １． Employed Lawyer ２． Managing Lawyer（Member of a Legal Professional Corporation included） ３． Other
5. Roughly how many lawyers belonged to the law firm when you began to work? Managing Lawyer（ persons） No-Managing Lawyer（ persons） 6. Roughly how many lawyers belonged to the law firm in your last year at the law firm? Managing Lawyer（ persons） No-Managing Lawyer（ persons）
7. Which is the management style of the law firm among the following? (Multiple choice is possible) １． Solo-practice ２． Cost sharing ３． Income sharing ４． Legal professional corporation ５． Other
8. Please choose one or more fields among the following if the income from the field accounted for one-third of your income or more (Except for item 1, you can choose up to three fields). １． No such field ２． Labor Law ３． Medical Malpractice ４． Traffic Accident ５． Family Law ６． Real Property ７． Multiple Debts ８． Personal Bankruptcy ９． Criminal 10. Intellectual Property 11. Finance 12. M&A 13. Bankruptcy 14. International Transaction 15. Tax Law 16. Other
9. When you began to work at this law firm, how much was your annual income before tax? A. Less than 3 million B. 3 million to less than 5 million C. 5million to less than 7 million D. 7 million to less than 10 million E. 10 million to less than 15 million F. 15 million to less than 20 million G. 20 million to less than 30 million H. 30 million to less than 50 million I. 50 million to less than 100 million J. 100 million or more
10. In the last year at this law firm, how much was your annual income before tax? A. Less than 3 million B. 3 million to less than 5 million C. 5million to less than 7 million D. 7 million to less than 10 million E. 10 million to less than 15 million F. 15 million to less than 20 million G. 20 million to less than 30 million H. 30 million to less than 50 million I. 50 million to less than 100 million J. 100 million or more

Please go to the last page A【law firm】.

VII. B

7th Career【Corporation】

If you have moved more than 7 times and the present position is in a corporation, please answer the questions below.

1. Year you began to work：in or Showa・Heisei
2. Location of corporation：1．Tokyo Pref 2．Osaka Pref 3．Aichi Pref 4．Other with a High Co 5．Other without a High Court
3. What is the main reason you moved here among the following? (Multiple choice is possible) 1. Better Income 2. Worthwhile Work 3. Human Relations 4. Work-Life Balance 5. Other
4. When you worked at the corporation, did you suspend your registration at the bar association? 1．Yes, I suspended 2．No, I did not suspend 3．Not registered yet
5. In which of the following did you begin to work? 1．Law department 2．Other than law department
6. At the beginning of your work, how many legal professionals worked at the corporation? (persons) 7. At the end of your work, how many legal professionals worked at the corporation? (persons)
8. At the beginning of your work, how many employees worked at the corporation? 1．1 to less than 50 persons 2．50 to less than 100 persons 3．100 to less than 300persons 4．300 to less than 500persons 5．500 to less than 1000 persons 6．1000 or more persons
9. Which among the following is the industrial field of the corporation? Please choose one main field of thecorporation. 1．Manufacture 2．Finance/Insurance 3．Construction 4 Information 5．Electricity/Gass/Water 6．Transportation/Mail Service 7．Wholesale/Retail sale 8．Real Property/Rental 9．Medical/Welfare 10．Other
10. When you began to work at this corporation, how much was your annual income before tax? A. Less than 3 million B. 3 million to less than 5 million C. 5million to less than 7 million D. 7 million to less than 10 million E. 10 million to less than 15 million F. 15 million to less than 20 million G. 20 million to less than 30 million H. 30 million to less than 50 million I. 50 million to less than 100 million J. 100 million or more
11. In the last year at this corporation, how much was your annual income before tax? A. Less than 3 million B. 3 million to less than 5 million C. 5million to less than 7 million D. 7 million to less than 10 million E. 10 million to less than 15 million F. 15 million to less than 20 million G. 20 million to less than 30 million H. 30 million to less than 50 million I. 50 million to less than 100 million J. 100 million or more

Please go to【the last page】B for Everybody.

VII. C

7th Career【Public Office（Judge/Prosecutor included）】

（Teacher at a national and public university is classified as 'Other'）

If you have moved more than 7 times and the present position is in public office, please answer the questions below.

1. Year you began to work：in or Showa・Heisei
2. Where in the following were you employed? 1． Court 2． Prosecutor's Office 3． National Ministry 4． Prefecture 5． Municipality 6． Other
3. What is the main reason you moved here among the following? (Multiple choice is possible) 1. Better Income 2. Worthwhile Work 3. Human Relations 4. Work-Life Balance 5. Other
4. Were you employed for a definite term? 1． Yes, for a definite term 2． No, not for a definite term
5. When you worked at your office, did you suspend your registration at the bar association? 4． Yes, I suspended 2． No, I did not suspend 3． Not registered yet
6. At the beginning of your work, how many legal professionals worked here? (persons) 7. At the end of your work, how many legal professionals worked here? (persons)
8. When you began to work in your office, how much was your annual income before tax? A. Less than 3 million B. 3 million to less than 5 million C. 5million to less than 7 million D. 7 million to less than 10 million E. 10 million to less than 15 million F. 15 million to less than 20 million G. 20 million to less than 30 million H. 30 million to less than 50 million I. 50 million to less than 100 million J. 100 million or more
9. In the last year in your office, how much was your annual income before tax? A. Less than 3 million B. 3 million to less than 5 million C. 5million to less than 7 million D. 7 million to less than 10 million E. 10 million to less than 15 million F. 15 million to less than 20 million G. 20 million to less than 30 million H. 30 million to less than 50 million I. 50 million to less than 100 million J. 100 million or more

Please go to【the last page】B for Everybody.

VII. D

7th Career【Other】

If you have moved more than 7 times and the present position is in [Other], please answer the questions below.

1. Year you began to work：in or Showa・Heisei
2. What was your job among the following? 1. Assemblyman（Politician） 2. University Teacher 3. NPO 4. Labor Union 5. Policy Secretary 6. Other
3. What is the main reason you moved here among the following? (Multiple choice is possible) 1. Better Income 2. Worthwhile Work 3. Human Relations 4. Work-Life Balance 5. Other
4. Were you employed for a definite term? 1. Yes, for a definite term 2. No, not for a definite term
5. When you worked here, did you suspend your registration at the bar association? 1. Yes, I suspended 2. No, I did not suspend 3. Not registered yet
6. At the beginning of your work, how many legal professionals worked here? (persons) 7. At the end of your work, how many legal professionals worked here? (persons)
8. When you began to work here, how much was your annual income before tax? A. Less than 3 million B. 3 million to less than 5 million C. 5million to less than 7 million D. 7 million to less than 10 million E. 10 million to less than 15 million F. 15 million to less than 20 million G. 20 million to less than 30 million H. 30 million to less than 50 million I. 50 million to less than 100 million J. 100 million or more
9. In the last year at this corporation, how much was your annual income before tax? A. Less than 3 million B. 3 million to less than 5 million C. 5million to less than 7 million D. 7 million to less than 10 million E. 10 million to less than 15 million F. 15 million to less than 20 million G. 20 million to less than 30 million H. 30 million to less than 50 million I. 50 million to less than 100 million J. 100 million or more

Please go to 【the last page】 B for Everybody.

A· Please answer the following questions if you work at 【law firm】.

Otherwise, please go to B.

1. In your present work, how much does dispute-related work (including consultation on a dispute as well as litigation) occupy in terms of your total income? 1. Almost all 2. More than half 3. Third or more but less than half 4. Less than a third 5. None at all 6. Do not know
2. Does your law firm have a site on the Internet? 1. It has 2. It does not have
3. Does your law firm advertise? (You can choose more than one) 1. Advertise on a train/bus/taxi 2. Advertise on the radio 3. Advertise on TV 4. Advertise in other way 5. Do not advertise
4. Does your law firm accept a client without introduction? 1. Accepts 2. Does not accept
5. How many full-time supporting staff work in your law firm? 1. None 2. 1 to 5 persons 3. 6 to 10 persons 4. 11 to 20 persons 5. 21 to 30 persons 6. 31 or more persons

B. Questions for All

1. Do you hope to change your present job? 1. I hope to change 2. I do not hope to change 3. Cannot say either way → End of Questionnaire
1-1. To those who hope to change the present job To which in the following do you hope to move? Please choose one. 1. Law Firm 2. Corporation 3. Public Office 4. Other
1-2. To those who hope to change the present job Why do you hope to change the job? (Multiple choice is possible) 1. Want to increase income 2. Want to do more worthwhile work 3. Because of human relations 4. Considering work-life balance 5. Want to have my own law firm 6. Other

Thank you for your cooperation

Index

M. Murayama (ed.), *The Japanese Legal Profession in Transition*, Economics, Law, and Institutions in Asia Pacific,
https://doi.org/10.1007/978-981-97-2692-9

The manufacturer's authorised representative in the EU is Springer Nature Customer Service Centre GmbH, Europaplatz 3, 69115 Heidelberg, Germany. If you have any concerns regarding our products, please contact ProductSafety@springernature.com

Printed and bound by CPI Group (UK) Ltd, Croydon, CR0 4YY

01/10/2026

02225852-0012